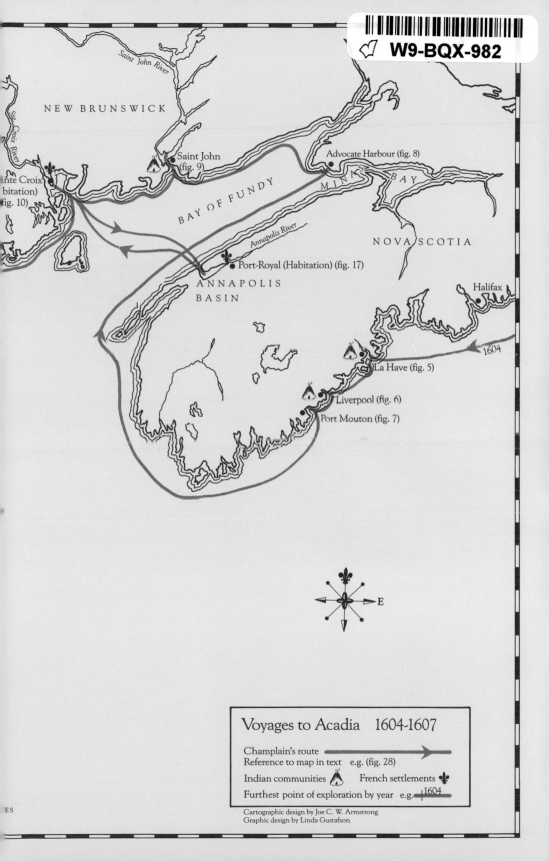

Saint John River

NEW BRUNSWICK

Ste Croix River

Saint John
(fig. 9)

Advocate Harbour (fig. 8)

inte Croix
bitation)
fig. 10)

MINAS   BAY

BAY OF FUNDY

NOVA SCOTIA

Annapolis River

Port-Royal (Habitation) (fig. 17)

ANNAPOLIS
BASIN

Halifax

1604

La Have (fig. 5)

Liverpool (fig. 6)

Port Mouton (fig. 7)

E

ES

Voyages to Acadia   1604-1607

Champlain's route
Reference to map in text   e.g. (fig. 28)

Indian communities 🛖   French settlements ⚜

Furthest point of exploration by year   e.g. 1604

Cartographic design by Joe C. W. Armstrong
Graphic design by Linda Gustafson

CHAMPLAIN

For Michael Bliss, A Champion for Canada
With Very Best Wishes,

"Champlain . . . . sets out with two vessels for New France, a country almost invented, one might say, out of his single brain . . . . This was a great adventurer, a tremendous energy, one of the foremost colonizers of our continent."

William Carlos Williams (1883-1963), *In the American Grain*, 1925

CHAMPLAIN

JOE C.W. ARMSTRONG

MACMILLAN OF CANADA

A Division of Canada Publishing Corporation
Toronto, Ontario, Canada

Canadian Cataloguing in Publication Data
Armstrong, Joe C. W.
   Champlain

Bibliography: p.
Includes index.
ISBN 0-7715-9501-8

1. Champlain, Samuel de, 1567-1635. 2. Explorers — Canada — Biography. 3. Explorers — France — Biography. 4. Canada — History — To 1663 (New France).* 5. America — Discovery and exploration — French.   I. Title.

FC332.A75 1987   971.01'13'0924   C87-094206-9
F1030.1.A75 1987

All inquiries regarding the motion picture or other dramatic rights for this book should be addressed to the author's representative, The Colbert Agency Inc., 303 Davenport Road, Toronto, Canada M5R 1K5. Representations as to the disposition of these rights are strictly prohibited without express written consent and will be vigorously pursued to the full extent of the law.

Design: Catherine Wilson for C. P. Wilson Graphic Communication
Endpaper maps graphic design: Linda Gustafson

Printed in Canada

For my son Geoffrey, with love

ACKNOWLEDGEMENTS

From Canada, France, Italy, and the United States, many people generously contributed information and assistance, and just a few of the names that deserve mention are: Denis Amyot, Serge Barbe, Chris Barron, John Berkart, Nancy Biehl, David and Ginny Butler, Morley Callaghan, Tim Campbell, Victorin Chabut, Louis Chippell, Father Denis Clement, Luca Codignola, Nina Cohen, Walt Collins, Father Coutant, Neil Currie, Edward Dahl, Susan Danforth, Father Edward Debono, Cynthia Dooley, Jacques Duval, Gerald Fox, Jacques Francoeur, Elisabeth Gross, Michelle Grouet, Angel Guerra, Rosemary Hache, Sister Rolande Hamel O.S.U., Gus Hurtubise, Jim Ingram, Tom and Beth Johnson, Walter Johnson, Patricia Kennedy, Wallace King, Mark Kinney, Sister Elaine Lachance O.S.U., André Laflamme, Mike Lavoie, Jean-Marie LeBlanc, Donald Lemon, Peter Levitt, Elizabeth Liszkowski, Neil McNeill, Bernard and Bea Martin, Diane Martineau, Martha Morden, Lucille Mulcahy, Kent Newcomb, Michael Newton, Paul Oxner, Alain Parent, Paul Patterson, Bruce Powell, Peter Pratt, Elisabeth Price, Michelle Quealey, Shirley Racine, Serge Sauer, Addie Shields, Lorne Ste. Croix, Carl Thorpe, Ron Tropea, Maija Vilcins, Philip and Elizabeth Walden, Everett Wilkie Jr., Ron Williamson, Michel Wycznki.

The author was also treated with courtesy in many libraries, art galleries, and museums, including: The Bibliothèque Nationale, Paris; The Reading Room, British Museum, London; The John Carter Brown Library, Providence, Rhode Island; The Charente-Maritime Archives, La Rochelle; The Library of Congress, Washington; The Thomas Fisher Rare Book Library, Toronto; The Metro Library of Toronto's Map Department, Canadian History Department, and Fine Arts Department; The Public Archives of Canada, Manuscript Division; Musée du Nouveau Monde, La Rochelle; The Widener, Harvard, Cambridge, Massachusetts.

The generous permission of The Champlain Society to quote extensively from their excellent edition of Champlain's journals is very gratefully acknowledged. The author is also grateful to the Ontario Arts Council for its support.

A very special note of appreciation is due to Stephen Sheridan of the Historic Sites Branch, Parks Canada, who joined in the Champlain treasure hunt concerning geographic points of interest; Kathleen Richards of Macmillan of Canada, a professional, who, as editor and friend, guided this work to final fruition, and finally, as before, my wife Barbara, the unwavering gentle force ever supportive of the commitment.

CONTENTS

PHASE FIVE: VOYAGES TO EXPAND THE EMPIRE WESTWARD: 1613-1616

PART II — THE FIGHT FOR THE FOUNDATION: 1616-1635

Maps and Illustrations

(NOTE: The dates shown indicate, as far as possible, the date of the drawing's creation unless otherwise noted)

PART I — THE VOYAGES: 1598-1616

PHASE ONE: WEST INDIES AND MEXICO

PHASE TWO: FIRST VOYAGE TO NORTH AMERICA

PHASE THREE: ACADIA

PHASE FOUR: THE ST. LAWRENCE: QUÉBEC, NEW YORK, VERMONT, ONTARIO

PHASE FIVE: VOYAGES TO EXPAND THE EMPIRE WESTWARD: 1613-1616

PART II — THE FIGHT FOR THE FOUNDATION: 1616-1635

Preface

SAMUEL DE CHAMPLAIN, THE SEAMAN FROM France, was the first great visionary to promote the development of the North American continent. Today, it is his dream that has survived as the French fact of America and more particularly as the nation of Canada. This work is about this man's life and it is also an examination of the cultural, social, political, and economic forces that formed the environmental bedrock for the first footsteps of the French in the colonial development of early America.

In 1976, many Canadians were awakened to the fact that Canada was threatened, as it still is, with political disintegration as a nation. It was on November 9 of that same year that the voters in Québec elected a provincial government dedicated to the separation of the Francophone heartland from the Canadian federation. Yet for most in North America, the English-speaking majority, this orderly result was a profound shock. Most Anglophones had lived their lives neatly walled from the French fact that now seemed to threaten political, cultural, and economic upheaval. Americans were concerned about this result, though they were more removed; not since December 20, 1860, when the State Legislature of South Carolina declared the American Union dissolved had an elected body on this continent endorsed the legal break-up of a nation through the democratic process. To me, a sixth-generation Canadian and an eleventh-generation American, there was one outstanding question: how was it possible that in Canada, a society universally considered one of the world's most fortunate, successful, and even happiest, such a dramatically retrograde step for a national federation could so nearly approach the threshold of political reality?

In the intervening years from 1976 to the present, nothing has happened to resolve this question. This cloud remains even though there was the defeat of a separatist referendum in 1980 in Québec and also the defeat of a separatist government in that province in 1985. Even though there was patriation of Canada's federal constitution in 1982, this legal step has concentrated primarily on the cultural confrontation of the English and the French. Then in 1987 all the first ministers of the land reached an accord that could lead to an apparent constitutional reconciliation of Québec as a partner on paper. Under this latest blanket proposal now known as the Meech Lake Accord, the legal authority to promote a distinct French society within a national federated state would, if legislated into law, be forever heralded as a democratic endorsement of Québec nationalism. This would be the unequivocal first legal step toward the realization of the separatist goal of Sovereignty-Association.

Deeply concerned in 1976, I made the decision to pursue a quest of my own for the origins of French colonization in Canada. It soon became evident to me as I started my research that the beginning of French culture in this country can be traced to the life of Samuel de Champlain, the seaman from Brouage, France. It is with him that those who pursue this quest of comprehension must first sail and then move onward in steadfast companionship.

Completing this journey has taken nearly a decade. In the course of my research, writing, and exploration, I have travelled some nine thousand miles in order to personally discover the memorials and monuments (over one hundred of them), voyage routes, and trails of Champlain in France, Canada, the United States, and the West Indies.

For the first time, the Olympian saga of the founding father of Canada is offered more in keeping with the format of the original Champlain journals. They are my major reference source for the biography. Here, too, is the entire Champlain inventory of cartography and illustrations pertaining to North America. Champlain provided extensive illustrative material in support of his own text, much of which has been either ignored or technically diminished and downplayed. Yet his graphics are essential to understanding: the maps and drawings establish a strong visual perspective and theatrical setting. Champlain often employs these drawings as stage props and cue cards of the drama against which he plays his many roles as the playwright, director, and principal actor in his story. By restoring the cartography and graphic art to its original, intended prominence, we are able to see Champlain the chronicler and diarist beyond the historical restraints of his age, the ancien régime of seventeenth-century France. Whether he depicted a porcupine as big as a mountain, a beaver on all fours, or a whale blowing water like a knocked-over fire hydrant, Champlain created captivating graphics that help to provide realism which enlivens the often saint-like drudgery of his more sober penmanship. (Where consideration of a map or other illustration pertains to the text, a reference to the illustration is provided; e.g. figure 26.)

In the main Champlain's own testimony as provided by his journals is the primary source material for any work about this figure, and I have taken them at face value. Yet I have done so with discretion. Infrequently, I have felt it necessary to pose an alternative perspective, challenge a longstanding tradition, question some new theory, or even simply to enlarge the point being presented. There is a dangerous range of conjecture open to the historian studying the complex period of the ancien régime. The distinguished American historian Barbara W. Tuchman claims that, in the writing of history, she does "not invent anything, not even the weather." However, regardless of one's good intentions, the very writing about any age long past involves a subjective organization of the historical material under consideration. The success of the historian is measured by the standard of the celebrated French philosopher of history Paul Veyne: "The first duty of the historian is to establish the truth and the second is to make the plot understood; history has a critique but has no method, for there is no method to understand." Such an understanding requires that the historian acknowledge the limits of his or her revelation and personal biases.

It will be clear to readers of this work that I view Champlain as a great heroic figure. Not all who write of this same period agree with my assessment and, according to a few recently published works, there are now more fashionable concepts boasted both from the academic arena and from journalists and generalists now digging in the dungeons of the past. In prologues and epilogues, and even within the body of any historical work, objectivity was in the past traditionally claimed by earnest professional historians. There is now all manner of new notions and liberal license from those who confidently espouse new standards, such as derivative regurgitation of the works of one's predecessors. Perhaps such a method implies that revelation is at last at hand through sheer tonnage of paper alone. But the business of the historian is not so simple. As always, the task remains exquisitely painstaking, tedious, and full of flaws. The historian's limits are legion: those inherent in the information itself as well as the frailties of its practitioners. The task is frustrating beyond measure, and exhilarating for those who relentlessly strive within its boundaries to reach the truth. One of the many reasons I wrote this book was to urge a return to the great historical tradition.

I am prompted to note three prominent published examples that have, in my view, trivialized the Champlain legacy. On the academic frontier, Bruce G. Trigger, Professor of Anthropology at McGill University, in a comprehensive and widely circulated work, *Natives and Newcomers: Canada's "Heroic Age" Reconsidered* (see Bibliography), substantially downgrades Champlain's position in history, and then, in a chapter note at the end of his work, draws the conclusion that all the Champlain historical biographies to date have been "for the most part works of hagiography" — saint worship! Trigger's work challenges a hefty chunk of the stonemasonry of the cultural foundation of the French fact in early America.

This negative attitude is not without glib support. No less a figure than the aspirant leader of the new nation he had in prospect, the founding father of Separatism, René Lévesque, ex-premier of Québec, offered this put-down in his 1986 published *Mémoirs*: "Champlain? Not very stimulating, the old founding father. His wife seems to have been a lot more fun. Poor guy, always stuck with the building of his Habitation at Québec with the English overrunning it time and again . . . ." Apart from the historical distortions of his remarks (e.g., Champlain's Habitation was only captured once by the English), with this lack of pride in the French heritage, no wonder the revolution failed!

Even the celebrated author and Canadian nationalist Pierre Berton has managed a dismissal notice for Champlain. In his popular book *My Country*, the Founding Father of the nation is shrugged off as merely "an assassin."

In Part I, *The Voyages: 1598-1616*, the French exploration vessels sailed the Atlantic Ocean between France and America for sixteen years. Champlain is both witness and guide to many trials and triumphs on the journey, through his frequent comments from the original journals.

Part II, *The Fight for the Foundation: 1616-1635*, deals with Champlain's lengthy struggle to seed and preserve the settlement foundation. This section examines the personal actions of the players and their social and political context.

The book is further divided into "phases" of Champlain's life, reflecting his changing interests in many fields — navigator, warrior, naturalist, political lobbyist, cartographer, administrator and ethnographer.

Original sources have been generously used and the explorer's testimony in his journals is of course ranked first. The Champlain

Society's *The Works of Samuel de Champlain* (6 vols., 1922–1936) edited by H. P. Biggar is the invaluable central authority. Other primary sources include the 73-volume set *The Jesuit Relations and Allied Documents: a selection* edited by R. G. Thwaites(1896–1901). (References to The Champlain Society edition of the journals are noted by volume and page; e.g. II: 273.)

It must be noted that Champlain's journals are replete with factual and publishing errors in their chronology and, on rare occasions, in the location of specific events and the specific dates that are noted. For clarification of most of these, another book would be required. Most of these errors are of a trivial nature and many of the more obvious ones have already been aptly identified as deserving scrutiny; changes for many have already been suggested in the Champlain Society's publication of Champlain's works. Where possible and convincing, however, more recent scholarship has been used.

The contribution of lawyer and poet Marc Lescarbot (c. 1570–1630), who wrote *L'Histoire de la Nouvelle France* (Paris, 1609), provides valuable insight for the short period covered, and as a source it is discussed more extensively in Chapter Nine. (Where quotes are taken from The Champlain Society edition of his works, the notation refers to the page (e.g., C[hamplain] S[ociety]-L[escarbot]: 111.) Other works such as *Long Journey to the Country of the Hurons* (*Le Grand Voyage du Pays des Hurons . . .*) by the Récollet lay brother Gabriel Sagard, also published by The Champlain Society (as are the works of Lescarbot), is another gem. As well, many manuscript documents — over 300 — ranging from bills of sale to pay receipts have been culled for new perceptions and hitherto skimmed-over detail. Along these lines, Volume 1 of *Champlain: son époque*, the 1967 centennial Government of Canada publication heralding the work of the Public Archives of Canada, is an essential tool which, one hopes, may some day be joined by a publication of the documents related to the latter period of the Champlain era and will also include some of the more recent finds that have since surfaced.

Among the treasures most certain to be included in any second volume about the Champlain era will be one very significant document — an affidavit executed in Cádiz, Spain, in 1601, by which Champlain inherited considerable wealth from his uncle, "Captain Provençal." This "Rip Van Winkle" find, which should have been included in the first of the Public Archives volumes, has explosive implications. In view of the document's importance and the fact that it has not been published before, it has been translated from Spanish into English for the first time and is included along with a detailed discussion in Appendix II.

The reader is also notified, especially in view of the general audience for which this work is intended, that many names have been shortened to facilitate the reading of this work. Hence the Sieur Jean Biencourt de Poutrincourt, for example, becomes simply the Sieur de Poutrincourt. Also some very minor changes have been made to the translation where necessary, particularly where archaic or even confusing terminology has been employed in the translation of the original journals.

In the discovery of North America, there is no adventure as grand as the epic saga of Samuel de Champlain. As well as being a heroic figure in the discovery and settlement foundation of North America, Champlain is one of the greatest sons of France. It is hoped that this tribute to a champion will further better understanding of his golden legacy as well as provide fun and adventure for all who live and dream of new horizons in life.

Je me souviens

PART I
THE VOYAGES:
1598 - 1616

CHAPTER ONE

The Setting of New France and the France of Champlain

"France has been so embroiled,
the last few years, that what is
chiefly sought is peace; and
there is no money to spend on [exploration]."

Champlain, *Les Voyages*, 1632

THE STORY OF FRANCE'S GREATEST EXPLORER AND voyageur begins in 1567 with the birth of Samuel de Champlain in Brouage, France. But beginning in the early years of the sixteenth century, long before Champlain's birth, fishermen from France had been making seasonal crossings of the Atlantic Ocean to the American continent in order to harvest the riches of the sea: trading with the Indians for fur pelts, and exploring the possibility of settlement. Then, in the last decades of the sixteenth century, while European nations were consuming themselves with war and waste, a few ambitious people began to prepare themselves for further exploratory ventures. These men and women yearned for a better and more peaceful way of life, and their search for that life led them to become the first voyageurs and habitants to seed a French empire in the New World.

Under the crown of France, those who mustered this vibrant trickle of humanity were the men of consortiums, corporations, church, and militia. Most who came, whether as freemen, or under contract, were of lesser rank and included carpenters, locksmiths, tailors and weavers, bakers, butchers, candlemakers, shoemakers, ironmongers, stonemasons, and even pin makers. In this lineup of hungering humanity were those without status, the legions of society's dislocated: the

2

impoverished, those uprooted by war, and countless numbers from cells and dungeons charged with all manner of crimes — from insult to murder. All these souls of Mother France, rich and poor, were veterans of deeply troubled times, and they believed that their search for a better way of life was a revelation of divine inspiration.

It was with this confident sense of purpose — and in the belief that God's commands were being carried out — that France in a dark age shuttled her sons to a world called New France. These veterans of the Old World were called upon to settle the land and make it fruitful and to seek souls and convert them to Christ.

But on arrival at this frontier of promise, the hopeful immigrants found yet another hostile environment. This land was not a panorama of rolling plains, grassy meadows, regal forests, and bountiful fields fed by a thousand nutrient streams, as was much of France. For the summer invader of this new empire in the raw, there were great riches, but also a price to be paid for wresting the wealth from the rugged surroundings. The newcomers were ever under the assault of the blackfly and mosquito. And for the winter intruder determined to endure, the offering of this wilderness was, in the main, an unending struggle against cold, whipping winds, and deep snow. For those who risked this frontier, there was a lonely life of anxiety, a poverty of needed provisions, and all manner of new and terrible ailments, which were a constant reminder of the frailty of man.

As well as pitting themselves against nature, these adventurous French were greeted on the shores of New France by Indians who, in order to preserve their own way of life, had to defy this assault, bargain for its restraint, and daily ply for its diminution. The Indians had possessory title to the land but lived without that concept. In bands or as nations, either bound in federations or not, loosely connected and otherwise, they confronted the trespassers who could only lay claim to ownership by contrivance or force. For, in the beginning, the only land deeds to North America were the wind whispers of the names given by the native nations. In the large Algonquin family, there were the lands of the Abenaki, Malecite, Micmac, and Ojibway; in the even larger Iroquois nation there were the lands of Cayuga, Mohawk, Oneida, Onandaga, and Seneca. For the French, much instructed in matters of religion, these names rang out like a biblical call-sheet of long-lost tribes from another millennium, and soon they too, in harmony, added their own names to these masters of the forest: the Huron of Ontario, the Montagnais of Québec, and the Almouchiquois of Maine and Massachusetts.

It was under these conditions that the seaman Samuel de Champlain, a French soldier of fortune with private means, disembarked for the first time on the North American continent at Tadoussac, the wilderness trading post on the St. Lawrence River in 1603.

Tadoussac was the first of many "meeting places" between European and Indian to be established on this gaping inland waterway named in the summer of 1535 by its discoverer, Jacques Cartier of Saint-Malo, France (1491–1557). Cartier was the same seaman who in 1541 had abandoned the region, allegedly remarking that it was "the land God gave to Cain." Yet Cartier's lack of success in seeding an empire for his King was not the only failure. In the years that followed, French attempts at permanent settlement on the continent were frequent and always unsuccessful. Jean Ribaut (c. 1520–1565) and René Laudonnière (fl. 1562–1582), who built Charlesfort on Parris Island, South Carolina, and Fort Caroline (now Jacksonville) at the mouth of the St. Johns River, Florida, also claimed these southerly lands for France: but as far as colonial development in this era was concerned, possession was 100 percent of the law, and their massacre by the Spaniards in 1565 quickly terminated their ill-conceived enterprise.

Even by the time that Champlain landed for the first time at Tadoussac, the more recent attempts at settlement were nothing more than additional episodes in a long litany of disasters. In an experiment just before the turn of the century, a penal colony was established in 1598 by the Marquis de La Roche (c. 1540–1606) on wind-swept Sable Island off the coast of Nova Scotia. By 1603, it had collapsed in an orgy of anarchy and murder after its residents were driven to madness by starvation and cruel neglect. At the end, on this desolate sandbar, only eleven of a band of fifty French ex-convicts and their Swiss soldier guards were alive to be rescued. The mercy mission that would carry the survivors back to France arrived just weeks before Champlain set foot ashore at Tadoussac.

Even at Tadoussac the settlement saga was not a happy tale. In 1599, Pierre Chauvin, a wealthy merchant from Honfleur, had obtained a monopoly in the fur trade and permission to build a trading post on the site. Sixteen settlers attempted to survive the first winter; but the result of this gamble was the loss of eleven hapless souls because of bickering and starvation. This tragedy occurred despite the support in the region of a trader experienced in dealing with the Indians: François Gravé (du Pont), or Pontgravé (c. 1554–c. 1629).

From 1504 — when French fishermen from Brittany were jettisoned onto the shore of America in a storm — through the voyages of Giovanni da Verrazzano (c. 1485–c. 1528) [the Venetian commissioned by the Renaissance King Francis I (reigned 1515–47)], and on into the opening years of the seventeenth century, there were no land winnings for France. In fact, as far as French colonial development was concerned, the North American continent for the entire sixteenth century was only a theater for bad dress rehearsals.

The arrival of Champlain, an experienced observer, chronicler, navigator, and soldier of fortune, signaled a change. It was this seaman who cultivated the idea of colonial development, and then persisted throughout his lifetime to personally and repeatedly ensure that this concept was transported from the ancien régime of France to the shores of New France. Champlain had a new perspective that called for the unveiling of the American continent rather than the simple continued exploitation of the coastal trade and offshore fishing grounds. It was because of his determined efforts — and those of a handful of his like-minded supporters — that the wealth of the continent was finally exposed and advertised for the legions to follow. From 1603 onward, as a result of Champlain's discoveries and written communications, continuous new settlement foundations took root: first in 1604 at Île Sainte-Croix (now Dochet Island) in Maine (fig. 11), succeeded by a relocation of this settlement in 1605 to Port-Royal, Nova Scotia (fig. 16), and on to Québec in 1608 (fig. 24), the first French settlement in North America to survive as an ongoing community.

From the beginning, the land grab in early America was a heated international race. In 1607, the year that the French abandoned the Acadian coast (including what is now the New England coast) after the cancellation of a legal trading commission, the English established both Jamestown in Virginia and the Popham settlement at Phippsburg, at the mouth of the Kennebec River in Maine. Two years earlier, Champlain had completed an extensive survey and completed a chart (fig. 12) of this area. By 1609, just a few weeks after Champlain had pushed southward from the St. Lawrence River into Iroquoia (New York state), Henry Hudson, sailing for the Dutch, had pressed northward up the river that would one day be named after him. The discoveries of these two men were less than a hundred miles (160 km) apart. In 1605, fifteen years before the *Mayflower* landed at Plymouth, Massachussetts, Champlain had produced a detailed chart of Port Saint-Louis (later Plymouth Harbor) (fig. 14). This chart had been published in Europe seven years before the New Englanders arrived.

The territorial struggle endured long after the French were defeated militarily at Québec in 1759, and after the English were defeated by General George Washington — with the aid of the French — in the American Revolution of 1776–1781. In 1782, Jean-François de La Pérouse (1741–1788) led a successful French naval attack and seized the York Fort and Prince of Wales Fort on Hudson Bay; and, as late as 1812, the Napoleonic Wars once again polarized alignments between English and French interests in North America.

Champlain was at the foundation of the French fact in North America. His legendary baton of discovery, exploration, and cultural germination was lifted by many in the years following his death in 1635. In 1673, Louis Jolliet (c. 1645–1700) followed the route described by the Indians and Champlain into the heart of the continent, and discovered the "father of waters," the mighty Mississippi. In 1743, the ubiquitous La Vérendrye brothers pushed through the great western plains of America to North Dakota to the foothills of the Rockies. One encyclopedia lists twenty-three out of fifty American states that were explored or discovered by the French, and in Canada the record includes all ten provinces.

The Champlain story is a Homeric saga of early America. Champlain crossed the ocean to and from North America twenty-nine times, and he voyaged over a hundred thousand miles (161,000 km) under sail. The list of his achievements is a triumphant march for first place. This is the first explorer who can be documented on site as having discovered the Great Lakes, and what are now New York state and Ontario. He is also the first to provide chronological and comprehensive visual imagery of the exploration process. As an illustrator, he furnished details of the geography, habitations, wildlife, and historical events experienced in territory that now comprises four states and five provinces. He produced the first urban plans and architectural drawings of America at Île Sainte-Croix, Maine (fig. 10), and Québec City (fig. 25). His maps of the Atlantic seaboard from Cape Cod, Massachusetts to Cape Breton, Nova Scotia are so clear they can still be used today. Furthermore, his detailed cartography of the interior of the continent was not only the first in the field; it established the standard of navigational and surveying science that prevailed for almost a century. In the course of his lifetime, Champlain published four books, one of which includes a treatise on seamanship. Champlain was a chameleon who played many roles: he took the part of naturalist, soldier, ethnographer, arbitrator, diplomat, administrator, promoter, and playwright. He was also the first to undertake feasibility studies of North America. In the span of just over three decades — from 1603 to his death in 1635 — this crusader enlarged the colonial perspective for his countrymen and others to a vista of the entire continent. In the history of geographic exploration and the colonial development of the North American continent, there is no other of his caliber.

Traditionally, and with a note of paternal affection, Champlain is recognized as the "Father of New France," but a growing number of people now recognize him as the "Founding Father of Canada." He is also recorded by some, following the practice of the Jesuits in the seventeenth century, as the first governor of Canada, although he was never officially or even informally given this rank.

❧

In the history of France, the name Samuel de Champlain is recorded for the first time at the end of the sixteenth century. But there is no contemporary record of Champlain's birth, and indeed, for the first thirty years of his life, there is almost nothing known of him save an isolated comment on his youth provided in his own journal.

In 1852, over two hundred years after Champlain's death, his birth was recorded in the biographical records of his home province of Saintonge. It was given as 1567, although no source for choosing this particular date was cited. Today, many scholars round off the year of his birth to the year 1570. For the purpose of this book, we will use 1567.

Champlain, the seaman from the port of Brouage, on the Bay of Biscay, was born into a turbulent period in French history — a period characterized by wars of religion and social upheaval. He lived his entire life during the period now known as the ancien régime. It is generally considered to be the most sterile in the nation's history. Most North Americans, including the vast majority of French Canadians, have a vaguely romantic and inaccurate perspective regarding the period of French history during which colonial development occurred. Previously, Canada's colonial legacy had been wedded to either the French Renaissance or the reign of the Sun King, Louis XIV (1638–1715). It occurred, however, in the period between — the period of the ancien régime. It was, as the French historian Pierre Goubert described it, "a society of positively cultivated confusion."

When Samuel de Champlain was born, the great Renaissance King,

Francis I (1494–1547) had been dead for twenty years. Francis I left two legacies. The first was a chain of incredible chateaus, palaces, museums, and libraries. The second was a repressive policy toward religious "reformers", which was adopted late in his reign when he was seriously ill and could no longer hold back the power of the Catholic Church.

John Calvin, the leader of these reformers, was exiled to Geneva where he continued to preach. By 1562, five years before the birth of Champlain, hundreds of Calvinist churches had sprung up in France to challenge both the Catholic Church and the monarchy. It is interesting to note that these Calvinists, or Huguenots as they were called, were strongest in the port towns of Normandy and Brittany, areas that would subsequently provide many of the colonists for New France.

The astoundingly rapid spread of Calvinism, apparently gave the Queen Mother, Catherine de Médicis, cause for grave concern. An insightful woman, who was ruling in the name of her young son, Charles IX (1550–1574), Catherine saw that repression was doing nothing to stop the growth of Protestantism. In fact, the more it was repressed, the faster it seemed to grow. In 1561, Catherine summoned the French clergy in an unsuccessful attempt to achieve a religious compromise with the Huguenots. The following year, she issued the Edict of January, which allowed the Huguenots a measure of freedom. But the Catholics, and primarily the noble House of Guise, the champions of Catholicism in France, reacted violently to the Edict. In 1562, partisans of François, duc de Guise (1519–1563), massacred a Huguenot congregation at Vassy, thus beginning the first of the religious wars. They would last until Samuel de Champlain was thirty.

France, with some twenty million people, was the most populous country in Europe. With 85 percent of its population engaged in farming, it was an agrarian nation that, despite years of disruption owing to war, had experienced no large demographic shifts. Even in times of war and social change, the French were fundamentally sedentary and conservative.

In this society, each individual not only came from some place identified by current residence or birth, but carried his geographic nomenclature with him, attached to his name as if branded. Captain Guillaume Hellaine, Champlain's uncle by marriage, was known as the Provençal uncle because he came from that region. Another example of this geographical identification was Champlain's patron, the nobleman Pierre du Gua de Monts (c. 1558–1628). He was identified only geographically, as the Sieur de Monts (not to be confused with another Sieur de Monts who was a royal commissioner in New France, c. 1662).

During this period, the countryside of France was dotted with hundreds of hamlets, villages, seaports, large and small estates, as well as with grand chateaus. All these areas of settlement were in some way fortified, and yet connected by roads, rivers, and coastal waters that fostered the formation of a national society. It has been estimated that today there are some twenty-seven thousand rivers in France; in Champlain's time there were even more rivers and, although these provided the major form of transportation, man also contributed by building roads. In the first decade of the seventeenth century, the duc de Sully (1559–1641), first minister to King Henry IV (1553–1610), could boast that France had eighteen thousand miles (28,000 km) of surfaced road, the most in all of Europe.

The geography of France has always been an open invitation to invaders. Only the mountain barriers of the Pyrenees and the Alps to the south and southeast have ever presented a topographic challenge to those bent on the conquest of what was once Caesar's Gaul. For those who have lived in this region over the centuries, there has always been a strong military presence in the country to serve as a reminder that this land is a land exposed. Three ocean coasts constitute two thirds of the country's perimeter: Normandy, Brittany, and the Bay of Biscay; and along the Latin shoreline to the south, the Mediterranean Sea. Had nature only gone one step further and scissored off Spain at the Pyrenees, France would have been just one large vulnerable peninsula attached to Europe. During Champlain's time, France was involved not only in civil conflict, e.g., the Wars of Religion, but in wars with Italy, Spain, and her perennial rival, England. The apron of Calais, it will be remembered, was once English territory, and England seldom failed to intervene in uprisings in French coastal areas. One such intervention in 1627, albeit one complicated by other factors including a tempestuous royal marriage, was to have a profound effect on Champlain's struggle to establish the Québec colony.

In Champlain's France, there were only a few sizable urban centers, but these were the nodal points of great legal, military, and commercial power. Paris, with a population of over 300,000, was the largest capital in Europe, and it was also the fulcrum of the nation's business. We know that after the age of thirty Champlain was a frequent visitor to Paris, where he came not only to do business with the Crown but to return as a citizen to his matrimonial home. In this city, the great colonial advocate was in contact with kings, princes of the Church, and members of the nobility, as well as with publishers, engravers, and all manner of merchants and their agents.

In Paris, Champlain also witnessed the great extremes of wealth and poverty. Although the fortress walls of the city rose to a height of twenty-eight feet (8.5 m) in order to withstand attacks from outside, the greater threat was the poor standard of living for those within who daily struggled to eke out mere existence. While Champlain reached out for financing during the height of his explorations overseas, there were not enough funds to combat the sewage problems that plagued the daily lives of the residents. Wooden clogs and leather halters for the noses of the noblemen and the better-off bourgeoisie were the minimum accoutrements needed to ward off the stench while venturing along many streets layered with filth. In Paris in these times, the destitute were so numerous they had to vie for the red and yellow crosses to wear on their sleeves as proof of entitlement to public relief. In spite of deprivation, however, the city was also a bustling center of commerce with a growing merchant class. Two years after Champlain's death (1635), one report prepared by the Spaniards in anticipation of conquering France, noted the existence of hundreds of arts and crafts guilds with a membership of some 38,000, a figure that did not include the 5,600 apprentices in service.

But all was not well in Champlain's France in spite of its commercial prowess. Francis I had nearly bankrupted the nation, and the civil strife and religious wars that followed his death caused rampant fiscal anarchy and technological obsolescence. France was a land of shortages, inflation, and undisciplined markets. The precious metals — gold and silver — were hoarded by the rich and were even woven into the grand tapestries of the great chateaus built in a prior age. During the entire ancien régime, however, from the Renaissance of Francis I through to the beginning of the French Revolution, any form of metal was scarce and unavailable to the vast peasant population. Most farm implements, e.g., the plow and the rake, were still being made of wood, and technologically all industry languished somewhere between the stone age and the iron age. In 1615, the noted dramatist, exiled swordsman, and founder of the French steel industry, Antoine de Montchrétien (c. 1575–1621) completed an industrial survey of the Netherlands and England. Both these countries were using metal in a variety of ways and prospering because their tools were vastly superior to the tools used by the French. Montchrétien urged reforms in France, but his plea was ignored.

In Champlain's youth, only the textile industry, which provided 5 percent of the national income, suggested the existence of any sizable enterprise.

In addition to its financial and technological problems, Champlain's France was not a country where rapid change could be easily accomplished. All change, especially in economic areas, was inhibited by an awesome bureaucracy. (See Notes for this chapter.)

The supreme arbiter in France was the king, and in these times the monarchy ruled according to the doctrine of absolutism. "Sovereignty is no more divisible than the geometric point," wrote the noted jurist Le Bret in 1632.

In France, the most direct vehicle of the monarch's authority was the royal edict — the imprimatur of the monarch's command. A royal edict, however, did not have the force of law until it was registered and published. In order for this to occur, it had to be approved by the appropriate *parlement*. The French word *parlement* is not to be confused with the English word "parliament", for, although they share the same root, *parlement* is a historic term referring to a specific institution quite different from the elected parliaments of today. During this period of French history, the *parlement* developed out of the *curia regis* (King's court), and was composed of principal nobles and prelates who met periodically to debate feudal and political matters, and to deal with legal cases submitted to the King as sovereign judge. In turn, the most powerful nobles of France's regions also had *parlements* composed of their own minor nobles and prelates. By the beginning of the seventeenth century, when Champlain was nearly thirty, there were no fewer than seven provincial *parlements* in France, in addition to the monarch's *parlement* in Paris. In no sense were the *parlements* legislative bodies, but they were powerful sovereign authorities whose primary duty was that of publishing and implementing the King's commands. Although they were in effect high courts of law, their powers of interpretation were limited. Nonetheless, within their respective jurisdictions, their powers of implementation upon registration were sweeping. In secular France, the order of the social structure gravitated around these darkly robed centurions of the Latin legacy.

Above the *parlements* in the various regions of France were the noble families who served the King. The nobility's own authority was under attack from a growing military and merchant class that would, over the next two hundred years, completely erode the authority of the *parlements*. But during Champlain's time, the battle against feudal control advanced and took hold.

Champlain's Mother France was neither a federation nor a republic; neither was it like the Roman Empire, under imperial rule. It was a monarchy in a state of disunity, fraught with religious wars. Powerful nobles rose to defend their faiths, and in so doing challenged the absolute power of the throne. The internal chaos of Champlain's France is highlighted by the following quotations. "Men never do evil so completely and cheerfully as when they do it from religious conviction," wrote the philosopher Blaise Pascal (1623–1662). "Recourse was had to arms for slight reasons or for no reason," testified the noted European jurist Hugo Grotius in 1625. "Warfare in Europe was so prolonged and so indecisive; smouldering away like wet blood, inflicting continuous damage on the countryside like some chronic disease to which the patient had philosophically, if miserably, resigned himself"; such is the summation of the English military historian Michael Howard.

Before Champlain's birth, the chaotic and deadly Catholic-versus-Huguenot struggle was further complicated by what came to be known as the Counter-Reformation. Like the Reformation, it also had its origins during the reign of Francis I. His liberal-minded sister, Marguerite de Navarre, who had once sheltered Calvin, called for a reformation within the Catholic Church itself to answer those who would pull away from it and leave forever by founding their own Protestant movements.

Marguerite de Navarre died in 1549, four years after the Council of Trent was convened to consider reform from within the Catholic Church. This Council continued its deliberations until 1563 when, as a result of its decisions, many abuses were abolished, such as the demand for money before the administration of the sacraments. The reforms did not, however, satisfy the Huguenot reformers; thus, the struggle continued. It must also be added that the reforms within the Church were not immediately adhered to by all. The reformation of the Catholic Church, both from within and by outside reformation, involved far more than a battle for men's souls. It was a struggle for economic power as well.

Ten years before the Council of Trent was convened, an important religious initiative had been taken in Spain. In 1534, the Spanish nobleman Ignatius of Loyola founded the Society of Jesus. Loyola commanded his following to "stand like an anvil when it is beaten upon." By the time that Loyola published his *Spiritual Exercises* in 1548, the order had gained a fierce following, and its members had come to be known as Jesuits.

The Jesuits were not alone. There were other missions that had been formalized to carry out the work of the Catholic Church; among these were the Récollets, a Franciscan order — an army of salvation known for its commitment to community. This order had been in existence for several hundred years and included orders for both men and women. To join either the Jesuits or the Franciscans, a candidate had to undertake vows of chastity, poverty, and obedience. Blind willingness to follow was not enough. There had to be subordination of all intellectual and emotional opposition in favor of enthusiastic support. The brethren of these orders were handcuffed in a lifelong partnership between God and His Church on earth. These were the crusaders for Christ who would accompany Champlain to America.

There was no peace in France for the first three decades of Champlain's life. In 1572, when Champlain was five years old, the Catholic Marguerite de Valois married the Protestant Henry III of Navarre (later to become Henry IV, King of France). Three thousand Huguenots gathered to celebrate the wedding on Saint Bartholomew's Day; they were massacred in an uprising of furious Catholics. And all over the country Huguenots, some ten thousand in all, were murdered.

Three years later, King Henry III (1551–1589) joined with the Catholic League to fight the Protestant heresy. Debauched, violent, and homosexual, he was stabbed to death in 1589. Under Salic law, which prohibited female succession, the will of this troubled King who died without heirs provided that the aforementioned Protestant Henry of Navarre (1553–1610) should be his successor, to rule as King Henry IV of France.

Not until Henry IV ascended the throne did the conflict subside with the issuance of the Edict of Nantes — a royal command that ordered a compromise. Henry IV reigned from 1589 to 1610, and was to be Champlain's first commander in chief.

Henry IV was a man of great personal charm, a handsome red-bearded rake, much loved by his people. He was reputed to have some fifty-six mistresses and many bastard children; but for all his philandering, his sharpest critic and first minister, the Duc de Sully, was satisfied that in affairs of state, the king also showed ample commitment: "He was candid, sincere, grateful, compassionate, generous, wise, penetrating . . . he loved his subjects as a father, and the whole state as the head of a family." The evidence is convincing that this was a King in search of higher purpose and one whose own prayer for "victory over passions and especially sensuality" had been answered by the Almighty. With the signing of the Edict of Nantes in 1598, engineered by King Henry, there was, for a brief period only, peace in the land as there was a concord between the Catholic and Huguenot interests. Although there were serious inequities as a result, this rare moment in the history of the ancien régime provided a tiny window of opportunity for leadership energies to be devoted to social and economic issues. Exploration and colonial development were the healthy consequences of this momentary respite in the religious conflict.

There are some comments that survive from those few who chose to remark on the values of the age in this land where only 2 percent of the population could read.

Champlain's contemporary for one year in Acadia, Marc Lescarbot, wrote that France was the "fair eye of the universe, nurse from of old, of letters and of arms, resource of the afflicted, strong stay of the Christian religion, dearest Mother." He was wrong; this was not a peaceful and pensive society and it was not ready, even in 1638, three years after Champlain's death, for René Descartes's (1596–1650) soft call to reason: "I think therefore I am." Rather, this was a time for defence and retreat. It was a cynical age. "Live now, believe me, wait not till tomorrow; gather the roses of life today" was the advice of the nation's poet Pierre de Ronsard (1525–1585). Outside the mainstream of Christianity, the Jesuit-trained lawyer turned dramatist Jean Bodin (1530–1596) instructed that any of seven different creeds offered an equal chance for paradise. It was an age for the quick turn of a phrase; "I treated him, God cured him" was the remark that won for Ambroise Paré (c. 1517–1590) more notoriety for his wit than for his medical skill. And for others disoriented and wandering in this world of mystery and madness, there were always the cosmic prognostications of Nostradamus (1503–1566), that career gadfly physician who before Champlain's birth allegedly discovered how to prevent the plague and whose prophecies ever since have been cited to predict everything from the murder of Champlain's royal patron King Henry IV in 1610 to the two world wars in the twentieth century. One reporter of the period noted: "No more than a few thousand people died for the crime of witchcraft between 1560 and 1570"; but another noted that in one case six witches "were held responsible for two to three hundred murders and then confessed to having eaten the hearts of children to quench their blood lust." These were bad times, and not until 1624 did the Paris *parlement* abolish the infamous water test. To undergo this test the accused was bound with weights and thrown into a tank of water. The "witch" who floated to the top in a tank of water was innocent, but those who drowned were proclaimed guilty. Few, if any, floated innocently. In France, for most, this was only the worst of times.

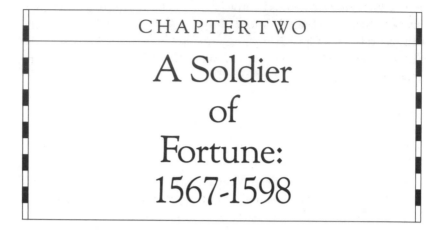

CHAPTER TWO

A Soldier of Fortune: 1567-1598

"From my childhood, the art of navigation has won my love."

Champlain, *Les Voyages*, 1613,
Letter to Queen Marie de Médicis

SAMUEL DE CHAMPLAIN WAS BORN IN BROUAGE, A thriving seaport on the salt-bed fens of the Biscay coast in the south of France. The community is located some eighteen miles (30 km) south of the great walled sea fortress of La Rochelle, which was a Protestant stronghold in Champlain's time. As a result of Champlain's only comment about his youth, there has been much romantic speculation as to the influence of this regional geography on his life, as well as to the influence that his father, a seaman, may have exerted. But the dominant factor of Champlain's youth was the religious persecutions and wars that consumed France and that were particularly fierce in the area where he lived. During his youth alone, there were no less than nine bloody confrontations in France, including the worst, which occurred when he was only five years old — the Massacre of Saint Bartholomew's Day in 1572.

Many of the hundreds of Huguenot leaders who had come to France from Switzerland before Champlain was born settled in the coastal areas. As a result of this thrust, the seaport of Brouage, and its larger urban neighbor to the north, La Rochelle, where Champlain was to inherit property, became Protestant strongholds over the years.

The salt, harvested in abundance from the surrounding marshlands, made Brouage a coveted community as early as the year

1047 when the marshlands belonged to a nobleman of the Saintonge district, Geoffrey Martel, and his wife Agnes. The land was then transferred to the Church. By 1374, the bay of Brouage, then of great interest to the Crown, was incorporated into the royal domain; in 1380 by letters patent, the treasured fens were donated by the French King Charles V (1337–1380) to the Seigneur de Pons as a handsome reward for the support that the feudal baron had rendered to his monarch during the wars against the English. Nearly two centuries later, Jacques de Pons of the same seigneury gave the community of Brouage its first name, Jacopolis.

By the middle of the sixteenth century, Brouage, as it was becoming known, was recognized as a major port where hundreds of ships from England, Portugal, the Netherlands, and Germany — as well as the "little sardines", those plucky undersized vessels from other French ports — came to barter for the cones of dried salt harvested from the largest saline marsh of Europe. The seamen came regularly to these fens, for salt was more than a dietary necessity at sea: it was the basis of brine, the all-purpose preservative for meat and fish, and the indispensable lubricant of ocean travel in a world without refrigeration. Perhaps in the summer of 1576, the nine-year-old Samuel de Champlain witnessed the arrival of Henry of Navarre, who would one day be his King, in his home town. Perhaps he also watched the arrival of seventeen ships commissioned by the Paris entrepreneur Claude Daubray, who had seized a commercial opportunity to replenish Paris's supply of the precious mineral. Writing at the end of the sixteenth century, the journalist Nicolas Alain described Brouage as "a port celebrated throughout all of Europe."

Throughout the sixteenth century, the monarchs, military leaders, and legions of France, ever more alert to the strategic and commercial importance of the port, visited Brouage on a regular basis. Sometimes they came to exert political influence or, if necessary, to carry out bloody business for the control of this port and its resource. Brouage was accessible to visitors by sea, or by the more leisurely route through the clam-bedded canals of the marshlands.

After the outbreak of the Wars of Religion in 1562, King Charles IX (1550–1574), a Catholic, paid a personal visit to Brouage in 1565, for he considered the security of this region essential to his military strategy. Early in the year 1570, when Champlain was three, the local commander in residence, La Rivière Puytaille, commenced the construction of the first ramparts of the Brouage fortress under the direction of the King's engineers. All this was in preparation against an attack in that same year by La Rochefoucauld, a general in the Protestant army opposed to the Catholic king. La Rochefoucauld, however, was not deterred by the fortress. Within six months, he had brought Brouage to its knees. On August 8, 1570, a treaty was signed at Saint Germain-en-Laye, and Brouage was returned to Catholic control — until 1574, when it was seized by the Huguenot general François de La Noue (1531–1591). Continuing this steady stream of blood letting, Charles de Lorraine, duc de Mayenne (1554–1611) laid siege to Brouage in 1577 with five hundred cannon shots directed over a period of two months; by the time the capitulation documents were signed on August 16, Brouage was on the verge of total destruction with her surviving population starving and plagued by disease.

In these early years, the Champlain family could have known no peace. For the young Samuel de Champlain, life at sea was more than an option; it was a necessary refuge from what Champlain years later was to refer to as those "usual disturbed conditions in France" (IV:350). Yet, for all the battles and sights seen in his youth, the only confirmation about his life in these early years was one provided in a letter that he wrote in 1613 to Queen Marie de Médicis, who was acting as regent for King Louis XIII:

> Madam, among all the most useful and admirable arts, that of navigation has always seemed to me to hold the first place; for the more hazardous it is and the more attended by innumerable dangers and shipwrecks, so much the more is it esteemed and exalted above all others, being in no way suited to those who lack courage and resolution (I:209).

The historical record yields only a fuzzy impression of Champlain's family. As far as is known, he was an only child, and although his parents, Antoine Champlain (a.k.a. Anthoine de Complain) and Margueritte Le Roy, are mentioned, with different spellings, in more than one notarial record, little is known about them. According to Champlain's marriage certificate of 1610, Antoine was a sea captain, and from recent evidence, it is now known that Champlain's mother, Margueritte, had a sister. (See Appendix IV.)

As far as can be determined, Champlain's most important relationship was with his uncle, Guillaume Hellaine, who was married to his maternal aunt. This mysterious fellow, about whom we are told nothing, had enough variations of his surname to justify the employment of a full-time genealogist. In the Spanish world that he frequented, Hellaine was known either as "Captain Provençal" (the southerner), because his home port was Marseille, or as Guillermo Elena — Elena being the Spanish version of Hellaine. This uncle was Champlain's greatest benefactor, and the contacts and personal wealth that Champlain inherited from this relationship proved crucial in furthering the career of Canada's founding father.

Historians have filled the record with many nonsensical theories about Champlain's religious background; but by the beginning of the journals in Champlain's mid-life, the reader is most certainly introduced to a devout Catholic. For all the guesswork offered, there is not a whit of evidence to suggest otherwise for the earlier years. Those who speculate that the name Samuel was a choice signifying Protestant persuasion offer no evidence for this notion, and although Champlain served a Protestant monarch, King Henry IV, it was also this same monarch who converted to Catholicism. As for Champlain's army service, his commander, Marshal Jean d'Aumont, was a Catholic monarchist who fought for the Catholic League as a supporter of King Henry IV; to add to the confusion, the Catholic Champlain served under a Protestant, the Sieur de Monts, his postwar patron and commander during his first voyage to New France.

Nothing is known of Champlain's education; but in print he reveals an increasing knowledge of discovery history and the science of navigation. In the Champlain journals, there is an assortment of confusing references that suggest that he had gained some knowledge about the customs of other peoples. This is not surprising in view of the many international vessels that stopped in Brouage to stock up on salt; it is rather odd, however, that the devout Champlain doesn't make a single Biblical reference in his entire written legacy. Yet, it seems that Champlain was not simply a self-taught man.

Whatever the source of his education, no issue is as frustrating as the mystery of Champlain's physical appearance. Over the centuries, historians and artists have conjured up a variety of impressions of what he looked like. The American biographer Morris Bishop has written that "Champlain was in fact a lean ascetic type, dry and dark." Another, the celebrated Samuel Eliot Morison, in just as confident a manner, theorizes, "as one who has lived with Champlain," that he was "blond and bearded."

Most people who encounter a portrait of Champlain will be treated to the most famous depiction of all, the one that looks more suitable

SAMUEL DE CHAMPLAIN

for a cereal package. This popular version shows a man of somber countenance, transfixed like a sturdy New England pilgrim, with long hair and wearing a large, plain white collar. Almost all the portraits seen today are derivations of this delight (see portrait).

Unfortunately, this widely circulated image, in whatever form, is one grand artistic hoax. Thought for years to be an authentic picture of Champlain, this portrait was attributed to the seventeenth-century engraver Balthasar Moncornet; but in 1904, a scholar by the name of

Victor Paltsits demonstrated that the artistry was most likely the work of the nineteenth-century painter Louis César Joseph Ducornet (1806–1856), whose work was first published in 1854. On the basis of the evidence, it now seems convincing that Ducornet did not portray Champlain, but rather made a copy of Moncornet's portrait of Michel Particelli (produced by Moncornet in 1654), King Louis XIV's comptroller of finance, who was a rogue and crook. Some have suggested the sun face in the compass rosette on Champlain's map of 1612 (fig. 29) was really a self-portrait; but it seems unlikely at best that this cherublike visage, with the rosebud lips to match, belonged to a rugged seaman.

The only certain images of Champlain are the crude self-portraits to be found in three of the four battle scenes; of these, the best is the lone figure standing in the middle of combat at Lake Champlain, New York, in 1609 (fig. 26). Here the warrior *is* self-portrayed: breastplated, with protective breeches, he wears the famous plumed burgonet helmet with an upturned edge like a small eavestrough. Champlain, thus encumbered in heavy armor, looks the perfect Spanish conquistador. As a warrior outfitted for battle, the costume is fitting, as it is in this manner that Champlain is introduced in history — as a soldier in full armor, in his mid-twenties, fighting for the Protestants in the Wars of Religion. The opening lines of Chapter 2 of his *Brief Narrative* confirm his military background:

> Having been employed in the king's army which was in Brittany, under Messieurs the Maréchal d'Aumont, de St. Luc, and the Maréchal de Brissac, in the capacity of quartermaster in the said army for some years, and until his Majesty, in the year 1598, reduced the said country of Brittany to obedience, and dismissed his army (I:3).

It is believed that Champlain served in Henry of Navarre's army from 1593 to 1598 and that this was a happy part of his life. Writing to King Louis XIII (1601–1643) in an unguarded moment years later, he fondly referred to his first commander in chief, King Louis's father, as "King, Henry the Great, of happy memory" (I:207). A note this cheerful was expressed by Champlain only once in an entire journal record of thirty years.

More in keeping with the times, Champlain's military service also had its gruesome moments; on one occasion his commander, Marshal d'Aumont, hanged twenty-eight of his own soldiers for disobedience;

on another sortie with this same army, the French drove some four hundred Spaniards to the edge of the ocean. By the end of the slaughter, there were only eleven Spanish survivors and only two that escaped injury. In this same conflict, the French and their allies — the English — lost nearly three thousand men. Coincidentally, and most likely unknown to Champlain, one of the Englishmen was the flashy pirate and commander of the first mining expedition to North America, Sir Martin Frobisher (c. 1535–1594), who died of an infection from the wound he received fighting on the same side as Champlain in this battle.

In 1598, with the formal, although temporary, cessation of hostilities in the Wars of Religion, there was a period of peace. Quartermaster Samuel de Champlain of Brouage, one of the King's victorious soldiers, was demobilized and pensioned for his loyal service.

Retirement? Perhaps for some, but not for this energetic man. This man about to journey to the New World was what would have been termed in the vernacular of his day, "a Corneillian" — a model for Pierre Corneille's (1606–1684) Le Cid. The champion knight of this famous play was ever committed to a cause, and his motto was: "To conquer without risk is to triumph without glory." The motto of this fictional character might well have been the motto of the soldier of fortune on the verge of his first great voyage.

CHAPTER THREE

Early Voyages: Spain, The West Indies, and Central America: 1598-1602

"What is life? An illusion, a shadow, a story?"

Pedro de la Calderón de la Barca, 1600–1681

And seeing myself thereby without any charge or employment, I resolved, so as not to remain idle, to find means to make a voyage to Spain, and, being there to acquire and cultivate acquaintances, in order, by their favour and intermediary, to manage to embark in some one of the ships of the fleet which the King of Spain sends every year to the West Indies . . . to make inquiries into particulars of which no Frenchmen have succeeded obtaining cognizance because they have no free access there, in order to make report of them to His Majesty on my return (I:4).

So began the *Brief Narrative*, in which Champlain chronicled his postwar experiences.

These were bold words from a retired billeting officer, who within weeks of terminating his military service had discovered a purpose worthy of a lifetime commitment. Champlain saw a way to serve and, in the process, to build a power base with the help of the French monarchy.

To accomplish my design then, I went to Blavet [a port on the Brittany coast], where at that time was a garrison of Spaniards, in which place I found an uncle of mine named Captain Provençal, who was considered to be one of France's first-rate seamen, and who, in that capacity, had been commissioned by the King of Spain as Pilot-General of their sea forces (I:4).

23

As time passed, this rendezvous with his uncle proved to be one of the most important events in Champlain's life. Captain Provençal had been contracted by the Spanish government to repatriate the defeated Spanish soldiers stranded at Blavet. Blavet had been heavily fortified and was the last place to be evacuated by the Spanish following the Treaty of Vervins (1598).

Seeing that his nephew was anxious to go to Spain, was enthusiastic about a seagoing career, and appeared to be talented, Champlain's uncle seized the opportunity and invited his nephew to join him aboard the *St. Julien*, "a great ship of five hundred tons' burden," Champlain noted (I:5).

On July 15, 1598, a fleet of ships, including the *St. Julien*, was officially contracted to make the southward journey to Spain. The *St. Julien* cast off in early August with her white sails billowing full with a good wind. Within ten days, the grand ship reached the northern coastline of Spain. Off the coast, an accident occurred; the flagship of the fleet was damaged during a dense fog, and the fleet remained fogbound for six days outside Bayona. Here, Champlain undertook the first of his surviving illustrations, a chart of the harbor and surrounding countryside. It was a crude and disappointing work compared with others in the *Brief Narrative* and compared with the finer illustrations in his later published works.

After repairs were completed, and after cruising the Spanish coastline for three more weeks, the ocean-tossed troop transport reached Cape St. Vincent on the southwestern tip of Portugal. Here, Champlain completed a second and equally primitive chart. Then, for some unexplained reason, the fleet reduced its speed and, as a result, did not reach Cádiz until September.

Located just a few miles from Gibraltar and the North African coast, Cádiz was Captain Provençal's home away from home. Here, in this proud regional capital and naval training center, the contract for the delivery of the soldiers was completed; the captured Spaniards were released and the French transport ships were sent homeward save one, Provençal's *St. Julien*. It seemed there were bigger plans in store for the sturdy galleon, which was once again chartered by Spain.

Awaiting orders and apparently unchallenged with duties, Champlain remained in Cádiz a full month before sailing thirty miles (48 km) northward on the Spanish coastline to Sanlúcar, at the mouth of the Seville River. There, three more months were seemingly idled away in the autumn sun. From the erratic scribblings in the *Brief*

Narrative, the purpose of this lengthy stay in the region of Seville remains a mystery. As for the city itself, there's not a word in Champlain's notebook about the beautiful beige ramparts covered with cascading greenery, the luxurious vineyards, the bullfights or the dark-haired ladies with flowers in their hair and shawls of lace. Nor is there mention of the music that filled the streets — such as the haunting folk ballads rendered on a mandolin. For Champlain, the layover seems to have been nothing more than a long siesta, a trivial interlude before the realization of his larger vision.

But perhaps Champlain was not as bored as his writings suggest. It is worth noting that in Seville Champlain would have had access to the Spanish General Archives of the Indies, the last surviving repository of all Spanish trade and naval records relevant to the Caribbean seas. Other such records had been destroyed by arson during the pillage of the capital city of the Caribbean, Santo Domingo (in the present-day Dominican Republic), on January 9, 1586, by the English navigator Sir Francis Drake. Champlain, who had already stated his ambition to inform his king well on matters relating to the West Indies, would have had good reason to research this precious cache of primary documents while in Seville.

During Champlain's lengthy stay there, news arrived from Puerto Rico, another of Spain's colonies in the West Indies. The English fleet had laid siege to the island and seemed bent on capturing it. With this latest threat to Spain's Caribbean holdings, there was immediate mobilization, and within twenty days vessels and two thousand Spanish troops were on standby awaiting orders to leave for the West Indies.

At first, the *St. Julien* was included, with Provençal in command. Just as Champlain is "very readily resolved to go with him" (I:8), however, a second communiqué arrived reporting that Puerto Rico had already fallen to the English. Champlain, obviously anxious to go to the Caribbean under any circumstances, was discouraged. Then, in storybook fashion, the journal records that "there came from the King a nobleman named Don Francisco Colomo, a Knight of Malta, to be general of the said armament; who seeing our vessel fitted out and ready for service . . . resolved to make use of it" (I:9).

Action at last! But there was a hitch. The local commander serving under Colomo had special plans that called for the separation of Champlain and his uncle. The captain from Marseille and his vessel the *St. Julien* were given a local mission that was of no interest to

Champlain. Again Champlain expressed his disappointment in his journal. But before his departure, Provençal ensured that his nephew was able to join Admiral Colomo's fleet and sail for the Caribbean. Thanks to his uncle, Champlain's dream of adventure on the high seas came to life.

In January, 1599, Samuel de Champlain, who at this time was thirty-two years of age, set out to cross the Atlantic Ocean for the first time. The pensioned-off soldier, observer, and painter was a French national on a lonely mission in the companionship of his former enemies, seconded into the charge of a foreign government.

Little is known of Champlain's exact role on this voyage, but he did note that his uncle gave him the "charge and care" of the vessel (I:10), the *St. Julien* and from this some scholars have concluded that he was in fact the ship's commander. Taking all the facts into account, however, it seems just as likely that he could have been not only an observer with artistic skills, but one empowered as a passenger to exercise considerable influence in voyage decisions during these tours of the West Indies.

In six days, "with a very steady cutting wind," Colomo's fleet was within sight of the Canary Islands off the African coast. Here once again, Champlain produced a crude watercolor to illustrate his text.

By mid-March, after an early season transatlantic sailing, the Spanish fleet had crossed the ocean, and Champlain, the seaman from Brouage, found himself in the Caribbean off the island of Guadeloupe (variously spelled by Champlain), where once again he produced a crude chart of the region (fig. 1).

From Guadeloupe, Admiral Colomo's fleet sailed past the Virgin Islands, where Champlain noted the "great number of good harbours and havens" (I:13), and then it seems that they voyaged onward to Isla de Margarita off the coast of Venezuela.

Modern navigational experts choke in disbelief at this claim, concluding that this visit to Isla de Margarita makes no sense in view of the time allotted for the distance covered. There are also timing contradictions in this record when compared with other logbooks of Admiral Colomo's fleet.

Perhaps what is needed to explain this discrepancy is a little imagination. It is certainly not impossible that the well-connected Champlain might have been on a privately financed side trip, traveling on any of the numerous Spanish vessels cruising the region. But regardless of how he got to Isla de Margarita, he was clearly there, and he left

1 GUADELOUPE, THE FRENCH WEST INDIES, c. 1599
Gardalouppe

In Champlain's day this Leeward Island, discovered in 1493 by Columbus and another island called La Desirade, also illustrated in the *Brief Narrative* was feebly colonized by the Spaniards until 1604 when suddenly they were abandoned. The French began a settlement on Guadeloupe a few months before Champlain's death in 1635.

Champlain's chart of Guadeloupe Island is typical of the crude surveys in the *Brief Narrative*. While the contour outline and artistry are only marginally successful, in terms of accuracy design reveals a pattern for future graphics. Wherever space is available, one can expect a variety of random wildlife sketches and selected information about the geography from Champlain, and often with distortions that are comical and seemingly frivolous.

---

something for the record: two delightful illustrations. One shows the pearl divers of the island earning their dangerous livelihood, leaping overboard in search of treasure, and the other is a chart of the island. (See Appendix III.)

From the coast of South America, the fleet traveled northward to Puerto Rico from which the English, according to the diary, had just departed. Here, they remained for an entire month.

At this point in his diary, Champlain described the pillage of San Juan according to one of the survivors, a Negro who spoke "tolerably

good Spanish." Descriptions followed of the island, its major agricultural products, its vegetation, its birds, and its animals. "[There] are a
great quantity of chameleons which it is said, live on air; but of this I
can give no assurance although I have seen them many times. They
have a rather pointed head, the body somewhat long for its thickness,
that is to say, a foot and a half long, and they have only two legs, which
are in front; the tail is very pointed, and of a colour between grey and
yellowish" (I:21). This potpourri of information is all recorded in the
formative style of the developing Champlain tradition. But again
there is another discrepancy: English naval records do not agree with
the dates in the *Brief Narrative* and the history is a bit muddled.

In Puerto Rico, Champlain made more sketches, including one of a
chameleon. Then the fleet prepared to depart. The admiral apparently
divided the fleet into three squadrons. Four galleons remained with
him; three were sent to Portobelo [on the coast of Panama, twenty-
three miles (37 km) from Colón], and three, including the vessel
Champlain was on, were sent to New Spain (Haiti and Dominican
Republic today).

Champlain reported that he sailed past the "whole island of Santo
Domingo on the north side" (I:23). While on this policing survey of
the north shore of the second largest of the Caribbean islands, searching for the enemy vessels of Spain — including pirate ships from
France — the three ships made a brief stopover at Puerto Plata, the
now famous tourist resort. Here, Champlain completed a chart of the
harbor to illustrate the *Brief Narrative*.

On this navigational route, Champlain was following in the footsteps of history as he traced the course of another cartographer,
Christopher Columbus, who had also mapped parts of this coastline
more than a century earlier. Champlain's ship continued westward
along the northern coastline, past the ruins of La Isabela, where there
were remnants of the first settlement attempted by Columbus. Next,
Champlain wrote an observation of Manzanillo Bay near the border
of present-day Haiti and the nearby island of Tortuga.

Circumnavigating this island without mentioning his brush with
the past, Champlain reported a visit to the capital city of Santo
Domingo on the north shore. But for the reader who yearns to know
his thoughts on this occasion, he says nothing that is historically
memorable. Indeed, Champlain treated his visit to this first capital of

the Americas with the same disdain he showed for all the capitals he ever visited, save Mexico City.

By Champlain's time the capital of Santo Domingo (also named Hispaniola) could boast the ruins of the New World's first cathedral as well as the majesty of its flourishing replacement. Santo Domingo, the capital, was a city walled at the shoreline with a great red stone buttress adjoining a summer fortress high above the harbor. The fortress stood in readiness to repel attack.

At the time Champlain visited, nearly one hundred years after the city was founded, the great white walls and ten Doric-columned archways of the palatial mansion of Alcázar were still standing. Alcázar had once been the home of the former Viceroy Diego Colón, the son of Christopher Columbus. A residence that had belonged to Hernán Cortés (the conquistador of Mexico in 1521) was also a prominent feature to be found on the main street in this city of "firsts." It was a city with a hospital and surgeons on staff. In this happy community, often ridiculed for its frivolities, there lived an eccentric poet and the city's noted artist in residence, Bernardo de Albornoz. The architectural historian, Eugenio Perez Montas, describes this ancient city as a community of "partying and vanities". In this first city of sophistication in the New World, carriages had traveled the cobblestoned streets when Champlain was a child of seven.

After duly noting that the island was "very fertile in fruits and abounding in cattle and good merchandise, such as sugar, cassia, ginger, molasses, cotton, ox-hides, and some furs," and that there are "numerous good harbours and good anchorages" (I:32), the division of Colomo's fleet, of which Champlain's vessel was a part, moved on again to Cuba and the Cayman Islands. Champlain explained that the islands offered several harbors; the ship anchored at one and he went ashore. In any case, he reported: "I walked a league inland through very thick woods, and caught some rabbits, which are very numerous, a few birds, and a lizard as thick as my thigh, of a grey and dark yellow colour" (I:33) (fig. 2).

Of all these meanderings in the Caribbean seas, the highlight of Champlain's first voyage across the Atlantic was his journey to Mexico. The first stop on this tour was Campeche on the Yucatán Peninsula. In its descriptions of "New Spain" (Mexico), for the first time, the *Brief Narrative* gathers some color and gusto. There are fish "the size of

2 Birds and Rabbits, The Cayman Islands, British
West Indies, c. 1599–1601
Oiseaux-Marin, Lapins

In his early maps, Champlain placed wildlife every which way on the
terrain with little concern for either proportion or location. The
untrained illustrator showed some skill, but he was hardly a
Renaissance master. The rabbits with ears like pine trees would have
been more suitable in a children's book. The two large seabirds look
like combinations of a dodo and a duck, and they are not unlike some
of the strange flying fowl that he drew years later in North America.

a dory, of a red colour, and very good if eaten fresh." And there was
some action:

one of our patches [boats] foundered without our being able
to learn the cause. The soldiers and sailors saved themselves by
swimming, some on planks, others on oars, others as they best

could, and from more than two leagues away made for our ship, which they encountered very seasonably, and we had them picked up by our boats which went out to meet them (I:35).

Leaving Campeche, the fleet crossed the Golfo de Campeche to Veracruz.

Fifteen days after our arrival . . . I set off, with the permission of our said Admiral, for Mexico City . . . and a more beautiful country could not be seen or desired than this kingdom of New Spain . . . . I admired the fine forests that are met with, filled with the most beautiful trees that one could wish . . . moreover, this whole country is adorned with very fine rivers and streams, which traverse almost the whole kingdom . . . the soil is very fertile, producing corn twice a year. . . . If the king of Spain would permit vines to be planted in the said kingdom, they would fructify like the corn [fig. 3].

Trudging about the Mexican countryside, Champlain's excitement was boundless when he reached Mexico City.

All the contentment I felt at the sight of things so pleasing was but little in regard to what I experienced when I beheld that beautiful city of Mexico, which I had not supposed to be so superbly constructed of splendid temples, palaces and fine houses; and the streets extremely well laid out, in which are to be seen the large handsome shops of the merchants full of all sorts of very rich merchandise. I think, as well as I could judge, that there are in the said city twelve to fifteen thousand Spanish inhabitants, and six times as many Christian Indians also dwelling there, besides a great number of negro slaves (I:41-2) (fig. 4)

After a month in Mexico, Champlain voyaged in a smaller vessel to Portobelo, Panama, where he joined other visionaries of the age who foresaw the Panama Canal, imagining "that, if these four leagues of land that lie between Panama and this river were cut through, a passage might be made from the South sea to that on this side, and the route thus shortened by more than fifteen hundred leagues" (I:69).

Champlain's voyages through the West Indies drew to a close and he again joined up with the main fleet. His excursion vessel sailed on to Havana, Cuba, a harbor described as "one of the finest that I have

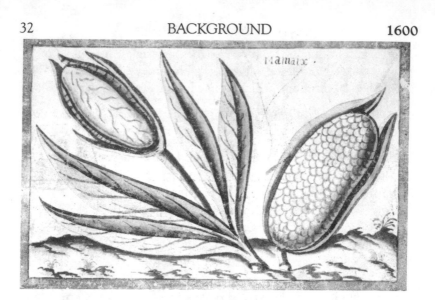

3 MAIZE (INDIAN CORN), MEXICO, c. 1599–1601
Maimaix

Few of Champlain's illustrations match this wonder of graphic art.
This was an artist who drew for dramatic effect, and the *Brief
Narrative* is filled with such cockeyed visuals. In another science
fiction-like illustration in the same journal, Champlain depicted a
palm tree with two coconuts on the ground, each of which is larger
than the entire foliage of the tree.

   During Champlain's time Indian maize was the dietary staple of the
North American continent and there are many references to this
grain in his journals.

---

seen in all of the Indies" (I:73). In passing, Champlain noted Morro
Castle. He spent four months in Cuba, but little more was written
about the island.

   Suddenly, without any forewarning or further explanation, Champlain's attention turned toward the northwest.

> I have spoken . . . of the land of Florida; I will say here again
> that it is one of the best countries that could be desired, for it is
> very fertile if it were cultivated, but the King of Spain takes no
> account of it because there are in it no mines of gold or silver.
> There are great numbers of savages, and these make war against
> the Spaniards, who have a fort on a point of the said land,
> where there is a good harbour. This low-lying land for the most
> part is very pretty (I:79).

4 THE SPANISH INQUISITORS AT WORK: MEXICO
c. 1599–1601
(Untitled)

There are thirty-seven illustrations of Mexico included in the John
Carter Brown copy of the *Brief Narrative* an average of more than one
a day produced during Champlain's visit. This was Champlain's
prolific period. For all his enthusiasm for Mexico, he was horrified by
the excesses of the Spanish Inquisition and the cruelty of the
Conquistadors toward their Indian slaves. This is the most gruesome
illustration he ever made, to show his contempt: "Such evil treatment
was the reason that the poor Indians, for very apprehension of it, fled
to the mountains in desperation, and as many Spaniards as they
caught they ate; and on that account the Spaniards were constrained
to take away the Inquisition for if they had purposed still to chastise
them according to the strict rule of the said Inquisition, they would
have caused them all to die by fire" (I:63-4).

His own dealings with North American Indians in the future
showed that he had learned a great deal from the Spanish example.
American historian Francis Parkman expressed the different attitudes
of three European cultures nicely: "Spanish civilization crushed the
Indian; English civilization scorned and neglected him: French
civilization embraced and cherished him."

These brief observations were a foreshadowing of the future, and although they are more detailed than those provided for many other locations described in the journals, there was no suggestion put forward that Champlain placed a foot on the peninsula. But did Champlain explore Florida? A number of factors favor an affirmative answer, including the lengthy duration of his travels in the relatively small Caribbean sea, the extent of his moving about reported, and of course his original self-imposed mandate: to gather information to pass on to the King of France. In future years, Florida, for the French, became an elusive dream, and there were many commitments made to settle this area as well as references citing its desirability. It is reasonable to assume that Champlain was a bona fide explorer of the Florida coast.

There is much argument about the date of Champlain's return to Spain and even more dispute about the time of his homeward trip from Spain to France. With certainty, however, Champlain can be placed back in Cádiz on June 26, 1601, though he may have returned to either France or Spain much sooner.

Champlain's homecoming was a sad one. His mentor, patron, and uncle, Captain Guillaume Hellaine, was dying at the home of Antonio de Villa. During the summer, in this private home, a group of five witnesses joined the principals — Champlain and his bedridden uncle — to legally execute a complex document that was a combination of a will and a living trust. The immediate legacy and subsequent events were milestones in Champlain's life. The testament affirmed both verbal and written covenants that had the effect in law of making Champlain the sole heir, the sole trustee, and, after his uncle's death, the irrevocable beneficiary of a substantial farming complex identified as the hacienda Real Del Rey Nuestro Señor at La Rochelle, the Protestant citadel near Brouage. (See Appendix II regarding the will.)

For Champlain, the pensioner, and now experienced voyageur, the newly acquired estate was a bonanza. Among the many assets that he would inherit were vineyards, orchards, and additional lands available for cultivation as well as numerous houses and storage buildings. In addition, there was substantial income from rents, income from cash crops, and valuable customs fees vested with this property. Moreover, there were funds held in trust in Spain, and in total the size of the legacy was sufficient to require there be a legal description stating that the bequest was in excess of "five hundred salaries." (A salary in this context likely represented the annual earnings of a laborer of the time.)

According to the trust, although Champlain was to have immediate power of attorney, the ailing uncle was to retain title for the remainder of his life. But there was a contradiction: the authority given was sweeping and totally without reservations. It was a rambling testament touching on every aspect of a dying man's wishes to hold on to, and at the same time let go of, a vast estate. But in effect, Champlain's uncle released his wordly possessions, "for much good work that he does for me in my illness, and came when I have needed him and also for the great love I feel for being married to his aunt, his mother's sister."

Within a week of the execution of the testament, Captain Provençal died, and through this instrument, regardless of birthright and without further formality, Champlain became a member of the landed gentry of France. Historian Marc Bloch, the expert on French rural history, painted a picture of what one might have expected to find during this period.

> The houses will be surrounded by gardens and orchards, all enclosed . . . the land inside the enclosure was sacrosanct, secured against intrusion from the communal herd. There will be some enclosed areas on the open fields where hemp or vines are growing . . . . The ground bordering the stream, if there is one, will be meadow; then come the ploughlands, interspersed with or surrounded by grazing.

It was to such a refuge on the outskirts of the fortress of La Rochelle that Champlain would return between voyages.

Champlain retained this estate in the south of France until December 29, 1625, and it was the wealth provided by the estate that gave him his independence. For all Champlain's accomplishments, he owed much to his uncle, who made it possible for him to be a man financially free to make a commitment in search of a destiny. That commitment was to be New France, and that is exactly where we next find Samuel de Champlain.

CHAPTER FOUR

The St. Lawrence: the River of Dreams and the Grand Alliance: 1603

"When everything has been carefully studied, weigh anchor, and set sail."

Champlain, *Treatise on Seamanship*, 1632

IN 1603, TWO YEARS AFTER HIS RETURN FROM SPAIN and the West Indies, Champlain rejected retirement and the life of a country squire. It was, he felt, time to take the next step toward fulfilling his ambitions. As evidence of his talents as an observer, he made a report on his West Indies journey to the vice-admiral of France, Governor of Dieppe and Viceroy of New France, Aymar de Chaste. De Chaste, in addition to long-established connections with trade on the St. Lawrence River, was also the affluent governor in residence at the seaport of Dieppe, a thriving center of naval commerce. The vice-admiral must have been impressed with the report because he agreed that Champlain could participate in the season's trading expedition to the St. Lawrence River. Doubtless King Henry IV had a hand in the matter as well, especially in view of Champlain's stated promise to further intrigue royalty with geographic matters.

Thus, Champlain was retained for a second time without a specific, or stated, role. He reported for duty at Honfleur on the Normandy coast in the spring for his first venture to North America. His new commander was Captain François Pontgravé.

Their meeting was the beginning of a longstanding friendship. For the next three decades, Champlain experienced the jovial Pontgravé's unflagging loyalty, his tantrums, his administrative blunders, his bouts with gout and a heart condition, and much laughter. Pontgravé was the Falstaff of French North American exploration, and Champlain would grow very fond of this substitute for his dead uncle.

On March 15, 1603, with the new team in readiness, the tiny 120-ton *Bonne Renommée* sailed out from the Norman coast to be joined by two other vessels. As before, Champlain commenced a journal. This time, however, the record was to be published by the author. *Des Sauvages*, Champlain's first publication, was a small handsome work that was licensed for printing and distribution on November 15, 1603. Other than the short notation about Florida in the *Brief Narrative*, this first published account contained Champlain's first impressions of North America. Unlike the West Indies diary, *Des Sauvages* included extensive field notes, which covered a wide range of observations on subjects as diverse as mineralogy and biology, ethnography and geography. As an observer, Champlain had matured. Adding to his skills as an artist and diarist, there is evidence in *Des Sauvages* of a cartographic scientist in the making who was developing the additional skill of methodically recording field-note observations.

At the opening of the book, a minor poet, the Sieur de La Franchise, unctuously invokes the muses to take note of Champlain's courage. Following this commissioned and self-serving entrée, the author set the proper tone for the work with a preface addressed to the Admiral of France, Charles de Montmorency (1537–1612): "My Lord, — although many have written somewhat concerning the country of Canada, I have not been disposed to abide by their descriptions, but have gone to the place on purpose to be able to give you faithful testimony of the truth which you shall read (if it please you) in the brief account which I give you" (I:85). (See chapter note.)

Each observation in the new diary is hammered methodically into place so that readers who continue to sail with Champlain must accept the price of long-term passage — a steady drubbing of bearings, place names, and all manner of geographical observations that at times may dull the senses of the most ardent adventure fan. Nonetheless, here is the hydrographer and surveyor par excellence of the seventeenth century, the first chronicler to establish the modern method of keeping field notes. Readers who pay attention to the journal are rewarded: intermixed with Champlain's file of facts is the adventure of his first voyage along the great "River of Canada" — the St. Lawrence.

The most important feature of *Des Sauvages* is Champlain's identification of future opportunities for settlement. In years to come, these opportunities identified on this first journey up the St. Lawrence would prove the imagination and wisdom of the author. Champlain returned to this first published account as a reference plan or blueprint for the next three decades. A study of this treasure also reveals the pattern of his future communication: he recognized geographic opportunity as the result of an accumulation of information, which included rumor, hearsay, speculation, and then, wherever possible, scientific information gained from his own on-site observations.

On this short excursion of only ninety days, the exploration party managed to set an impressive record. Champlain recorded the first European awareness of Hudson Bay (fig. 30): "The Indians from the North say they are in sight of a sea which is salt. I hold that, if this be so, it is some gulf of this our sea, which overflows in the north into the midst of our continent and indeed it can be nothing else." While the route to this third ocean of America was incorrectly estimated to be the Saguenay River northward from Tadoussac (fig. 23), the overall perception was remarkable. Even after discovering his Mare Magnum, Henry Hudson did not have as sound a concept of the bay in 1610 as Champlain did seven years earlier (I:124).

Just as intriguing are Champlain's comments, the first on record, concerning the Great Lakes — Ontario, Huron, and Erie. And for the first time, Niagara Falls was noted: "At the end of the said lake [Ontario], they pass a fall which is somewhat high . . . they carry their canoes by land about a quarter of a league in order to pass this fall." In another information coup, Champlain persuaded the Indians to sketch an outline of the Ottawa River. "I made them draw by hand [where] . . . they go up the river in their canoes . . . to a river which extends to the dwelling-place of the Algonkians." This is the first account to confirm the mapping skills of the Indians (I:153-55).

The military information gained on this first journey ranked equally with the geographic promise. The strategic location of the Iroquois Indians in what is now upper New York state was identified. Champlain also pinpointed the site of their fortress on the St. Lawrence River at what is now Sorel, Québec (fig. 27), at the mouth of the Iroquois (Richelieu) River. The fortress controlled the river access to their main encampment on Lake Champlain in New York state (fig. 26), and even at this very early stage, Champlain heard about far-off inland waterways, including a "river which leads down to the coast of Florida." This is the earliest account of the interior linkages to the

Susquehanna River of Pennsylvania, leading to Chesapeake Bay, where years later, in 1615, Champlain sent Étienne Brûlé (c. 1522–c. 1633) on a military mission (I:143).

On this first voyage into the continent, Champlain also learned of the river that would be discovered and explored by Henry Hudson within a few years, a river that would bear the name of the English explorer in the service of the Dutch in years to come. And in a final accounting, for the moment more intrigued with these northern lands, Champlain altered his unqualified opinion of Florida's merits first expressed in the *Brief Narrative*: "The country and coast of Florida may have a different climate, and be more abundantly productive of fruits and other things than that which I have seen; but there cannot be lands more level nor of better quality than those which we have seen." For the time being, the St. Lawrence River was the winner (I:171).

After an uneventful crossing, Captain François Pontgravé and his curious passenger reached Tadoussac on the north shore of the St. Lawrence River on May 26, 1603. Here, for the first time, Champlain set foot in New France.

Champlain reported that on the 27th he and Pontgravé went ashore to accompany two Montagnais Indians who had returned home to Tadoussac after having spent the winter in France on what might be called a "cultural indoctrination" program. It was time for the French to cash in on this investment in propaganda.

The foursome went directly to the "lodge of the grand sagamore, named Anadabijou." Here they found Anadabijou (fl. 1611) with "eighty or a hundred of his companions." Champlain reported that one of the homecoming natives made a speech telling the assemblage how he was received at court and how he had been entertained in France. He concluded with the following words: "His majesty wished them well, and desired to people their country, and to make peace with their enemies [the Iroquois] or send forces to vanquish them." The Indian also described the fine buildings in France, the palaces, and the living conditions. Following the speech, which was heard in absolute silence, Champlain and Pontgravé were invited to smoke with the gathering (I:99).

Champlain then related the reply of the grand sagamore Anadabijou: "[He] began to address the whole gathering, speaking with gravity, pausing sometimes a little, and then resuming his speech, saying to them, that in truth they ought to be very glad to have His Majesty for their great friend. They answered with one voice, saying Ho, ho, ho, which is to say, yes, yes. Continuing his speech, he said that he was well content that His said Majesty should people their country, and make war on their enemies, and that there was no nation in the world to which they wished more good than to the French" (I:100-01).

Following this, there was a feast given to celebrate the alliance as well as a recent victory in battle over the Iroquois. "And they began to hold their *Tabagie* or feast, which they make with the flesh of the moose, which is like beef, with that of bear, seal, and beaver, which are their most ordinary meats, and with great quantities of wild fowl. They had eight or ten kettles full of meats in the midst of the said lodge, and these were set some six paces apart, and each on its own fire" (I:101).

Dogs were thrown to the ground in a display that was not explained. Iroquois scalps were displayed and paraded around the campsite, and there were dances, as Champlain recorded the scene.

Champlain described what happened on the following day. At daybreak Indians began to gather around the harbor of Tadoussac and as they came in families, he placed the number at a thousand persons, "men as well as women and children" (I:105).

The result of the previous day's meeting was an awesome alliance between the French, the Algonquin, the Montagnais, and Etchemin Indians. Excepting occasional interruptions, this alliance was to last for over 150 years until the French had lost New France at the end of the Seven Years' War, in 1763. But at the time, the terms seemed simple enough: the French were to be allowed to settle the country without hindrance in exchange for a commitment to join a triumvirate of Indian nations and to fight their enemies, the tribes of the Iroquois nation.

Later in June, Champlain recorded another feast of victory. Similar to the first, this one included a ritual dance in which women participated. "Suddenly all the women and girls proceeded to cast off their mantles of skins, and stripped themselves stark naked, showing their privities, but retaining their ornaments. . . . After they had made an end of their songs, they cried all with one voice, Ho, ho, ho" (I:106-07). This appeared to be Champlain's first real cultural shock, and it was to haunt him for the next thirty years.

As the summer passed, Champlain sought out the grand sagamore and recorded in his journal some of their conversations concerning religion. In one such exchange, Anadabijou told Champlain the following story.

Once upon a time there was a man who had a good supply of
tobacco . . . . God came to this man, and asked where was his
tobacco-pipe. The man took his tobacco-pipe and gave it to
God who smoked tobacco a great while: after HE had smoked
enough, God broke the pipe into many pieces: and the man
asked HIM, "Why hast THOU broken my pipe? Surely Thou
seest that I have no other." And God took one of HIS own, and
gave it to him, "Here is one that I give thee, carry it to thy
grand Sagamore, say to him to keep it, and if he keep it well, he
shall never want for anything whatever, nor any of his companions . . . but afterwards the said Sagamore lost his pipe and
this is the reason of the great famine which sometimes comes
among them" (I:114).

According to Champlain the story was fully believed by the Indians; in this savage world, man's punishment for losing the Creator's
peace pipe was famine or the visitation of some plague.

Champlain seemed fascinated with this newly discovered and
spellbinding world of mystery, monsters, and mythology. It was a
world that was both frightening and hellish. There were medicine
men "who speak to the devil face to face and he tells them what they
must do . . . , Moreover the Indians believe all the dreams they dream
are true" (I:117-18).

Champlain seems to have swallowed this world of black magic
holus-bolus. At the end of the summer, just before the return voyage
to France, after a final stopover at the Gaspé (fig. 40), he wrote a
fanciful entry in his journal, one that resulted in his being ridiculed
unmercifully.

There is another strange thing worthy of narration, which
many savages have assured me was true; this is, that near Chaleur bay [south of the Gaspé Peninsula], towards the south,
there lies an island where makes his abode a dreadful monster,
which the savages call GOUGOU. They told me it had the
form of a woman, but most hideous, and of such a size that
according to them the tops of the masts of our vessel would not
reach his waist, so big do they represent him; and they say that
he has often devoured and still devours many savages; these he
puts, when he can catch them, into a great pocket, and afterwards eats them; and those who had escaped the danger of this
ill-omened beast said that his pocket was so large that he could
have put our vessel into it. This monster which the savages call

the GOUGOU, makes horrible noises on that island, and
when they speak of him it is with unutterably strange terror,
and many have assured me that they have seen him. Even the
above mentioned Sieur Prévert from St. Malo told me that,
while going in search of mines, . . . he passed so near the haunt
of this frightful beast, that all those on board his vessel heard
strange hissings from the noise it made, and that the savages he
had with him told him it was the same creature, and were so
afraid that they hid themselves wherever they could for fear it
should come to carry them off. And what makes me believe
what they say, is the fact that all the savages in general fear it,
and tell such strange stories of it that, if I were to record all they
say, it would be considered untrue; but I hold that this is the
dwelling-place of some devil that torments them in the manner
described (I:186-88).

After exploring to the limits of Jacques Cartier's penetration of the
St. Lawrence to the Lachine Rapids at Montréal (fig. 28) on July 4,
1603, the voyageurs returned to Tadoussac (fig. 23) where, for five
weeks, they rested at the post and were caught up on the latest news of
the workings of the new pact and the latest skirmishes with the
Iroquois. If there were trading matters of interest, Champlain recorded
nothing, and commercially the season ended with a question mark.

Six weeks later, the *Bonne Renommée* was readied for the homeward
journey to France, and as planned she sailed for Île Percée, off the
Gaspé coast. It was a safe and quick journey that took only two days;
but then, on arrival at the Atlantic outpost and just before departure
for France, something strange happened to Champlain's dreams of the
inland, something that had been discovered only a few days earlier
and held promise for the future. At the Gaspé, Pontgravé and Champlain met up with a devil quite unlike the one spoken of by the
Indians. This devil was the silver-tongued promoter Jean Sarcel de
Prévert (d. 1622) of Saint-Malo in Brittany. Prévert was an experienced
and well-connected trader who had logged considerable mileage along
the Acadian coast. Prévert was the grand huckster of the saga; he
flogged secondhand stories of a copper bonanza to be found farther
south on the Acadian coast and he added his own experience to the
"monster" story.

Trader Prévert's motives were thoroughly suspect. He was a compet-
itor out to discourage southerly exploration by his compatriots. Apart
from tales of man-eating monsters, which he related without a blush,

he repeated the traditional and uninformed babblings of the French chronicler Pierre Cayet (1525–1610), who claimed that the Massachusetts Indians "are savages of quite monstrous shape . . . very agile and resolute . . . settled in the best land of all Acadia."

Champlain and Pontgravé listened with interest as Prévert described in great detail substantial deposits of copper and other minerals to be found within Acadia. They were so charmed by Prévert that they postponed their plans to further explore the St. Lawrence and made new plans for a mining venture.

With a successful summer on record and many prospects in mind for the future, the expedition home from the Gaspé began on August 24. As in the previous year, busy Pontgravé had a special cultural mission in hand. On the recommendation of Anadabijou, the son of another chief was offered the chance to see those "fine castles, palaces [and] houses" in France (I:100). The pattern of cultural exchanges initiated by Jacques Cartier over sixty years earlier was now an integral part of the plan to build New France, and, in this year especially, there was a major payoff — the grand alliance for the future.

CHAPTER FIVE

The First and Second Excursions, and the First Settlement: Île Sainte-Croix, Maine: 1604-1605

"If I did not ask [God] for anything but bread, I would be without moose-meat or fish."

Chief Membertou's rebuff to Father Biard in response to the line from the Lord's Prayer — "Give us this day our daily bread." — *Jesuit Relations and Allied Documents, 1896–1901*

THEIR HEADS WERE FILLED WITH NEW IDEAS WHEN Pontgravé and Champlain returned to France on September 20, 1603. Unhappily, they soon learned that the Viceroy, Admiral de Chaste, had died in their absence.

Fortunately, King Henry IV turned to his old friend, another noted Huguenot, Pierre du Gua de Monts, to replace the Admiral. Like Champlain, the Sieur de Monts had been a loyal servant to his monarch and, having served with distinction during the Wars of Religion, had been rewarded with a pension of 1,200 crowns and the governorship of Pons, in Saintonge. As this was the same region where Champlain was born and owned land, there can be little doubt that in the small world of the nobility and the upper strata of the merchant class these two former comrades in the same army either knew of each other or at least had some contact prior to the exploration period.

The Sieur de Monts was an ideal choice. He was a nobleman of considerable wealth and seagoing experience. His experience already included several trading expeditions to the St. Lawrence basin during the latter years of the sixteenth century. A man of property, de Monts was a fiercely independent maverick who remained a Huguenot after

his King had converted to Catholicism. He was possessed of an entre-
preneural spirit, too, that ensured his continued support for a permanent colony in New France.

For the exploration of Acadia, the Sieur de Monts was granted a
Royal Commission on November 8, 1603, just seven days before the
publication of *Des Sauvages* on November 15. The new commission
was a command performance for a Christian crusade. In the royal
document it was stated that "men barbarous, atheists, without faith or
religion" were to be converted, and for these results the venturers were
commanded to "instruct, provoke, and incite the Indians to the
knowledge of God."

What de Monts had been granted was a monopoly on the fur trade,
and in Champlain's opening outline of the voyages, the reasons for the
grant were made clear: "For he [the Sieur de Monts] realized that what
had ruined the former undertakings had been a lack of assistance to
the promoters, who, neither in a single year nor in two, had been able
to become acquainted with the regions and the peoples who inhabit
them, or to find harbours suitable for settlement. He proposed to his
Majesty a method of meeting the expenses without drawing anything
from the royal exchequer, namely, that he be given a monopoly of the
fur trade of that country" (I:230). So, the plan was irresistible: de
Monts would establish a company of investors who would have a
monopoly. Ninety percent of returned profits would pay the investors,
and it seems it was understood that it would take two or more years
before the investments began to pay off; 10 percent would go to the
Crown, and, best of all, France would have a colony in the New World
at absolutely no expense to the royal treasury.

The King must also have been influenced by the fabulous tales from
the mining promoter Prévert, for in granting de Monts his commission he called on all the principals: "for the great and apparent profit
which may be drawn [those in charge should] make carefully to be
sought and marked all sorts of mines of gold and of silver, copper and
other metals, to make them to be digged, drawn from the earth,
purified and refined for to be converted by us, to dispose according as
we prescribed by Edicts and orders."

The Sieur de Monts moved quickly to take advantage of his grant.
He formed a trading company, and five ships in total were to be
provisioned: three to leave early in the spring of 1604 to conduct the
season's fur trading on the St. Lawrence, and two vessels with a
complement of 120 workmen were to head southward on a new

mission to explore along the Acadian coast toward Florida. They were all to rendezvous at a specific location, perhaps near where Canso, Nova Scotia, is today. Two men of the cloth were drafted into service and included on the voyage roster: Nicolas Aubry (d.c. 1611), a Catholic priest from Paris, and a Protestant clergyman, who was not identified by Champlain, to serve the needs of the Huguenots.

The Sieur de Monts also considered the security of the mission. Knowing that three years earlier, de La Roche's men had mutinied at Sable Island, de Monts deemed it wise to take along a contingent of Swiss mercenaries who would protect him against internal mutiny or assist in case of attacks by unfriendly Indians.

Another notable was invited to participate after making his wishes to come along as an observer known to the King. This personage, the Sieur Jean de Biencourt de Poutrincourt (1557–1615), a somewhat impoverished nobleman, was nonetheless highly regarded by the King. Like Champlain, Poutrincourt had served in the Wars of Religion with the King and had been in the King's personal service since 1593. Just as Champlain's interests were in mapping, writing, and colonizing, Poutrincourt seemed to have a special interest in farming. He wished to assess the arability of the land in New France. Like Champlain, too, Poutrincourt would earn a place in Canadian history books. Not as large a place as Champlain, but a significant place. His love of the land would cause him to remain in Acadia and to establish a settlement that remained until 1607. Then Poutrincourt returned to Acadia in 1610 with his son, Charles, and took advantage of a seigneurial land grant at what is today Annapolis Royal. This small settlement remained until it was devastated by English traders in 1613. A few colonists remained, however, and thus a continuous French presence in Acadia was maintained.

For the first time, some insight was provided into Champlain's role on this, his third transatlantic journey. "The said Sieur de Monts asked me if I would care to take this voyage with him. The desire I had on the last voyage had increased so that I agreed to his request, provided I had His Majesty's permission, which I received on condition I should always make him a faithful report of all I saw and discussed" (III:321). It is clear from this statement that Champlain kept his original vow and submitted his journal to the King, either as soon as he returned in September or when it was published in November. It is also clear from the King's answer that Champlain's role went beyond that of cartographer.

Filled with promise and with a company of the old and some new players on board, the grand voyage to Acadia sailed from the French port of Le Havre-de-Grâce on April 7, 1604, and after an uneventful crossing arrived at Green Bay and the La Have River mouth in Nova Scotia on May 8, 1604. (See also figs. 5, 6 and 7.)

From Advocate Harbour (fig. 8) the expedition sailed onward, creeping southward ever so slowly, to round the southern tip of Nova Scotia. On the way, each inch of the shoreline was scrutinized as the voyagers sought not only a safe harbor but a suitable location for a settlement. Champlain frequently mentioned areas with dangerous rocks and incredibly strong tides.

On or about May 25, the expedition put into what was named St. Mary's Bay. They explored some small islands and this was the site of "Master Aubry's adventure." Nicolas Aubry, the priest from Paris, referred to in the diaries as "Master Aubry," lost his sword while a small group from the expedition were off exploring their surroundings and hunting waterfowl. While searching for his missing sword, Aubry became lost in the bush for seventeen days and "being at his wits [*sic*] end, without hope of ever seeing us again, feeble and weak, he found himself on the shore of French Bay, as it was named by the Sieur de Monts" (I:254). Alone on foot, without supplies, and frightened, Aubry had managed to cross the peninsula wilderness to the Bay of Fundy. He waited a long time to be rescued; by then, the main party had turned the southern "horn" of Nova Scotia, and on proceeding northward they caught sight of the terrified soul on shore waving his hat on the end of a pole. On this one rare occasion, the fates were kind to the French.

With Aubry safely aboard and recuperating, the voyage continued, this time in a counter-clockwise scan of the entire inside shore of the Bay of Fundy. Port-Royal (fig. 16), in the Annapolis Basin, was sighted and named; but for the moment it was passed over as the site for a settlement. In any case, it was too early in the summer for the party to commit itself to any one site. This mistaken judgment was the first strategic blunder in the Acadian adventure.

The expedition then turned southward along the Atlantic coast, and on June 24 de Monts, Champlain, and Poutrincourt arrived at "one of the largest and deepest rivers we had yet seen, which we named the R. St. John [fig. 9], because it was on that day we arrived here" (I:266).

Now, for the first time, Champlain's excitement was reflected in the

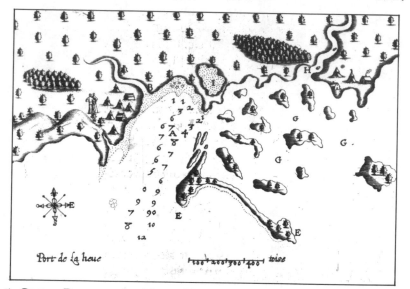

Port de La heue

5 GREEN BAY AND LA HAVE, NOVA SCOTIA, MAY 1604
Port de La heue

The chart of La Have on the Nova Scotia coast was Champlain's first
survey in North America and the first modern survey of any part of
the North American continent. As in the charts in the *Brief
Narrative*, his West Indies diary, the cartographer drew an outline of
the shore and the topography of the land mass. This time, however,
he added many more small illustrations that enliven the setting.
These were similar to his first painted sketches of the Caribbean.
Champlain demonstrated his ability to portray not only the physical
features of the area mapped, but some cultural information about the
region shown. In the first design, two Indians are shown, as well as
trees, sandy beaches, and offshore islands. Among the topographical
features like the hillocks and marshes around Port Mouton (fig. 7) are
various types of Indian houses, all meticulously detailed, with tiny
curls of smoke rising from home fires, and trees with their shadows
fixing time like tiny sundials.

In one corner of the Liverpool Bay map, the figure of an Indian
stands near the water's edge with what seems to be a spear. In another
area of the same map, there are lines of men armed with spears or
guns who seem to be a hunting party. Between campfires and crude
houses, trees and hunting parties, a bay filled with large fish whose
facial expressions vary from vacant to thoughtful, the map
encompasses careful specifics of man's place in the environment.
Though the drawings are crude, any viewer can see clearly where the
hills are, and can recognize that this was a sparsely inhabited land
peopled by hunters and gatherers. The viewer could also surmise that
the fishing was very good indeed, though the few fish look very bored
in the Liverpool Bay map.

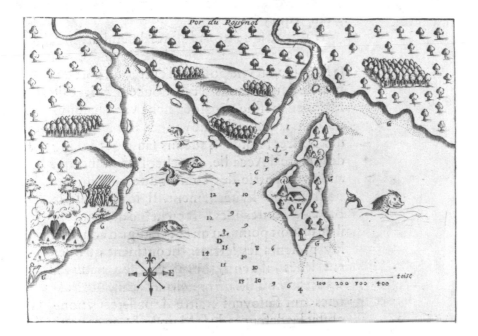

6 Liverpool Bay, Nova Scotia, May 1604
por du Rossynol

---

pages of his daily journal. He was ecstatic at this magical theater of tides, and he was the first to illustrate the famous Reversing Falls of Saint John. A "waterfall between two lofty cliffs, where the water runs with such great swiftness that if a piece of wood be thrown in, it sinks and is never seen again" (I:267). Intrigued by the sights and promises of riches farther inland, Jean Ralleau (fl. 1604–1615), personal secretary to de Monts, was assigned to go upstream and locate the Indian Chief Secoudon (d.c. 1616). The party hoped that this mighty sagamore of the Micmacs would help track down the famous copper mine first praised by the fast-talking Sieur de Prévert. No luck. Ralleau returned to the mouth of the river empty-handed, but the trip was not a complete failure. Ralleau returned with invaluable information on the inland water routes and pathways from the Bay of Fundy to the St. Lawrence River, and south to Penobscot River in Maine.

The giant jigsaw puzzle of American geography was being pieced

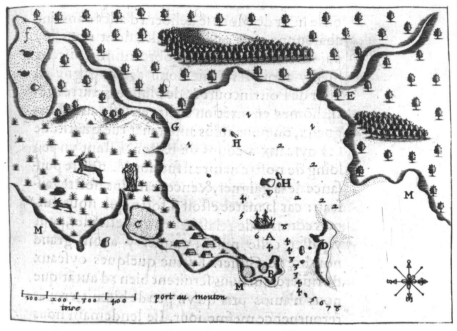

7 PORT MOUTON, NOVA SCOTIA, MAY 1604
port au mouton

---

in detail for the first time. More importantly, the area seemed criss-crossed with rivers. As pointed out in Chapter One, France too was a nation of rivers and of river transport. Early Canadian history confirms the fact that the French must have immediately seen the possibilities for trade with the interior, as they wasted no time in turning Canada's vast river system into a highway for transcontinental exploration.

Continuing to move along at a relaxed pace, the surveying party emerged from St. John harbor to again head southward along the coast. It was now the end of June, and not much progress had been made in terms of exploration. Florida was a long way off.

The next natural feature to command attention was Passamaquoddy Bay. Turning inland there, and sailing through the cluster of islands that were the feeding grounds of whales, the expedition entered the meandering river that today separates the state of Maine from the province of New Brunswick. A short distance upstream, the voyageurs discovered their long-sought sanctuary for the first winter. The Sieur de Monts, the expedition commander, named the island

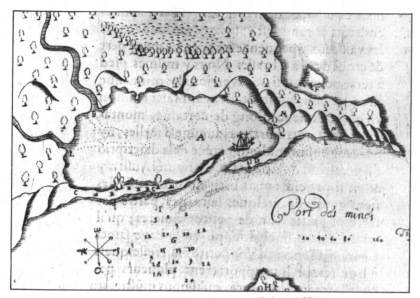

8 ADVOCATE HARBOUR, NOVA SCOTIA, MAY 1604
Port des mines

Île Sainte-Croix, in a gesture of unwitting irony. In the months ahead, the appellation would come to signify a burial ground rather than a haven of salvation.

The choice of this remote island seems to have been based on its apparent abundance of resources: "So great is the catch here of herring and bass that vessels could be loaded with them" (I:273). But the real reasons for the selection of the island were fear of Indian attack and the realization that time was running out if a settlement was to be made ready before freeze-up.

Thus far the expedition seems to have fallen short of the King's commission, which called for a broad range of activity including recovery of the Florida lands lost in 1565 by Ribaut and Laudonnière to the Spaniards, finding gold, silver, and other metals, and the conversion of a legion of souls for Christ. Apart from the discovery of Port-Royal, duly noted but passed by, little was accomplished before the explorers had to settle down and ready themselves for winter.

Security, shelter, and food supplies were the primary concerns of the expeditionary party, and they set about immediately to see to all three. The first step was to ensure that there would be "a sheltered spot where vessels of eighty to one hundred tons can lie . . . and we began to erect a barricade on a small islet a little removed from [the main island] and this served as a platform for mounting our cannon. Each worked so efficiently that in a very short time it was put in a state of defence, though the mosquitoes (which are little flies) gave us great annoyance while at work, and several of our men had their faces so swollen by their bites that they could scarcely see" (I:271-74).

At last, with the arrival of the supplies from France, "without loss of time, the Sieur de Monts proceeded to set the workmen to build houses for our residence, and allowed me to draw up the plan for settlement [fig. 10] . . . . Work on the buildings went forward steadily and vigorously" (I:276-77). In terms of morale, it was a proud beginning in spite of the site selected. There was clearly a small hamlet in the making. It included a storehouse, oven, grinding mill, and several houses. By early September, the construction of the settlement was so well advanced that de Monts was able to release Captain Champlain for his first exploration command, a "duty which I found very agreeable" (I:280).

Unfortunately, it was already fall and there were neither supplies enough nor time for any major undertaking. Late season weather had already begun, and heavy fog delayed Champlain's exit from the river and the treacherous tides of Passamaquoddy Bay.

But even if it was to be a short exploratory trip, Champlain was anxious for action. On September 5, he managed to exit the Ste. Croix river mouth and sail southward to the entrance of the Penobscot River in what is now Maine. An impressive sight greeted him at the entrance. Dominating the broken geography of this region was an island transected by a striking mountain range, "very high and cleft in places" (I:282). Champlain named it Mount Desert Island, the name it has retained.

It was near Mount Desert Island that the little group suffered its second accident of the voyage. The pinnace ran aground and Champlain, on his first command, ended up with a hole in the ship's hull next to the keel. Repairs were effected immediately and the voyage was successfully launched again. But the time for safe sailing was nearly over.

The explorers had only time enough to sail a few miles farther into the entrance of the Penobscot River (fig. 21). Since its discovery nearly four decades earlier, this river region of mystery had been noted on the mariners' maps as the Norumbega. As early as 1569, Gerhardus Mercator (1512–1594), the famous cartographic scientist, had pinpointed

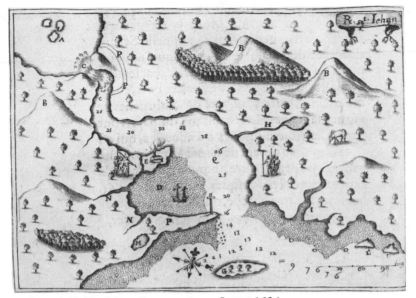

9 SAINT JOHN, NEW BRUNSWICK, JUNE 1604
R. St Iehan

the river mouth as the "Kingdom of the Future." "The river is beautiful," Champlain enthused as the happy band bobbed over the shoals upstream, where they found a waterfall (I:291). En route inland, Champlain crammed his diary full of observations and conversations with friendly natives that he encountered. Upriver, Champlain learned, "there is a great town thickly populated with skilled and clever Indians who use cotton thread [native hemp]" (I:285). Champlain had discovered the first known settlement on the site of what is today Bangor, Maine.

As at Tadoussac in 1603 (fig. 23), the voyageurs were given a great *Tabagie* in celebration. They smoked the pipe and partook of a huge banquet of fowl and venison. The happy atmosphere was infectious, and the travelers gave gifts in exchange for geographic information. The French offered to teach farming to the Indians and, as on the St. Lawrence, Champlain demonstrated a skill for local politics.

The mini-excursion ended after only three weeks. Out of provisions, the expedition had no alternative but to return to the sandy island settlement in order to assist with the preparations for winter. But this was to be no ordinary winter. The first snowfall occurred in

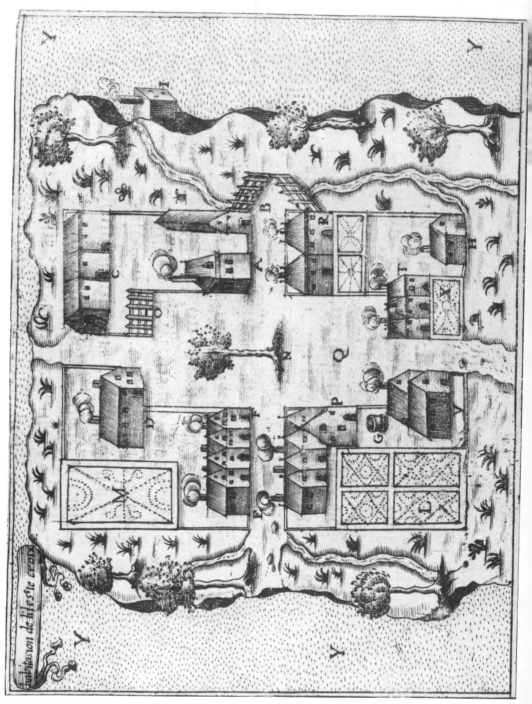

10   THE HABITATION, ÎLE SAINTE CROIX, MAINE, 1604-1605
habitasion de 1 ile s^{t}te croix

11 ST. CROIX REGION: MAINE AND NEW BRUNSWICK, JULY
1604
Isle de sainte Croix

early October, and Champlain reported: "Winter came upon us sooner than we expected and prevented us from doing many things we had intended" (I:301).

Only two weeks after his return from Mount Desert Island, Champlain reported: "The cold was severe and more extreme than in France, and lasted much longer" (I:302-03). Owing to the lack of fresh fruit and vegetables, the would-be settlers were beset with scurvy, adding to their misery. There are few passages in the annals of world discovery that match Champlain's vivid descriptions of this dread "land-sickness," as the disease was often called. "There was engendered in the mouths of those who had it large pieces of superfluous fungus flesh (which caused a great putrification)" (I:303). He described in graphic detail autopsies performed in hopes of finding the cause of the disease, and he commented sadly that not even the surgeons could prevent themselves from becoming ill. Of the seventy-nine men, thirty-five died over the winter, and twenty more were severely ill. The cider froze and could be given out only in blocks, and only the poor-quality Spanish wine was fit to drink. Bad water, insufficient wood for fuel, and other hardships plagued the men. The group was trapped on the island, unable to traverse the mountains of ice that had built up on the river. Champlain's matter-of-fact observation at the end of it all is a favorite of historians: "There are six months of winter in that country" (I:307).

The weeks of winter continued to grip the settlement. Anxious for the relief ships from France, which were due in April, Champlain plaintively noted that by the end of April there were still two or three feet (c. 1 m) of snow on the ground. By the end of May, there were still no ships in sight. Plans were made to escape in the pinnace if no help arrived by the end of June. Just when all seemed lost, François Pont-gravé arrived from France to report that the supply vessel was due. Champlain sighed in relief that "God helped us better than we had hoped" (I:310).

After the supplies were delivered, de Monts decided to "go in search of a more suitable site for a settlement, and one where the climate was milder" (I:311). At first, their target was the Gaspé, but as with past decisions, this one too was changed.

CHAPTER SIX

The Third and Fourth Excursions, and the Second Settlement: Port-Royal, Nova Scotia: 1605

"Most of the maps of this coast made for a long time after betray their indebtedness to Champlain. He was a skilled navigator, a man of science."

Henry David Thoreau (1817–1862): *Cape Cod*, 1849

ONCE THE PROVISIONS FROM FRANCE HAD ARRIVED in early June, the second season of coastline surveys commenced on June 18. Champlain reported two priorities. The first was the revival of plans to sail to Florida; the second, mentioned previously, was to find a more suitable site for the settlement. Perhaps the lesson that settlements on windswept sandy islands such as Sable and Île Sainte-Croix were doomed to failure had finally been learned.

On this next excursion, Sieur de Monts assumed command of the expedition, which included Champlain, "some gentlemen, twenty sailors, and an Indian Panounias, with his wife, whom the Indian is unwilling to leave behind" (I:311).

The party sailed southward past Mount Desert Island (fig. 21), the farthest point reached during Champlain's mini-voyage the previous year. From Mount Desert Island, the exploration party pressed on to the island-studded mouth of the Kennebec River (fig. 12). Once again, the original destination of Florida was superseded by interest in this new area. A detailed survey of the Kennebec River and its islands was undertaken, although the region had already been declared unsuitable for a settlement. In this case, the reasons for the area being declared undesirable had nothing to do with its geography, climate, or potential for development. The Kennebec River was the border of the Almouchiquois country, a nation with whom neither the French nor their Indian friends had an alliance. Wisely, the French realized that a settlement in this area might well place them between two warring nations. Champlain and his compatriots took care to map the area, carefully giving names to seemingly unimportant rocks such as Tortoise Island. With the border established,the French and their Indian friends hoped to minimize the risks of attack. Nonetheless they were still optimistic about an alliance with the Almouchiquois in spite of their meticulous surveying.

The Micmac chief, Panounias (d. 1607), began extensive negotiations with the Kennebec Indians. This was the reason that he had insisted that his wife be included on this voyage: she was herself an Almouchiquois. Her services as an interpreter proved indispensable, as she alone was able to negotiate with the Kennebec chief of the Almouchiquois, Manthoumermer. In the only credit Champlain ever gave a woman for anything other than doing domestic chores, being a decoration, or a whore, he reported that it was "she [who]explained to them [the Almouchiquois] the reason of our coming. We made friends with them and with the Indians of that river who acted as our guides" (I:314-15).

In the course of the discussions, it became evident, however, that although the Almouchiquois sought an alliance with the French, the accord was not to be along the same lines as the grand alliance negotiated with the Algonquins and Montagnais at Tadoussac in 1603. Now, the French agreed that the Indians could, "through our [French] mediation[,] . . . make peace with their enemies" (I:316). Champlain was so enchanted with this twist that twenty-five years later, in 1629, when he was forced to seek a refuge from the English who were about to seize Québec, he remembered the Kennebec region with much affection.

For the student of the Europeans' early dealings with the Indians — during all this interplay between surveying and negotiating — there is insight to be gained by examining the bargaining process. Firearms, powder, and halberds were never bartered, but small knives or even axes were considered worthwhile and safe items to be used as leverage for goodwill; but as much as possible the "Sieur de Monts had biscuits and peas given them, wherewith they were very much pleased" (I:316).

In spite of the evident goodwill and accord on both sides, the French still rejected the area as a possible site for their settlement. "This river Kennebec, for half a league from its mouth is very dangerous for vessels, because of the shallow water, great tides, rocks and shoals found both outside and inside. There is, nevertheless, a good channel if it were well explored. The little of the country I saw along the banks is very bad; for it is nothing but rocks everywhere." There was "very little cultivable land" — the ultimate comment signifying their lack of interest. The fact that Champlain found that the "place abounds in fish" was by no means sufficient justification for further consideration of this as a settlement site (I:320-21).

While considering the alternatives, the de Monts expedition lingered eight days on the Kennebec, and Champlain concluded his regional observation with a description of the Indian ritual conducted at Hockomock Point: "Each [Indian] left an arrow near a rock before which all the Indians pass. They believe that unless they do this, misfortune will befall them, for so the devil persuades them. Such superstitions and likewise many others do they practise" (I:317).

Although only two days' sailing time from Île Sainte-Croix, the de Monts expedition had been gone nearly three weeks from the settlement when, on July 8, it left the Kennebec River and headed south past Casco Bay, or baye de Marchen, as Champlain identified it on his map of 1607 (fig. 21). After having noted the snow-capped mountains of New Hampshire to the west, the expedition then moved on to an island described as very beautiful, "on account of what it produces . . . fine oaks and nut trees and an abundance of vines which in their season bear fine grapes. These were the first we had seen on any of these coasts from cape La Have [fig. 5]. We named it the island of Bacchus [now Richmond's Island]" (I:323).

Continuing at a leisurely pace, the voyageurs reached safe anchorage at the mouth of the Saco River in Maine (fig. 13), where they observed a large party of Indians dancing on shore. On this occasion, unfortunately, Chief Panounias was without his interpreter wife: she had gone home. When the Chief tried to take her place, linguistic difficulties developed.

Champlain, unable to understand or communicate, was reduced to physical observations: "Their chief [of the Almouchiquois] was good-looking, young and active . . . . These Indians shave off their hair fairly high up on the head, and wear the remainder very long, combing and twisting it very neatly behind in several ways, with feathers which they fasten on their heads. They paint their faces black and red" (I:325-26). On his summary map of 1612 (fig. 29), Champlain presented a handsome illustration of the Almouchiquois — "these active people with well-formed bodies" (I:326).

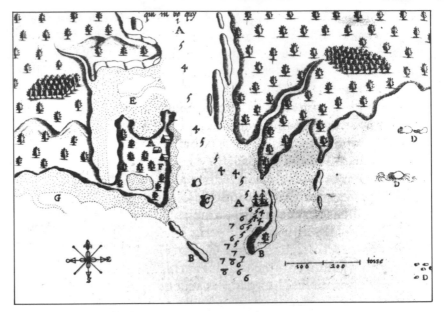

12 KENNEBEC RIVER MOUTH, MAINE, JULY 1605
qui ni be quy

The voyageurs arrived at the Saco River mouth on July 9, and here, for the first time, the French took the time to study Indian farming techniques:

> They till and cultivate the land, a practice we had not seen previously. In place of ploughs they use an instrument of very hard wood made in the shape of a spade . . . . I saw their grain, which is Indian corn [fig. 3]. This they grow in gardens, sowing three or four grains in one spot. The shell of the horseshoe crab is used as a trowel . . . . As for the beans, they were beginning to burst into flower, as were likewise the pumpkins and squashes (III:374; I:328).

For the French in New France, these were not casual observations, but the most important aspect of their fact-finding mission. In France, as in most of Europe, the attitude toward land was almost sacred. "I want death to find me planting my cabbages," penned the poet Michel de Montaigne (1533–1592). In Champlain's time, the heroic figure of the age was the shepherd boy Vincent de Paul (1581–1660). This is the lad who one day would be elevated to sainthood! Everyone praised

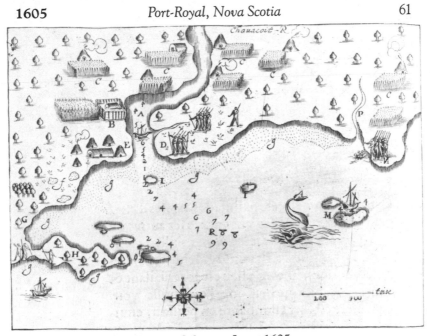

13 SACO AND BIDDEFORD, MAINE, JULY 1605
    Chauacoit R.

commitment to the soil. Historian and voyageur Marc Lescarbot, who spent a year in Acadia at Port-Royal, for all his interest in history and theater, was another who was in tune with the pastoral chorus: "Let us return to our tillage; for to that we must apply ourselves: it is the first mine that must be fought for." For the sons of France, there was no escaping this primordial call, stated so clearly by King Henry IV's first minister, the duc de Sully: "Tilling and grazing are the twin breasts that feed France."

Agricultural observations were the basis of Champlain's journals. At the Saco River, the next stop on the search for a suitable settlement site, Champlain noted that the Indians had "a large wigwam surrounded by palisades formed of rather large trees placed one against the other . . . . This place is very pleasant, and as attractive a spot as one can see anywhere. The river, which is bordered with meadows, abounds greatly in fish. At its mouth lies an islet adapted for the construction of a good fortress where one would be safe" (I:330). Although it was praised at the time, there was no further mention from Champlain again about the Saco River, except in a passing reference to the horseshoe crab. One of the most intriguing curiosities of the ocean world is the horseshoe crab, or the Siguenoc, as Champlain referred to it and illustrated it on his great map of 1612 (fig. 29). This particular crab looks like a combination of a crab and a tortoise, but is neither. It is actually a cousin of the scorpion, and biologically it is in a class by itself. Champlain noted the shell color, which is "like a dead leaf," the four pairs of "legs," and the fact that the creature eats with two of its "walking" appendages. He also confirmed the earlier observation made at the Saco River (fig. 13) that the tail of the Siguenoc was used by the Indians to tip arrows, and they were found by the de Monts party from Kennebec to Cape Cod.

Carefully scanning the shoreline, the voyageurs continued to sail southward. Just south of the Saco River (fig. 13), on Sunday, July 12, Champlain noted the miles of salt marshes at Wells, Maine. The party espied two Indians along the shore, who at first were mistaken for Canada geese, as they "flew" for cover. Champlain was apparently content with these trivial observations, and one wonders if there was any serious consideration given to this third coastal expedition originally intended to sail to Florida.

The expedition reached Cape Ann, the large promontory just to the north of present-day Gloucester and Boston harbor. On seeing smoke signals, the ships dispatched a small shore party with knives and biscuits for the Indians. The encounter was cordial, and Champlain seized the opportunity to draw a map with charcoal to show their hosts. In reply, the Indians added to the chart, with the same charcoal "another bay which they represented as very large" (I:335).The combined effort resulted in the first known regional map of Boston harbor, which was eventually incorporated into Champlain's survey of 1607 (fig. 21).

Proceeding south to "Massachusetts Bay," as mapped by the Indians, a single canoe party was sent ashore with knives and rosaries to test the atmosphere. Again, there were language difficulties; but perhaps equally important, the explorers found a large, well-entrenched native population. Unlike the landing at Kennebec, the de Monts party was not encouraged by their reception. The Indians seemed suspicious, and de Monts was quickly persuaded to press farther south.

Before leaving Massachusetts Bay, Champlain observed that the canoes were no longer made of birch bark but were instead carved out of whole trees. He pondered the work involved, the "great trouble and . . . time [spent] in felling them with hatchets of stone." This far south, the Indians made dugouts, and Champlain gave the details of tree selection, de-barking, and the hollowing out of the center with a water-controlled fire. "The stones from which they make their cutting tools are like our musket flints" (I:338-39).

By July 17, de Monts was fearful of an Indian attack and the French had still made no progress in selecting a permanent site. The expedition sailed farther south to the next area selected for study, named Port St. Louis by the French (fig. 14). Fifteen years later, in 1620, this same harbor was renamed Plymouth, the landfall of the first Pilgrims. In this pre-New England history, however, Champlain reported that a "great number of Indians came out to us in their canoes . . . and we perceived several smoke-signals, but on proceeding thither our pinnace grounded upon a rock, placing us in great danger" (I:340). After quick maneuvering all was recovered and contact was made with the numerous Indians, "who began to exhibit great signs of joy, and to make various kinds of harangues which we in no wise understood."

Again de Monts's distribution of gifts was welcomed, and the Europeans were delighted to receive in return "little squashes as big as your fist, which we ate as a salad like cucumbers, and they were very good . . . and we saw in this place a great many little houses, which are

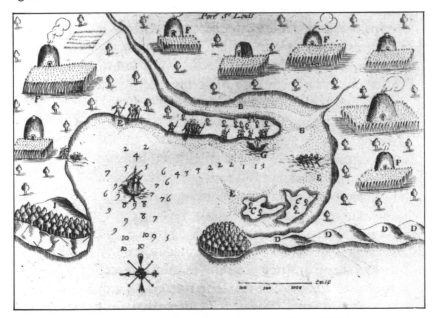

14 PLYMOUTH HARBOR, MASSACHUSETTS, JULY 1605
Port St Louis

situated in the fields where they sow their Indian corn" (fig. 3) (I:340-41). The fish were plentiful: "These [the Indians] catch with hooks made of a piece of wood, to which they attach a bone shaped like a harpoon, which they fasten very securely for fear lest it come out. The whole thing has the form of a little crook. The line which is attached to it is made of tree-bark . . . . I went on shore, where I saw many more Indians . . . . I went to explore the river" (I:344-45). At Port St. Louis (Plymouth) they did not fear an Indian attack, and the agricultural experts led by Poutrincourt were back to the business of scouting the geography for a permanent settlement.

Leaving Port St. Louis on July 19, the explorers headed directly into the inside arm of what is now called Cape Cod; Champlain named this giant curved sandbar the "White Cape." He was delighted with the surroundings. "This coast has fairly high sand-banks which are very conspicuous from the sea . . . and there is a great extent of open country along the shore before one enters the woods, which are very delightful and pleasant to the eye" (I:348-49).

In the next episode, having turned south at the "fist" of the Cape, a lookout spied Indians on the shoreline at Nauset Harbor (fig. 15), and once again, as at Massachusetts Bay, the explorers suspected there might be difficulties. So, without an interpreter, they did not put a landing party ashore; but it was noted that the residents made a hasty retreat, either out of fear or to report their sightings to others.

On the next day, the voyageurs were more intrigued than ever by the Indians' odd behaviour, and they decided to risk a closer encounter. Uncertain as to what reception they might receive, they also found the harbor to be "a very dangerous port on account of the shoals and sand-banks, where we saw breakers on every side." During the Frenchmen's onshore investigation, the Indians returned: "They come to us from, all sides, dancing" (I:349-50). In spite of this greeting, however, the explorers were uneasy about being surrounded, and their observations over the next few days confirmed their original caution. Nonetheless determined to press on, the explorers still deemed an agricultural assessment a priority, and a party was put ashore to visit the Indian village. Armed and wary, the men proceeded while their comrades guarded the pinnace. At first, the atmosphere seemed friendly, and the observers noted that the Almouchiquois were excellent land managers. "There were also several fields not cultivated, for the reason that the Indians let them lie fallow. When they wish to plant them they set fire to the weeds and then dig up the field with their wooden spades" (I:352). Not only were there luxurious cornfields in evidence, Champlain also reported there were "an abundance of Brazillian [sic] beans, many edible squashes . . . roots, tobacco . . . " (III:395) and woods that were full of oaks, nut trees, and red cedars, which had a "very pleasant smell." These Indians were also good builders. "Their wigwams are round, and covered with heavy thatch made of reeds. In the middle of the roof is an opening, about a foot and a half [46 cm] wide, through which issues the smoke of their fire" (I:352).

Residents of the village and the newcomers approached each other circumspectly. At first, even with the language barrier, both sides communicated with what seemed considerable success. As an example, Champlain gathered simple information, such as the annual amount of snowfall, by indicating his white collar and wiggling his fingers downward. The Almouchiquois signaled back that the winter on the cape was not as severe as the conditions remembered by the veterans of Île Sainte-Croix (fig. 11).

The observations were going well when a sudden storm hammered the midsummer visitors. Champlain reported that "the sun was hardly visible at all . . . . It was very cold, so that we were obliged to put on our greatcoats which we had entirely laid aside" (I:353). The bad weather served as a timely reminder that the mission had other objectives. It was also an ill omen, as the voyageurs in late season penetrated farther into less friendly country.

The underlying uncertainty and tension between the Almouchiquois and the French flared up on July 23, when five sailors went ashore on Nauset beach with large copper kettles to replenish the water supply. One rambunctious Indian snatched a kettle "by force out of the hands of a sailor who had filled his . . . first and had no weapons" (I:353). Fighting broke out when a comrade rushed to aid the shaken water-bearer. The sailor chased the Indian in order to recover the bucket and, seeing what had happened, the sailors aboard the pinnace fired shots to ward off an attack by the residents. Meanwhile, on board the boat, the many Indians who had been bartering and poking about with curiosity dove overboard, save one who was captured. Within seconds the skirmish was out of hand, and the sailor on the beach, unarmed and terrorized, was summarily executed by a volley of arrows fired by the Indians. His body was then assaulted by

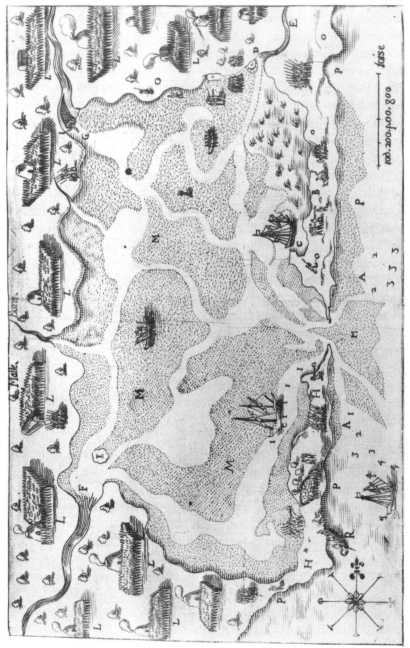

15 NAUSET HARBOR, MASSACHUSETTS, JULY 1605
Malle-Barre

numerous attackers armed with knives. Luckily — and with speed — the others made their escape to the boat.

During this fast flare-up, the rest of the French were secure but helpless aboard ship. With trepidation, a small party undertook a rescue mission, while others fired their muskets from the ship to hold the Indians back. But Champlain's weapon failed: "Mine exploded in my hands and nearly killed me" (I:354). (This was the first of many wounds he was to receive in the New World.) The Indians were like "swift footed horses," and in a flash they were gone from the scene.

There was no further conflict, and the rescue party buried their mutilated shipmate. Then, after a half-hearted apology was offered from one band of Indians who made an "outward show that it was not they who had done this evil deed but others farther off in the interior," de Monts released his only bargaining chip — the hostage grabbed at the outbreak of hostilities. With the unsatisfactory business over, Champlain gladly returned to his role of geographer, ethnographer, and naturalist: "All these Indians . . . wear no skins nor furs, except very rarely; but their clothes are made from grasses and hemp, and barely cover their bodies, and come down only to the thighs . . . the men have their privy parts concealed by a small skin. It is the same also with the women, who wear it a little lower . . . all the rest of the body is naked. When the women came to see us they wore skins open in front" (I:355).

After five weeks of voyaging through increasing "fogs and storms," Champlain recorded that "the Sieur de Monts decided to return to Ste. Croix island [Île Sainte-Croix], in order to find another spot more suitable for our settlement; for we had been unable to find such a place on any of the coasts we had explored on this voyage" (I:362). Supplies were nearly exhausted, and in the end, to finish off this second year of aimlessness, on July 25, the pinnace was nearly lost on a sandbar as it exited Nauset cove near the harbor entrance. The two inexperienced men acting as pilots, Champdoré and Cramolet, were accused of botching up the marking of the passage out of the harbor.

The retreat homeward continued, with a stopover at Saco (fig. 13), where de Monts took the opportunity to reinforce the goodwill initiated three weeks earlier by giving the Indians more gifts. In gratitude, the Saco Indians handed over a captive Micmac Indian to be returned to his own people by the northbound voyageurs. On this visit, however, the pleasantries were interrupted. News arrived that there was an

English vessel in the vicinity and, worse yet, that its crew was busily ravaging the entire area. The English, it was reported, had already killed five Saco Indians, and this news alarmed the peaceful French explorers with good cause. Whatever good will the French had built to date in this region was now in jeopardy. The threat of the Saco Indians on the warpath was reason enough to hurry home and get on with moving the settlement.

The voyageurs returned to the Île Sainte-Croix settlement (fig. 10) on August 2, and were relieved to learn that the provision ship from France was also on time. All that remained was the final decision on the relocation of the settlement, and for a change de Monts's ruling was swift: "To remove elsewhere, and to build another settlement to escape the cold and the dreadful winter we had experienced at Ste. Croix. . . . we loaded with the woodwork of the houses at Ste. Croix, to transport it to Port Royal . . . where we judged the climate to be much more agreeable and temperate. Pontgravé and I set out for this place" (I:367).

The task was a mammoth one. Having failed for months to find a suitable site, the colonizers had to take down their old settlement piece by piece, transport it to Port-Royal, and reconstruct it on the site that they had bypassed fifteen months earlier. And all of this had to be done before winter.

Despite the hasty move, Champlain wrote with a new optimism at Port-Royal. These words brought his record of the second Acadian excursion to a close: "We began to clear the ground, which was full of trees, and to erect the houses as quickly as possible. Everybody was busy at this work. After everything had been set in order and the greater part of the dwellings built, the Sieur de Monts decided to return to France to obtain from his Majesty what was necessary for his enterprise" (I:369-70).

The habitation at Port-Royal (fig. 17) was completed in short order with high spirits and marvelous teamwork. One result was an impressive multipurpose structure 216 feet (66 m) in circumference, which would serve as a storehouse, cellar, courtyard, and workmen's quarters. A platform on the western side was designed to hold "four pieces of cannon; and at the other corner, towards the east, is a palisade fashioned like a platform" (I:373).

As in the previous year, the little community made a major effort to be agriculturally self-sufficient; some of the forty or forty-five who stayed behind began to make gardens" (I:371). In lines reminiscent of those opening phrases of the West Indies journal, Champlain made his personal commitment:

> I also, in order not to remain idle, made one which I sur-
> rounded with ditches full of water wherein I placed some fine
> trout; and through it flowed three brooks of clear running
> water from which the greater part of our settlement was sup-
> plied. I constructed in it near the sea-shore a little sluiceway, to
> draw off the water whenever I desired. This spot was completely
> surrounded by meadows, and there I arranged a summer-house
> with fine trees, in order that I might enjoy the fresh air. I con-
> structed there likewise a small reservoir to hold salt-water fish,
> which we took out as we required them . . . . We often resorted
> there to pass the time, and it seemed as if the little birds there-
> abouts received pleasure from this; for they gathered in great
> numbers and warbled and chirped so pleasantly that I do not
> think I ever heard the like (I:371-73).

Such unguarded reflections are rare in Champlain's writing. Clearly, he was pleased with the new site and with himself. He had reason to be. It was a remarkable accomplishment and as in the previous year, time was left for another quick expedition before freeze-up.

With more energy than good judgment, Champlain struck out to look for the elusive copper mine of Prévert's stories. It was, after all, the magnet that had first pulled the French away from the St. Lawrence River two years earlier. This little band proposed to return to the Saint John River (fig. 9) in search of Chief Secoudon, who had guided Prévert's men "to the copper mine, for which I had already searched in company with the Sieur de Monts when we were at the Port of Mines [Advocate Harbour] but all to no purpose" (I:374).

Secoudon was located and easily persuaded to guide the deter-mined Champlain and his party over the same territory covered by de Monts and Poutrincourt in May and June of 1604, a year and a half earlier. At least this time the French found some promising signs: "We found there, embedded in greyish and red rocks, a few small bits of copper about as thick as a sou, and others thicker." The men realized that this minute outcropping of copper at Black Point, near Advocate Harbour, Nova Scotia (fig. 8), however, was neither sufficient nor accessible enough to justify commercial exploitation, and "the truth is that if the sea [i.e., the Fundy tides] did not cover these mines twice a day and if they did not occur in rocks of such hardness, one might

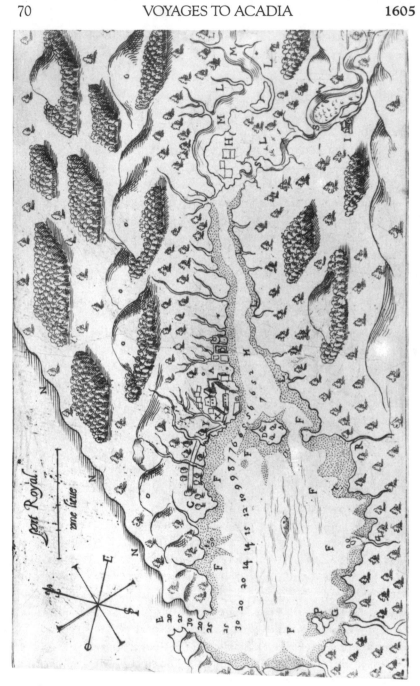

16 ANNAPOLIS BASIN, NOVA SCOTIA, 1604–1605
port Royal

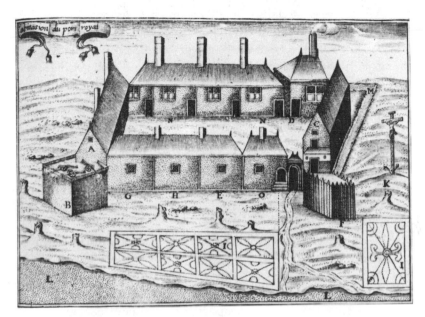

17 PORT-ROYAL, NOVA SCOTIA, 1605–1606
abitasion du port royal

Champlain's architectural drawing of the Port-Royal habitation (fig. 17) is a more detailed rendering than the completed illustration of the habitation at Île Sainte Croix (fig. 10). In this case the sketch of the habitation on the regional chart (fig. 16) is likely the plan that was originally intended. The letter D marks the residence of Champlain and Pontgravé. The workmen's quarters are located looking out toward the ocean (A), nicely protected on the river by the cannon (B). The gardens that are rimmed with what appear to be fences are marked I, and the surrounding palisade is identified as F. The four rooms at the front (H), (E) and the two marked (G) and (O) are respectively the kitchen, the blacksmith shop, and the rooms for the ship's rigging.

Today the Habitation stands as the only reconstructed Champlain settlement in North America.

---

expect something therefrom" (I:374-75). Another Prévert myth was laid to rest. Mining this lode wouldn't have been a viable proposition.

With another season wasted, the band returned to Port-Royal, where there was even more depressing news. Again, the dreaded scurvy was sweeping the settlement, and although conditions were not as bad as at Île Sainte-Croix, twelve of the forty-five settlers died and five more were seriously ill. Again, medical research was undertaken, and the surgeon, Des Champs of Honfleur, "a man skilled in his profession, opened some of the bodies to see if he could discover the cause of this illness better than had those who had tried in the previous year . . . . He could find no remedy for curing them any more than had the others" (I:376).

With the beginning of 1606, the weather was kinder to the settlers than it had been the previous year. Excepting one destructive wind storm, the snow had changed to frequent rains by February 20. The French had learned well how to manage their time in the milder seasons: in the spring they had to get down to the business of relocating to a more favorable climate. On March 1, 1606, at the first opportunity, Pontgravé readied the pinnace for a fifth expedition, and this time their goal was focused: "to proceed on a voyage of discovery along the coast of Florida" (I:377).

The Sieur de Monts never again returned to the shores of America, but his efforts were in part responsible for what would become the success of New France. De Monts returned to France to encourage new and continued investment in colonization on the part of both the Crown and his business associates.

With de Monts's departure, Pontgravé, who had just arrived from France with the supplies, was placed in command. Champlain was "at the same time, determined to remain there as well, in the hope of making new discoveries towards Florida; and of this the Sieur de Monts highly approved" (I:370).

Here again, Champlain expressed a long-term objective — a dream of new discoveries and the eventual colonization of the Carolinas and Florida. For three decades, Champlain repeated this theme. Long after plans for taking Florida were practical, Champlain devoted an entire chapter to the history of French colonial efforts in Florida and the Carolinas in the edition of Les Voyages published in 1632. In the intervening years, however, while the French dabbled with surveys and small settlements in Québec and along the Mississippi, dreaming of agricultural self-sufficiency, there were other nations pursuing the business of settling America (figs. 16 and 17).

CHAPTER SEVEN

More Excursions: False Starts, Retreat, and Reprieve: 1606

"I respectfully urge adequate appropriation for the Sieur de Monts National Monument on the coast of Maine."

President Theodore Roosevelt 1858–1919:
To the House Appropriations Committee regarding the creation of Acadia National Park, Mount Desert Island, April 10, 1918

F AMILIAR BY NOW WITH THE SWIFT DESCENT OF winter, the French had yet to learn of the vagaries of a Canadian spring. The early departure brought disaster. One day's sail away from Port-Royal, with bad weather closing in, Pontgravé hastily chose a poor anchorage site, and during the night the ship's moorings gave way. The pinnace was

> driven toward the coast at the mercy of God and the waves, which were . . . furious and dangerous . . . . In the surf, the wind and waves threw us upon a small rock and we only awaited the moment when we should see our boat break up, to save ourselves if we could upon some wreckage. In this desperate situation, after we had withstood several other waves, there came one so huge and fortunate that it carried us over the rock and threw us upon a little sandy beach which preserved us for the night from shipwreck (I:377-78).

The battered vessel was "speedily repaired by the diligence of Champdoré her master," and four days later the crew returned to the mainland. They encountered headwinds, fog, and a "great quantity of snow" and ice (I:379) in the Ste. Croix River, and the expedition was forced into a holding pattern at "po aux coquille" on the northeast corner of Campobello Island (fig. 21). By the end of March all seemed hopeless. Frustrated at every turn, Pontgravé gave up the year's first effort and ordered a return to Port-Royal. Shortly thereafter, the emotional and distressed man suffered a heart attack.

Pontgravé did not allow his physical condition to delay the planned trip to Florida. After only ten days' rest, François Pontgravé was in no condition to travel, let alone command. Still, he clambered on board again and stuffed himself into a sickbed below decks. Before doing so, however, he appointed Champdoré master of the vessel. For some reason, the more experienced Champlain was passed over.

On the first day, the frightened carpenter, miscast in his role as ship's master, was forced to seek advice from the stricken Pontgravé, who irritably tossed the options right back to his befuddled substitute. Left alone to decide, Champdoré gambled on the weather and again lost.

> The weather was very thick, being rainy and very foggy, with more prospect of bad weather than of good. As he sought to pass through the entrance of the port, we were suddenly carried by the tide out of the passage, and were upon the rocks . . . . Pont-Gravé and I, who were in bed, heard the sailors crying out and exclaiming, 'We are lost,' which soon brought me to my feet to see what had happened. Pont-Gravé was still ill, and this prevented him from getting up as quickly as he wished. I was no sooner on deck than the pinnace was thrown upon the coast . . . . At the first bump of our boat upon the rocks the rudder was broken, part of the keel and three or four planks were stove in, and some ribs were broken. This astonished us, for our pinnace immediately filled, and all we could do was to wait until the tide ran out to get ashore (I:380-81).

This time the result was disastrous. The vessel was lost and Champdoré "accused of having run our pinnace ashore with malicious intent, and after his examination he was imprisoned and handcuffed, in order to be taken to France" (I:383). Such a charge seems absurd and the question remains as to why the shipwright was given command of the ship in the first place. Poor Champdoré was obviously a scapegoat. Those in command of this venture were only too aware of Champdoré's limitations. They were all present the previous year at Nauset, Cape Cod, when Champdoré accidentally misplaced the buoy markers at the harbor entrance.

The recriminations over Champdoré's command continued for a week. Then, with no sign of the relief vessels — long overdue from France — the abused carpenter was given the opportunity to redeem himself. He was told to reconstruct the pinnace. There was good reason for this change of heart: as it had been arranged a year earlier, the colony was to close down in the event that the ships from France did not arrive by the July 16 deadline. If the colony was to be abandoned, seaworthy vessels were essential in order to make the homeward journey.

No ships were sighted by the deadline date and supplies were exhausted. The broken pinnace was restored to service and another urgently readied for the first stage of withdrawal. The plan was to retrace the voyage route back to the contact base-camp at Miscou Island (fig. 40) at the Gaspé, or if necessary to go much farther and north to Canso or Cape Breton, all in the hopes either of connecting with the French trading vessels en route homeward or, with luck, to encounter the overdue supply ships en route to Port-Royal.

On July 17, the deadline passed, and with no ships sighted the entire company abandoned the habitation, leaving only a token force of two colonists who were bribed with a hundred crowns of silver to risk another winter at Port-Royal. Gambling their lives, the two agreed, and the others departed for France.

The defeated colonists, beaten by mismanagement and the wicked environment, sailed from Port-Royal on schedule, and again bad luck followed them. For the third time in one month, and as before on the first day out from Port-Royal, disaster struck.

> We came to anchor in Long Island strait [fig. 21], where during the night our cable broke, and we were in danger of being lost . . . . there arose a heavy squall which broke our rudder-irons and placed us in such a predicament that we did not know what to do; for the fury of the sea did not permit us to land, since the breakers ran mountains high along the coast . . . . As each was thinking for himself what could be done for our safety, . . . Champdoré, who had again been handcuffed, said to some of us that if Pont-Gravé were willing, he would find means of steering our pinnace . . . Pont-Gravé . . . did not

refuse this offer and the others even less. Champdoré was accordingly set free for the second time; and thereupon, taking a rope and cutting it, he very cleverly mended the rudder . . . . In this way he makes amends for the mistakes he had committed on the first pinnace . . . and through entreaties . . . he was freed from the accusation against him (I:385-87).

In full retreat, the colonists sailed south from Port-Royal and then eastward around the tip of Nova Scotia. Near Sable Island the voyageurs miraculously encountered Jean Ralleau, personal secretary to de Monts, who had come ahead of the *Jonas*, a 120-ton supply vessel, in a shallop. Aboard the *Jonas* were three notables: the Sieur de Poutrincourt, Marc Lescarbot, and Louis Hébert (c. 1575-1627). To act in de Monts's absence, the Sieur de Poutrincourt had been appointed the Lieutenant General of New France. Having participated in the first explorations of Saco, the Kennebec, and Nauset, Poutrincourt was known to all, and his experience was welcomed. Strangely, Champlain neglected to mention the arrival of Marc Lescarbot, de Monts's personal lawyer. It was a curious omission, and it may have been the start of a feud. Louis Hébert, the third arrival, was to become the founding father of agricultural self-sufficiency in New France. The *Jonas* also carried badly needed fresh supplies and additional men, fifty of whom had already landed farther north at Canso. By July 30, Poutrincourt, Lescarbot, and the colonists, with Champlain and Pontgravé, had all safely returned to Port-Royal.

Their new commander, fully aware of the lost weeks in the season, moved quickly. The next day, "the Sieur de Poutrincourt proceeded to explain what ought to be done, and with the approval of everyone," the decision was made to "remain at Port Royal for this year, inasmuch as nothing had been discovered since the Sieur de Monts' voyage" (I:388-89). The colonists returned to their primary goal of finding suitable places for settlements, and under the stewardship of the grand dreamer Jean de Biencourt de Poutrincourt, morale was high and the colonists felt hopeful.

With the new priorities established, even though it was late in the season for planting, Poutrincourt made a major commitment to the Port-Royal settlement. He initiated his own pet agricultural project by sending "some laborers to cultivate the land at a spot he considered suitable, which is up river a league and a half from the settlement at Port-Royal [fig. 16] where he had thought of making our abode. There he had wheat, rye, hemp and several other seeds sown to ascertain how they would thrive" (I:390). At Annapolis Royal, Poutrincourt seeded the grainfield now recognized as the first in Canada, and the wheat fields of America had their beginnings in Nova Scotia and on Île Sainte-Croix, Maine (fig. 10).

While Poutrincourt farmed, Champlain struggled with cartography. "I also remained with the Sieur de Poutrincourt, in order with God's help to complete the map I had begun of these coasts and countries" (fig. 21). When everything in the settlement had been put in order, "The Sieur de Poutrincourt had provisions placed on board for our voyage to the coast of Florida" (I:391). Despite this often spoken-of trip, it was obvious that Champlain wanted to make maps and Poutrincourt wanted to farm and poke about in the world of agronomics. As for Florida, it was once again too late to venture forth on such a long journey.

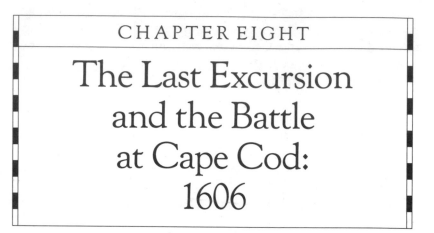

CHAPTER EIGHT

The Last Excursion and the Battle at Cape Cod: 1606

"All signs of discourtesy and disdain, as was possible for any brute creature to invent such as exhibiting their bare behinds and laughing immoderately."

Giovanni da Verrazzano, c. 1485–c. 1528: *Navigationi*, 1556 (Observation on the Indians of the New England coast.)

O N SEPTEMBER 5, ALTHOUGH IT WAS LATE IN THE season, Poutrincourt launched the pinnace on another exploratory expedition. As usual, the smaller vessel, the shallop, was put on board for inland surveying, although once again there was precious little time for any real exploration. A round trip to Florida was out of the question.

At first, the expedition headed for Île Sainte-Croix (fig. 10) to evaluate the condition of the gardens planted two years earlier. "We found some wheat which had fallen to the ground and had come up as fine as one could desire, and a quantity of garden vegetables which had grown up fair and large. It gave us the greatest pleasure to see that the soil there was good and fertile" (I:393). Wasting time, Poutrincourt, always the dreamer, delayed the party at the former colony for an entire week.

But before leaving Île Sainte-Croix, the Lieutenant to the Viceroy retained the services of Secoudon, Chief of the Saint John River Indians (fig. 9), and Messamouet (fl. 1604-1607), Chief of the Indians at Advocate Harbour (fig. 8). According to the journals, these were the same chiefs who had guided Champlain the previous year when he had searched for Prévert's copper bonanza. Like the Indian emissary at the great conference at Tadoussac in 1603, Messamouet had been to France for indoctrination in European ways. This native seemed likely to prove useful as he dazzled audiences with tales of great chateaus and carriages drawn by strange-looking "deer."

Having examined the gardens and acquired the Indians as interpreters, they once again set sail. It took nine days to reach the Saco River (fig. 13). Here they decided to make a return visit to Bacchus (Richmond's) Island. Apparently, this side trip was made in order to check the grapevines found on their previous trip. They encountered Chief Onemechin who had another native prisoner for them to take north. They also exchanged kettles, axes, knives, and other articles for corn, squashes, and beans.

Soon, however, the colder weather signaled the dying weeks of summer. Even though it was mid-September, the little expedition dallied on the northern outskirts of Massachusetts Bay at Cape Ann. Then the storms of early fall struck with fury. In a moment of reflection, Champlain remembered a happier passage in these waters: "Whilst we were in this predicament, I remembered that when following this coast with the Sieur de Monts, I had noted on my map at a league's distance a place which appeared suitable for vessels, into which we had not entered, because at the time we were passing, the wind was favourable for holding our course . . . . We proceeded to anchor at the entrance, and the next day went inside" (I:396-97) (fig. 21).

The harbor at present-day Gloucester, Massachusetts (fig. 18), was Champlain's favorite on the Acadian coast. He called it the "Beautiful port" (Le Beau Port) and Poutrincourt, the agricultural expert, also had reason to celebrate: it was harvest time and after a very mild winter there were magnificent crops of "very fine grapes," and beans, corn, squashes, and roots, as well as a luxurious forest. But this paradise was inhabited. There were some two hundred nervous natives in this community, and the explorers had no way of communicating with them. The Indians brought along on the mission were beyond their linguistic borders and could not make themselves understood.

A year earlier, when the explorers had found themselves in a similar position, they had hastily departed. Poutrincourt, however, felt no need to move along, and the record of trivia maintained by Champlain reveals that there were no new accomplishments, though there were a few good stories. For example, Champlain related how Chief

Onemechin from Saco had managed to beat the French ship to Gloucester by running ahead on foot. The inclusion of this tale seems more a confirmation of Poutrincourt's pace than of the Indian's speed. In another such aside, the reader is informed that:

> At this place we also saw an Indian who wounded himself so badly in the foot, and lost so much blood, that he fainted. A number of other Indians gathered about him, and sang for some time before touching him. Afterwards they made certain motions with their feet and hands, and shook his head; then while they breathed life upon him, he came to. Our surgeon dressed his injuries and afterwards he was able to go off in good spirits (I:399).

Meandering along in this manner and without communications with their stationary force, the French exploration party overstayed their welcome during the Indian summer doldrums. Without explanation, it appears that the situation between the explorers and the natives had deteriorated: "While we were caulking our shallop, the Sieur de Poutrincourt caught sight in the woods of a great many Indians, who with the intention of doing us some injury were on their way towards a little brook in the strait at the causeway leading to the mainland, where some of our men were washing their clothes" (I:399). Catching sight of a masquerading vanguard ready to attack, Champlain pretended that he saw only a ceremonial welcome and like a band leader he conducted the Indian performance. He encouraged more dancing, buying seconds for Poutrincourt and a company of musketeers who positioned themselves into an ambush position behind the trees. A bloody confrontation was narrowly averted as both sides retired and pretended that their friendship was unbroken. Poutrincourt was unperturbed and Champlain even managed a happy note on departure: "This port is very beautiful and a good one, with water enough for vessels, and shelter behind the islands . . . we have named it the Beautiful port" (I:401) (fig. 18).

With the anchor finally hoisted at Le Beau Port on September 30 and, with an unexplained sense of urgency, the voyageurs sailed all night past Massachusetts Bay (fig. 21) and Plymouth (fig. 14), onward to Cape Cod. Two days later — and after nearly a month out from Port-Royal — they reached Nauset Harbor (fig. 15), the limit achieved a year earlier, under de Monts.

At first, Nauset Harbor appeared to be a promising refuge and

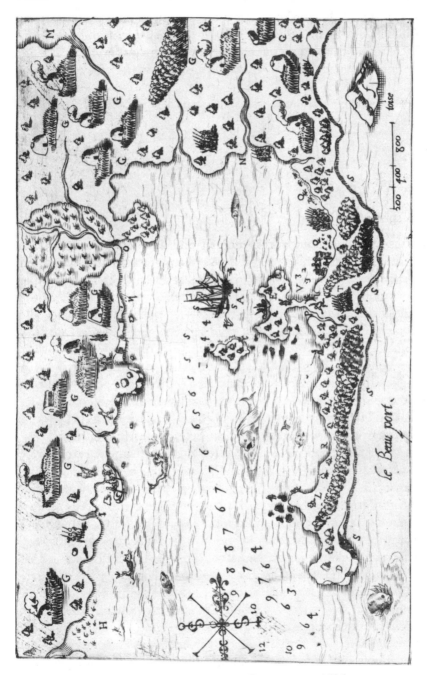

18 GLOUCESTER, MASSACHUSETTS, SEPTEMBER 1606
Le beau port

Poutrincourt, "accompanied by twelve to fifteen men, paid a visit to the port in the shallop" where they were met by "some 150 Indians, singing and dancing, in accordance with their custom. After . . . we returned to our vessel, and, the wind coming fair; [we] made sail along the coast steering south" (I:405). It seemed that the incident of the previous year, the murder of the baker on the beach, had been forgotten.

Safe navigation was, however, the most pressing concern. The Indians encouraged the explorers to press onward round the "hand" of the Cape and then southward. The search for a safe channel continued until "Finally by God's favour we succeeded in passing over a sandy point which projects about three leagues into the sea . . . making it a very dangerous place" (I:407). Having arrived at the elbow of Cape Cod, the pinnace was edged around a huge sandbar — with great difficulty — into two fathoms (1.8 m) of water at Port Fortuné (now called Stage Harbor) (fig. 19), and for a second time this season the rudder was broken and had to be repaired with ropes. To ensure a quick escape route through the shallows, the buoy markers were again dispensed and for this task, shipwright Pierre Champdoré was excused.

The more scientific minded of the party had time to savor their surroundings as repairs were completed. "All the inhabitants of this place are much given to agriculture, and lay up a store of Indian corn for the winter which they preserve in the following manner. In the sand on the slope of the hills they dig holes some five to six feet [1.5 m to 1.8 m] deep more or less, and place their corn and other grains in large grass sacks, which they throw into the said holes . . . . It is preserved as well as it would be in our granaries." It was here on the sheets of white sand of Cape Cod that Jean de Biencourt de Poutrincourt found his earthly paradise, and Champlain also enthused: "At this place we saw some five to six hundred Indians who were all naked except for their privy parts, which they cover with a little piece of deer or sealskin. The women are the same, and, like the men, cover their parts with skins or leaves. Both men and women wear their hair neatly combed in various ways." The French voyageurs found the antics of the witch doctor especially intriguing: "They are not but scamps who inveigle them [the other Indians] as the Egyptians and the gypsies do the simple village folk [in France]". Champlain also described the Cape Cod wigwam as "lofty, circular, and covered with matting made of grass or husks of Indian corn. Their only furniture consists of a bed or two raised from the floor, and made of a number of saplings laid one

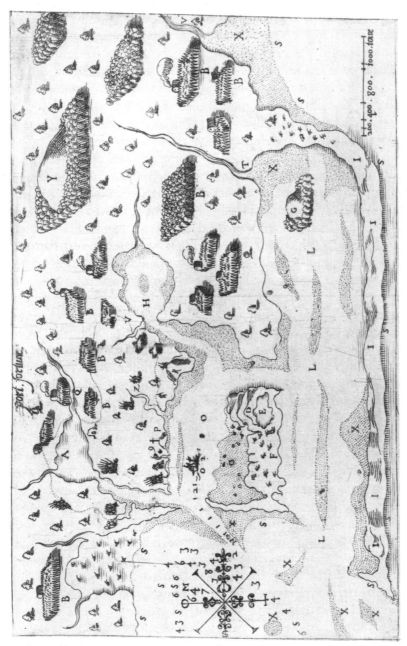

19 STAGE HARBOR, CHATHAM/CAPE COD,
MASSACHUSETTS, OCTOBER 1606
Port fortuné

against the other, whereon they place a reed-mat in the Spanish manner (which is a kind of thick mattress two or three fingers in depth), and upon this they sleep" (I:410-13).

In spite of the dangerous navigating conditions, the party's first impressions of Stage Harbor were hopeful: "This would prove a very good site for laying and constructing the foundations of a state, if the harbour were a little deeper and the entrance safer than it is" (I:414-15). After a quick overview, it was decided to stay longer; but additional safety measures were needed and "five or six" voyageurs set out in the shallop with one local Indian guide. The guide, fearing that he would be suspected a traitor for assisting the French, fled when they neared the ship. This was the first signal that something was wrong, and the shore party was recalled at once in preparation for a hasty departure.

Oblivious to danger and still ashore, however, Lieutenant-General Poutrincourt, with a dozen or so musketeers, continued to investigate the land. He did so in spite of the fact that time was running out for his farm-research program, and that, at that very moment, everyone was at great risk.

An anxious complement of voyageurs had watched the mood of the Indians change from guarded tolerance to hostility: "Indians were taking down their wigwams and were sending into the woods their wives, children and provisions, and other necessaries of life. This made us suspect some evil design." As at Gloucester, the pretence of friendship was maintained by stalling tactics and there was an appeal to the Indian women "to whom we gave bracelets and rings, in order to keep them quiet and from becoming afraid of us, while to the majority of the prominent and older men we gave axes, knives, and other articles of which they stood in need." The tactics worked, but Poutrincourt was enchanted with the area and had no intention of leaving. All those on shore were ordered to board the pinnace. But the baker — forgetting his predecessor's demise — wanted to finish making bread, and two others wished to remain with him. Duly warned, and armed, the three were advised to return to ship as soon as the bread was made. At sundown, the shallop was sent to pick up the three. Two of the three still refused to return to the ship despite the "remonstrances made to them on the risks they were running and the disobedience they were showing to their chief." Then, to make matters worse, two more sailors jumped ship to join the two recalcitrants on shore. As they were unwilling to return to the ship, the shallop returned without them, "but without informing the Sieur de Poutrincourt who was asleep, and who believed they were all on board the vessel" (I:416-20).

The next day, October 15, hundreds of Indians, apparently fearful that these curious newcomers had designs on their land, served the first notice to the French that they were prepared to defend their village and hunting areas. Quietly, in the early hours of the morning "the Indians did not fail to come and see in what state were our men, whom they found asleep, except one who was before the fire." In all, four hundred warriors

> came quietly over a little hill, and shot such a salvo of arrows at them [the Frenchmen] as to give them no chance of recovery before they were struck dead. Fleeing as fast as they could towards the pinnace, and crying out, "Help, help, they are killing us," some of them fell dead in the water, while the rest were all pierced with arrows, of whom one died a short time afterwards. These Indians made a desperate row, with war-whoops which it was terrible to hear (I:420-21) (fig. 20).

The night deck watch on the pinnace raised the alarm first, "To arms! They are killing our men!" Having heard the cry, the crew grabbed their weapons at the "same time some fifteen or sixteen of us embarked in the shallop to go ashore." The rescue failed. The French were forced to jump from the shallop when it ran aground on the sand shallows; then they had to wade the "distance of a musket-shot" to the beach. In this moment of chaos, the Indians fled with ease: "To pursue them was useless, for they are wonderfully swift" (I:421).

With their attackers gone, the French sent a burial party ashore. The bodies of their four fallen comrades were interred and a cross was reverently placed to mark the site. Then the shore detail returned to the pinnace. After three hours, the Indians returned and, on sighting them, the French fired several shots "from our little brass cannon . . . . Whenever they [the Indians] heard the report, they threw themselves flat on the ground to avoid the charge. In derision of us they pulled down the cross, and dug up the bodies, which displeased us greatly, and made us go after them a second time." Again, the cross was erected and the bodies reburied, "which they had scattered here and there among the hearths, where they had kindled a fire to burn them . . . . There was hardly any chance of taking vengeance for this blow" (I:422-23).

The next day, October 16, the French retreated after naming the battle site "Misfortune" harbor. Humiliated and no doubt angry, they sailed southwest to the vicinity of Martha's Vineyard (fig. 21). They were not gone for long. Unforeseen bad weather forced the French to return to Stage Harbor, which to their amazement, had been abandoned by the Indians who had so hotly contested it.

Uncertain of their continued safety, the French took advantage of improved weather conditions and, on October 20, maneuvered around the sandbars, once more in search of a permanent haven. Again, they navigated the forearm of the Cape Cod coast, this time reaching a river that Champlain named after himself. This was the first time Champlain used his own name to identify a slice of geography. Today it is identified as the Mashapee River.

During a new spate of bad weather, the explorers surveyed the locale. The weather then forced the expedition to return reluctantly for a third visit to the site of their encounter with the Indians. The mood on this forced retreat was glum. Plans to relocate before winter were in a shambles because the season was at an end. After three years of aimless exploration in Acadia, there was still nothing promising in sight, and furthermore, for a third season, it was too late to reach Florida and locate a suitable site. Such a venture would have required time to return to Port-Royal to pack up the habitation and supplies, and then seek a new site hundreds of kilometres away. As a final reminder of the bad luck that had plagued the expedition, within hours of arrival back at Stage Harbor, Pontgravé's son, Robert, lost a hand while "firing off a musket, which burst into many pieces" (I:426).

Bad weather continued to prevent an escape from the harbor, and morale was low. Moreover, nothing had been done to avenge the death of the five crew members. Being entrapped gave the explorers time to stew over the idea of reprisals. Their grievances festered.

A plot for retribution was developed. Initially, the strategy called for capturing a "few Indians of this place, in order to take them to our settlement and make them grind corn at a hand-mill as a punishment for the murderous assault committed" (I:427), but while mulling over their injuries, the idea of punishment turned into something infinitely more odious, a murderous ambush. To succeed with this new plan, the runaway enemy had be enticed out of hiding.

Laden with armor and unable to maneuver quickly enough on foot, the French planned an ambush in the water. Champlain observed that: "This was very well carried out as arranged." Flashing gifts to entice the victims into the water and using the "stoutest and strongest men we had, each with a chain of beads," the French strangled and stabbed the unwary who were deceived by the plot. For this action, the little brass cannon aboard the pinnace was used to keep the frantic Indians from assisting their comrades who were being slaughtered in the shallows (I:427-28).

This was not the end of the matter. Days later, there was a third episode: a small band of Indians, backed up by considerable manpower, waited in ambush in the sandhills, trying to coax the French into a similar trap. In response, Poutrincourt, this time more warrior than farmer, landed a well-armed shore party "resolved to fight them if occasion arose." The ambush was foiled; but for the French, there were no captives for "rehabilitation" to take to Port-Royal: "We withdrew to our pinnace, having accomplished all that we could" (I:429, 431).

On the homeward journey, there were as many as five wounded from the battle who were failing fast "through lack of ointment, for our surgeon had brought but very little. This was a great mistake on his part, and a grief to the sick men as well as to us, inasmuch as the stench from their wounds in a small vessel like ours was so great that we could scarcely bear it" (I:431).

This fighting between the French and the Almouchiquois Indians of Massachusetts, the first skirmish in the Indian Wars of America, is an event largely unnoticed by historians. The skirmishes at Stage Harbor, Massachusetts, were significant incidents affecting French colonization in America. They indicated a bleak prospect for conquering lands to the south, and Champlain never again returned to explore this coast. Moreover, for the French all but a small section of west Florida was lost to them forever. That area was never settled by the French, though their claim stood and it was included in the Louisiana Purchase (fig. 20).

On October 28, after a brief layover at Nauset (fig. 15), Poutrincourt's agricultural feasibility study of the Acadian coast was terminated and the voyageurs turned homeward to Port-Royal. "That day the air was quite cold and there fell a little snow." At this point, the "accomplishments" of the season defied positive evaluation. De Monts's instructions had not been followed: Poutrincourt had covered less than half the distance from Port-Royal to Florida, and a "more suitable place for a settlement" had not been found (I:432).

On the last day of October, the pinnace reached the area near Mount Desert Island (fig. 21) and for a third time this summer the

rudder was broken; but this time "into several pieces without our knowing the cause. Each expressed his opinion about it" (I:433). Defeat had blotted out the memory that the rudder had been damaged and then had to be repaired twenty-eight days earlier when the pinnace first ran aground on entering Stage Harbor. Exhausted and whipped, having seen ice and snow and experienced a raging storm, the crew made the final push for Port-Royal.

---

20 THE BATTLE AT STAGE HARBOR, CHATHAM,
MASSACHUSETTS, OCTOBER 1606 (PORT FORTUNÉ/
"MISFORTUNE")
(Untitled)

While some challenge the accuracy of Champlain's battle illustration, the work is easily recognizeable as his own. In style and execution this scene indicates his future depictions of such battle scenes, particularly at Lake Champlain, New York and at Sorel, Québec (figs. 26 and 27). The concentrated chaos and the clusters of Indians with arms akimbo are distinctive features. As in modern time-lapse photography, Champlain illustrated a number of incidents that occurred over the space of several days. While one can discern the four foolhardy crew members (A), each bristling with arrows, one can also see their graveyard with the burial cross in full view (E). There is also the scene of the Indians burning the dead bodies of the same men they had just dug up (C).

The most intriguing aspect of the battle scene at Stage Harbor, however, is the depiction of the French reprisal, in which the Indians were lured to the shallop and then strangled (L and M). It is as vaguely portrayed here as it was described in his journal. Champlain disguised this act of barbarism by showing the French only as shadowy background figures under attack by the Indians. Only one Indian is shown being hauled aboard and strangled.

There are many reasons why Champlain would have preferred to forget this harbor. He named it "Port Fortuné," as if he only had pleasant memories whereas he describes it in his journal as "Misfortune." It is also worth noting that in all other battle illustrations: at Lake Champlain, New York; Sorel, Québec; and at Syracuse, New York (figs. 26, 27 and 34), Champlain included himself in a crude self-portrait as an active participant and pointedly notes his own role in the legend. This is not so at Stage Harbor. His attempt to disassociate himself from what happened there was one of the lowest points in his career.

CHAPTER NINE

The Last Winter
and Farewell
to Acadia:
1606-1607

"Adieu, then, pretty hills and mighty mountains dear
Which like a double wall surround this port so near."

Marc Lescarbot (1570–1642), *Muses de la Nouvelle France*, 1609

ON NOVEMBER 14, POUTRINCOURT'S DISORGANIZED
and unsuccessful mission to Cape Cod returned to Port-Royal
and to the irony of a hero's welcome, "Hail to you, Sagamos, rest and
remain awhile. Come listen to a God that welcomes with a smile."
These are the opening lines from *The Theatre of Neptune*, an elaborate
presentation created by one of the new arrivals, Marc Lescarbot. The
greater significance of this dramatic episode was that it marked the
beginning of a personal conflict between Samuel de Champlain and
Marc Lescarbot which would have a profound effect on both of their
careers and the reputation of each in history. (It is a complicated tale,
and is discussed more fully in Appendix V.)

Marc Lescarbot had arrived with Poutrincourt's relief vessel on July
30, and remained at Port-Royal while Poutrincourt and his band
traveled southward. Lescarbot was energetic, ambitious, and talented;
certainly he did not mean to be an idle appendage to the exploratory
undertaking. He was anxious to be active; and he was in a preferred
position to achieve this goal. He was not only de Monts's private
solicitor and barrister, but he had previously provided legal services to
the expedition commander, Poutrincourt.

Winter closed in on the little settlement of Port-Royal in November
of 1606, with Poutrincourt, Lescarbot, and Champlain all in residence. Champlain wrote of his fellows that: "Having landed, and

recovered breath, each began to make small gardens . . . in preparation
for the spring, in order to sow several kinds of seed which we had
brought from France . . . . The Sieur de Poutrincourt on the other
hand had a water-mill built" (fig. 16). Wasting few words in his journal,
Champlain dismissed the fall season and then noted simply that:
"During the winter, in order not to be idle," the company constructed
a road (I:438-40).

Sad news interrupted the long frozen season as the voyageurs
huddled into close quarters for another winter. A party of Indians
arrived from Saco (fig. 21) to report that they had brought home the
body of Chief Panounias, the hero whose wife had been so helpful to
the French as an interpreter. He had been killed by the Almouchiquois for no apparent reason. The incident was a jolting reminder of
the many problems Europeans faced in the new land and of the way
tragedy touched everyone: "After a great deal of weeping, they took a
quantity of tobacco and two or three dogs and other things belonging
to the deceased, and burnt them upon the shore some thousand paces
from the settlement. Their cries continued until they had returned to
their wigwams . . . . They placed the body on its knees between two
stakes, with another supporting it under the arms; and about the
body were his mother, his wife, and other relatives and friends, both
women and girls, who howled like dogs." The murder led to even more
serious repercussions. The fragile framework of the alliance negotiated
the previous spring by the two interpreters, Secoudon and Messamouet, had been completely crushed after a mere two months, while
Poutrincourt pursued his agricultural tour of the Maine coast. The
great Chief Membertou of the Etchemin Indians in the Port-Royal
area "made a speech to his companions upon the death of the
deceased, inciting each to take vengeance . . . . All promised him to
do so in the spring" (I:444-45).

Champlain lightly dismissed the mild winter that followed with a
weather report on one day for each of the months of December,
January, and February. During this period of listless boredom, Champlain introduced his own theatrical creation to the community:

> We spent the winter very pleasantly, and had good fare by
> means of the Order of Good Cheer which I established, and
> which everybody found beneficial to his health, and more prof-
> itable than all sorts of medicine we might have used. This
> Order consisted of a chain which we used to place with certain
> little ceremonies about the neck of one of our people, commis-

sioning him for that day to go hunting. The next day it was conferred upon another, and so on in order. All vied with each other to see who could do the best, and bring back the finest game. We did not come off badly, nor did the Indians who were with us (I:447-48).

Lescarbot's description of this same, now-famous event, documented in his *History of New France*, provides an opportunity to compare the writings the two men: "Never at breakfast did we lack some savoury meat of flesh or fish, and still less at our midday or evening meals . . . having had everything prepared by the cook, marched in, napkin on shoulder, wand of office in hand, and around his neck the collar of the Order, which was worth more than four crowns; after him all the members of the Order, each carrying a dish. . ." (CS-L:343).

The murder of Panounias, however, had shattered the newfound congeniality within the settlement. War in the spring was not a welcome prospect, especially after the defeat at Stage Harbor (fig. 20). The French knew from their recent experience the cost of such adventures as the proposed Micmac revenge against the Almouchiquois. The surprise arrival of an agent from de Monts on May 24 removed any lingering indecision. Poutrincourt's instructions were to close down Port-Royal immediately and return to France.

Through the King's Minister, the Duc de Sully, merchants competing for the fur trade had engineered the revocation of de Monts's commission. As a result, the principal backer was now insolvent and faced with horrendous losses. The causes were easy enough to identify. To hold this royal privilege, it had been necessary for the licensee to make repeated, long-term and unrealistic colonial development commitments to the Crown in exchange for exclusive, but short-term trading rights.

Exploration had not proved a viable trade-off — nothing of value was found — and there was no justification for a trade monopoly. To date, there had been five fruitless excursions in three years within Acadia alone. The Sieur de Monts, noble patron of the first colonial

---

21 CHAMPLAIN'S SUMMARY SURVEY MAP OF ACADIA, 1607
(REVISED FROM 1606)
(*descripsion des costs/p[or]ts rades Illes de la nouvelle/france
. . . 1607*)

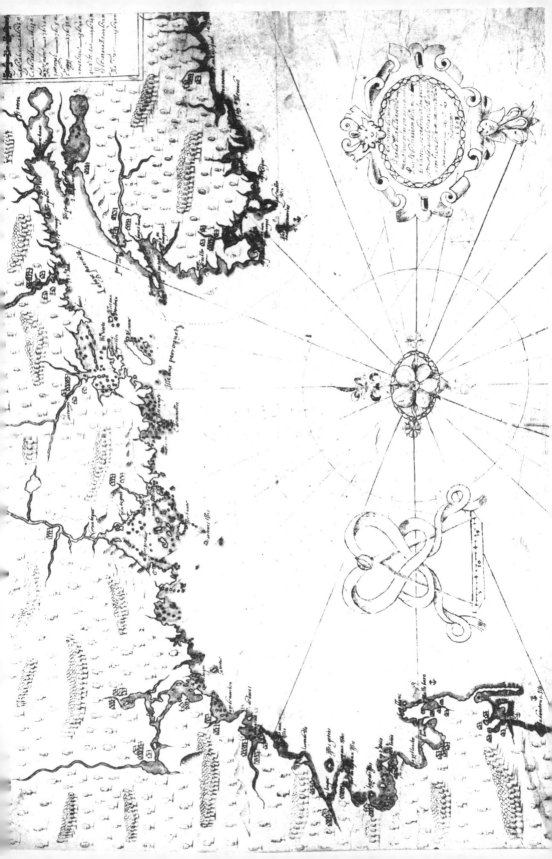

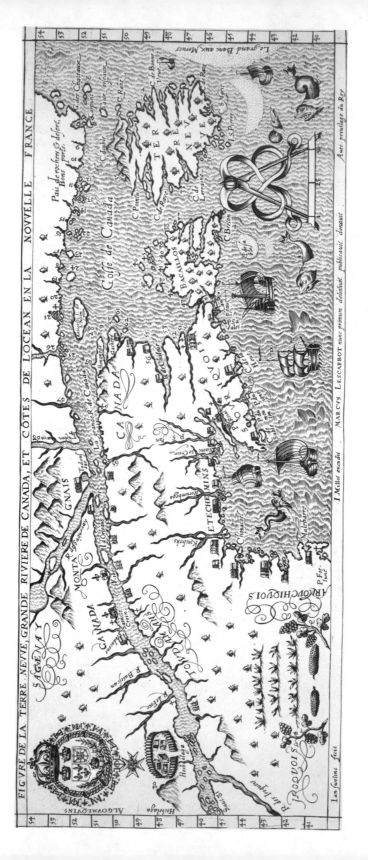

FIGVRE DE LA TERRE NEVVE, GRANDE RIVIERE DE CANADA, ET CÔTES DE L'OCEAN EN LA NOVELLE FRANCE

development initiatives for New France in the new century, did not have the financial means necessary to continue. The news was a bitter blow for such an unflinching supporter as Champlain, who would personally sustain much of the financial cost of maintaining the developing colony for his nation simultaneously with a competitive trading business for more than three years.

On August 11, the settlement was abandoned, and on September 3, 1607, after skirting the straits of Canso and the coast of Cape Breton Island, Nova Scotia, the weary voyageurs headed eastward across the Atlantic. For the French, it was farewell to Acadia. Of this band, only Poutrincourt would return, three years later, in May of 1610, to attempt the revival of a colony at Annapolis Royal. Here, a continuing French presence was maintained despite ensuing English conquests. For Samuel de Champlain and Marc Lescarbot (figs. 21 and 22), however, it was farewell to Acadia forever.

22 Marc Lescarbot's Map of New France, 1609
(DATE OF PUBLICATION)
Figure de la terre neuve, grande riviere de Canada, et côtes de l'ocean en la nouvelle France

CHAPTER TEN

The Founding
of Québec
and the Mutiny:
1608

"The third day of July 1608, when Champlain stepped ashore at Quebec and unfurled the fleur-de-lys, marks the birth of that city and province, and indeed of Canada as a nation."

Samuel Eliot Morison (1887–1976), U.S. historian,
Samuel de Champlain: Father of New France

WITH A CANCELED COMMISSION IN HAND AND orders to abandon Acadia, the voyageurs arrived back at Saint-Malo at the end of September 1607. In spite of many disappointments, Champlain was able to report that he wasted no time in briefing de Monts who then "discussed with me his plans in detail." At this time, Champlain also confirmed that it was on his own recommendation that de Monts was convinced that the French should turn their attention once more "to settle on the great St. Lawrence river, which from my journey up it [in 1603] I knew well, giving him convincing reasons why it was more convenient and fitting to establish himself there rather than elsewhere" (IV:31).

Accordingly, de Monts "to that end spoke about it to His Majesty, who agreed and granted him a commission to settle in that territory." What an about-face! After three years of half-hearted attempts to reach the promised land of Florida, the French had now decided to revert completely to the original program. Surprisingly, even with the huge financial losses of his New World ventures to date, de Monts was still prepared to hold "on to this business at any price" (IV:31-32, 35).

Even with this determination, it took more than three months to overcome the bickering of the merchants of La Rochelle and Normandy. Negotiations were also held with the Basques. These groups had already engineered the cancelation of the previous monopoly so they could continue their seasonal fur trading with the Indians uninhibited by law. Champlain was disgusted with these parochial interests, and claimed "that this [the fur trade and fishing rights] was a national matter, an advantage to be shared by the people at large" (IV:33). Years later, in the 1632 journal, his last, in a post-mortem review, he lashed out at the living and dead:

> It was an impossible task and more costly than the receipts . . .
> for the said Sieur de Monts received hardly anything, and was
> obliged more or less to let this decree go. This is how these mat-
> ters were treated in his Majesty's Council. May God forgive
> those whom He has called to Himself and put a better heart
> into those who are alive! By Heaven! What more can one
> undertake if everything is revoked in this way?   . Those who
> know the least shout the loudest, and pretend to know better
> than those [that] have had full experience (III:326).

Finally, he assaulted the memory of his long-deceased patron, who "should have sent [someone] to discover a suitable spot for founding a colony," and not researched areas "with which no one had any acquaintance . . . though the said Sieur de Monts's commission had been revoked, the settlement [Port-Royal] would not have come to an end . . . and the English and Flemings would then not have enjoyed the places they have filched from us and where they settled at our expense" (III:328).

Champlain was not being entirely fair in 1632. By that time, he knew full well that the lands in Acadia acquired by other nations from 1607 on had originally been abandoned by the French, and that their loss was partly a direct result of his own recommendation to de Monts at the time. Perhaps he also hungered for revenge — this belated attack being a result of de Monts's support of Marc Lescarbot.

In spite of the maneuvers of the city merchants, the new license was granted on January 8, 1608; but it covered only one year. Thus far, the colonial venturers had only lost some credibility as explorers. In terse formal language, the new commission spelled out the King's position: "We have resolved to continue the settlement which had already been begun in those parts." The statement meant nothing given the fact that Port-Royal was completely shut down, Île Sainte-Croix was dismantled, and Acadia and Florida were rejected as settlement sites. Unlike the first commission, the second boasted no vision of a route to Cathay, a great crusade for souls, or even the promise of a great commercial mining venture. Actual exploration had somehow modified French expectations of boundless riches from the New World at a nominal cost.

On a more positive note, in the move to implement the new plan, Champlain, as de Monts's lieutenant, was appointed to his first colonial command. In another curious turn of events, his former commander, François Pontgravé, was appointed to serve under him.

At no time were reasons ever given for downgrading the boisterous captain or for promoting Champlain. Perhaps Pontgravé's health precluded his appointment as commander, for at this time he was in his mid-fifties and ailing.

Armed for the first time with complete authority for a major expedition, Champlain speedily made arrangements for departure. Only two vessels were outfitted for the excursion, one under Pontgravé's command and the other commanded by Champlain.

For centuries, the noted sawyers and famous axmen of Honfleur, the French seaport, had fashioned clock towers, ornate belfries, and porticos, and in the fifteenth century they had constructed the magnificent timber church of Sainte-Catherine. The newly built Governor's house stood like a sentinel at the main dock. It was the fortress for the King's regional lieutenant. It also marked the beginning of a future naval empire.

When Champlain arrived at Honfleur, April 5, the harbor groaned with activity. Both vessels were being loaded to the gunwales with a complete fortress habitation to be constructed at Québec. The carpenters of Honfleur were experts at this early form of "pre-fabricated" housing. In addition to the fortress, the ships were loaded with the necessary food, lumber, window casings, cannon, and all manner of armaments and carpenter's tools.

Samuel de Champlain, the new Lieutenant of the colony, and Pontgravé — their ships loaded — set sail a week apart. After five years' absence, Champlain arrived back at Tadoussac (fig. 23) where he had first set foot in New France in 1603. He returned a seasoned officer who knew about frontier wars, Indian customs, physical deprivation, and political intrigues in France. As a commander, he had yet to be tested; but his opportunity came soon enough.

Having sailed a week earlier, Pontgravé arrived first. By the time Champlain arrived, Pontgravé had already managed to place de Monts's newly granted commission in serious jeopardy: "I was much annoyed at the brewing of a quarrel we could well have dispensed with" (II:12). The resulting conflict was more than a squabble. Instead of waiting for Champlain, the tempestuous seaman had antagonized the feisty Basque whalers who were squatting at the post and who challenged the French monopoly on the seas. Before Pontgravé's arrival, one Frenchman had been killed; on arrival, Pontgravé was seriously wounded, and virtually made a prisoner. His vessel and supplies had been hijacked and would be restored only, according to the Basques, on condition that the French departed. In one stroke, the Basques had reduced de Monts's commission to a joke. With their own ships and now one of the two French ships in their possession, they could blackmail at will. Champlain was, no doubt, infuriated.

Five years earlier, while serving at the same post, Champlain had had to deal with a similar incident. His past experience now enabled him to remain calm and assess the situation. He quickly employed his considerable diplomatic skill and bargained for access to his captured comrade. He and Pontgravé agreed that there was only one course of action: to negotiate terms for peace. Champlain then met with Captain Darache, the Basque leader. It was agreed that the whalers could continue their activity if Pontgravé was released. More importantly, however, was the fact that Champlain and Darache agreed that future arguments, should they arise, would be settled by the courts in France.

Some historians have concluded that Champlain was bested in these negotiations. This is not entirely correct. Realistically, Champlain concluded that a monopoly license given by the King of France or any other European monarch regarding trading or fishing in the New World was only as valid as the power to enforce it. As France was across an ocean, the monarch's power was clearly limited. Furthermore, Champlain's agreement with Captain Darache established a precedent for dealing with future disputes, and it enabled the year's mission to be salvaged.

With peace restored, Champlain turned to other priorities. For one month, numerous observations were recorded and the plans to move the construction supplies up river to the proposed settlement site at Québec were implemented (fig. 24). Champlain found that he even had time for a repeat voyage to the lower regions of the Saguenay River. But his impression of the Saguenay region was not changed, and he wrote of the "very disagreeable country on both sides of the river; in short a very real wilderness uninhabited by animals and birds." And, just as in 1603, other possibilities filled Champlain's imagination. He dreamed of what lay west, and of the "great inland

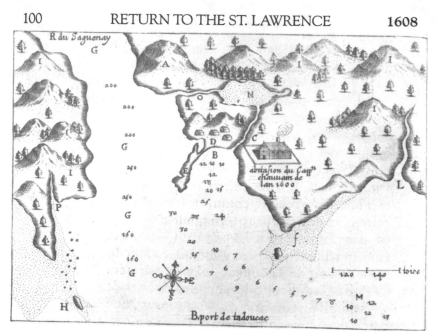

23 Tadoussac, Québec, June 1608
port de tadoucac

sea" that might be found to the north – a "sea" that Henry Hudson was about to discover (II:17) (fig. 30).

At the end of June, Champlain left Tadoussac, as planned, and headed for the new settlement site at Québec with the building supplies needed for construction.

As far as Île d'Orléans was concerned, he seemed a bit negative and wrote: "All this coast, both on the north and south sides, from Tadoussac to the island of Orléans is hilly country, and very poor, with nothing but pine, spruce and birch, and very ugly rocks, which in most places one cannot penetrate" (II:22).

Champlain's arrival at the site selected for the Habitation at Québec on July 3, 1608, marks the founding of Canada as a nation. No other date in the history of the French in America is as important. Québec is the oldest continually inhabited settlement to survive in North America, but the founder's words on this occasion indicate that he foresaw nothing of the historical importance of the moment:

> I looked for a place suitable for our building but could not find any more suitable or better situated than was the point of Québec, so called by the savages, which was covered with nut-trees

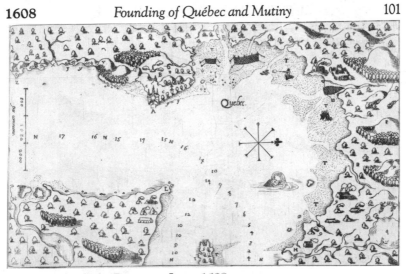

24 THE QUÉBEC REGION, JULY 1608
Quebec

and vines . . . . I at once employed a part of our workmen in cutting them down to put our buildings there, another in sawing planks, another in digging the cellar and making moats, and another in going to Tadoussac with the pinnace to fetch our effects. The first thing we made was the storehouse, to put our supplies under cover and it was promptly finished by the diligence of everyone (IV:48-49) (fig. 24).

The settlement was made into a miniature bastille and consisted of three main buildings. Each structure had two stories, and around the outside there was a gallery for viewing and for the placement of arms and men. Around the perimeter, for further protection, a moat 15 feet wide and 6 feet deep [4.6 m by 2 m] was dug. At the front and back there were open spaces for the gardens (fig.25).

Despite the successful construction of a more permanent settlement, however, the new colony faced serious problems. As the new settlers discovered that they were not to share in the profits of the colony, their discontent grew. Rumors of mutiny spread through the little community in autumn of 1608. Antoine Natel, originally one of the leaders of the revolt, finally had second thoughts and reported the planned uprising to Champlain. Both he and the ship's pilot were exonerated in exchange for their information.

With an uprising and possible murder afoot, Champlain wasted no

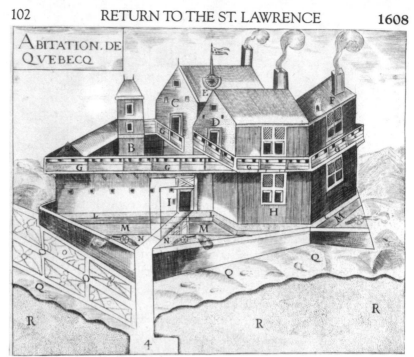

25 The Québec Habitation, July 1608
Abitation De Qvebecq

> This illustration of the completed settlement was one of the first
> architectural drawings of early North America. Those with a critical
> eye may be disturbed by the perspective problem evident in the
> drawing of the gardens. The same artistic flaw is in evidence in the
> illustrations at Île Sainte-Croix and Port-Royal (figs. 10 and 17). It is
> important to note, too, that Champlain drew planks and not logs.
> The French in the seventeenth century were master carpenters and
> sawyers in the art of building.

time. He had six sets of handcuffs made and a panel of judges convened to quickly conduct a speedy trial.

The situation resulted in the first recorded trial in North America.
Jean Duval, the master-mind behind the conspiracy, was convicted
quickly. He was to be "hanged and strangled at Québec, and his head
placed on the highest spot in our fort" (II:34).

With one of the conspirators hanged and two exonerated, the
problem of what to do with the three others remained. Keeping the
prisoners in Québec was both costly and dangerous. On the other

hand, taking them back to France would set a bad precedent for the long term and would help to arm de Monts's critics. In the end, the three were sentenced to death and turned over to Pontgravé to be returned to France for further disposition at de Monts's pleasure. This decision was not the best, though neither of the two options was desirable.

The little settlement also faced other more basic difficulties. The winter that year was harsh and not unlike the first terrible winter spent on Île Sainte-Croix. As early as mid-September, the Indians, short of food supplies as a result of the poor hunting season, moved into the settlement. Eel fishing had been a disaster since August, there was frost in October, and by mid–month most of the leaves had fallen. Gales came early in November and on the 18 there was a heavy snowfall. Two of the settlers died of dysentery, including Natel who had bargained for his life earlier. Anxiety gripped the settlers and the Indians when the last beaver hunt of the season failed because the heavy snowfall had raised river and lake levels and caused flooding.

By Christmas Champlain was forced to release the emergency provisions which the Montagnais had entrusted to him, but the supplies lasted them only a month. Champlain recounted the suffering of the Indians during the terrible winter and his descriptions are both vivid and moving. He spoke of one band trapped on the south shore of the St. Lawrence River:

> So hungry were these poor wretches, that being at their wits' end, they, men, women and children, resolved to die or to cross the river, in the hope that I would succour them in their dire need. Accordingly . . . the men and women seized their children and got into their canoes, thinking they would reach our shore by an opening in the ice which the wind had made; but no sooner were they caught in the middle of the river, than their canoes were trapped between the ice floes and broken into a thousand pieces. They maneuvered so well that they jumped with their children, whom the women were carrying on their backs, upon a large block of ice. While they were upon it, we could hear their screaming so much that it was pitiful . . . . But fortune favoured these poor wretches so much that a large ice floe struck the side of the one upon which they stood with such force that it threw them upon the land (II:54).

Rescued by fate, the Indians were given bread and beans at the settlement, but they were so starved, they could not wait to cook, even had there been enough food. In desperation, the French hung a dead dog in a tree to lure game, and on this occasion the Indians, without enough strength to climb and retrieve the "stinking and rotten" remains had only enough reserve to chop the tree down and eat the carcass.

The new year brought no immediate relief. In February, there was a two-day blizzard and by the 20, the entire encampment was on the verge of starvation. The dread scurvy moved in to take another terrible toll: eighteen were afflicted and ten died. Fear stalked the encampment even as spring grudgingly arrived.

Champlain left no doubt that the year Québec was founded was a bad one, and that the small settlement faced an uncertain future. On January 7 de Monts's one-year commission lapsed and the isolated community could only wait for the arrival of spring and the relief vessels from France. It was to be a very long wait.

CHAPTER ELEVEN

The First Battle Against the Iroquois: Lake Champlain, New York, and Vermont: 1609

"To conquer without risk is to triumph without glory."

Pierre Corneille (1606–1684), French dramatist

ALTHOUGH THE WINTER HAD BEEN HARSH, SPRING arrived early in April. Scurvy, which had plagued the band of settlers over the winter, disappeared; but there was still deprivation and discontent as the settlers waited anxiously for the relief vessels from France. Finally, on June 5, after many long days of waiting, Pontgravé's nephew, the Sieur de Marais, arrived with news that his uncle was on his way. More importantly, de Marais brought instructions that Champlain was to report to de Monts in France.

But what was Champlain's report to contain that would satisfy the investors and encourage them to continue supporting the fledgling colony? He could report only another devastating winter and a high death toll. There had been no further explorations, and to make matters look worse, the only thing returned to France thus far had been three troublesome prisoners. Champlain needed some success and he needed it before returning to France: "For, according to the orders of the Sieur de Monts in a letter he had written to me, I was to return to France, to inform him of what I had done and of the explorations made in that country [Québec]" (II:64).

Bent on some successful venture, Champlain appointed de Marais caretaker of the habitation, and set sail to greet his old friend Pontgravé who was en route from France. When they met at Tadoussac, the two of them considered their options; their first choice was a preliminary excursion west designed to intrigue their backers. They put their

105

plan into motion and combined manpower and resources from Tadoussac and Québec. To this they added a complement of men from Pontgravé's vessel. This would have brought the number of men to be included to twenty; but plans were changed, and in the end it was decided that Pontgravé would remain at Tadoussac to manage the post.

On June 18, Champlain left Québec. Champlain himself must have found this voyage up the St. Lawrence just the right tonic after the grim winter. "The country becomes more beautiful as you advance," and the river is "very rich in many varieties of fish, . . . everywhere [the countryside is] covered with great, high forests" (II:65). Rolling hills, trees covered with new leaves, tall grasses, and wild flowers must have been seductive indeed, but Champlain had more on his mind than pastoral pursuits.

Champlain's first step was to meet in council with the chiefs of the Indian nations that had originally formed the grand alliance. It had been six years since the agreement of May 27, 1603, at Tadoussac when Commander Pontgravé and his younger observer, Samuel de Champlain, negotiated with the federation of Montagnais, Algon-quin, and Etchemin nations. Then, the French had agreed to make war against the Iroquois in exchange for the right to settle there. But so far, the French had had no battle with the Iroquois, and they had done nothing to fulfill their promise to the grand sagamore, Chief Anadabijou. Furthermore, another Indian nation had joined this federation. These were the Hurons who lived south of Georgian Bay on Lake Huron. They were a populous nation of farmers who tilled the soil to harvest the gold of Indian maize. The Hurons, like the other tribes allied with the French, were also in danger of Iroquois attack.

To win the support of all these warriors, Champlain put on a one-man show with his musket, and, for an encore, he promised a bigger and better performance back at the settlement. The Indians were clearly impressed:

> They also asked me as a token of great friendship and rejoicing
> to have muskets and arquebuses fired off, whereat they would
> be much pleased. I did so and they uttered loud shouts of
> astonishment, especially those who had never heard or seen
> the like before. After listening to their speech, I made answer,
> and to please them I was glad to go back to our settlement for

their greater satisfaction, and that they could see that I had no other intention than to make war; for we had with us only arms and not merchandise for barter (II:70-71).

The above entry in Champlain's journals has caused some scholars to conclude that Champlain was a warmonger!

Ready for conflict, two shallops were provisioned on June 28 with Champlain in command of the first vessel. But again, the plan was changed. Pontgravé came out from Tadoussac to take command of the second shallop, then again was directed back to Tadoussac. The confusion was not explained; but what emerged was far less than the great armada promised to the Indians six years before. Instead of facing the Iroquois enemy with a full force, the French went forward with one shallop, four officers — including de Marais — and nine colonists.

An armed group of French and Montagnais gathered on July 3, the first anniversary of the founding of the Québec settlement (fig. 25), and moved westward to Trois-Rivières (fig. 40) to join the additional Indians assembling for battle. The French and the Indians prepared to face the enemy, but then for some inexplicable reason, the momentum slowed. Here the record is obscure; somewhere within the purpose and the events to follow lies the answer to one of the larger questions concerning Champlain, and indeed North American history. Simply, who really wanted this battle against the Iroquois in the first place?

Did Champlain want it so he could report back to France that the Iroquois had been contained? Did the Indians force him into battle by calling in their I.O.U.s and enforcing the terms of the alliance? Or, was it all originally planned as a show of strength?

Whatever the reason, there was a delay. Champlain could not have known the strength of the enemy; it is possible that his Indian allies had strong second thoughts as they drew closer to Iroquois territory.

As far as the passage of time was concerned during this southward journey up the "River of the Iroquois" (Richelieu River), the delay did not seem to bother Champlain. He examined streams, took soundings, studied the vegetation, and fished. The journals make it seem as if he were enjoying a simple summer vacation. Even after the war party arrived at the mouth of the river entrance to Iroquoia (New York state), the relaxation continued: "We stayed two [more] days and refreshed ourselves with choice game, birds, and fish which the Indians gave us" (II:76).

At this point, the Indians began to argue among themselves about the reason for going to war in the first place, and this led to a split in the ranks: "Only a part of them decided to come with me, whilst the rest went back to their own country with their wives and the goods they had bartered" (II:76). As Indian resolve faded, Champlain became discouraged: What success could he report to de Monts?

Nonetheless, Champlain and the Indians continued south into Iroquoia. But geography was to add to their difficulties. The war party became stalled at the upstream rapids (Chambly, Québec) as the shallop proved too large for further portages.

Champlain complained that he had been misinformed about the access route to the Iroquois encampment and he quickly retreated from the original grand plan and sent the shallop back to Québec with de Marais and the men.

The operation had been scaled down to the absurd. There were only two French soldiers left, "eager to go." Champlain himself was no longer the leader of a large confederacy of Indians and French, but rather had become an instigator leading a band of zealots. With only this token commitment left, the Indians considered leaving, but Champlain urged them on "to persist in their first design . . . for I wished to show them that for myself I would not fail to keep my word to them, even if I went alone" (II:81).

Still, there seemed to be some advantage to leading this much smaller war party. If it succeeded, Champlain would become the hero responsible for the downfall of the Iroquois menace, and if they were defeated, the French could not be blamed too harshly because they could complain that they were misinformed about the geography, and far more relevant, were misled to believe that their allies were firm in their resolve. "Having thought it over well, I decided to proceed thither to carry out my promise and also to fulfill my desire" (II:79-80). Champlain might have added, "destiny."

Traveling by canoe, Champlain reached the upper rapids on the river into Iroquoia (Rouses Point, which is now on the Québec–New York border), and entered the lake that would come to bear his name. In so doing, he became the first European that could definitely be said to have discovered what would become New York state and Vermont.

While Champlain took the lead, his two companions traveled by land with the war party of sixty Montagnais, Algonquin, and Huron Indians. They carried twenty-four birch-bark canoes. As they neared the place of battle, Champlain was — as so often happened — distracted. At Cape Cod, it had been the horseshoe crab; here, on Lake Champlain, he discovered the Chaousarou, or garfish, and was clearly impressed with the ugly and monstrous creature;

> the largest of them, as these tribes have told me, are from eight to ten feet [2.5 m to 3 m] long. I have seen some five feet [1.5 m] long, which were as big as my thigh, and had a head as large as my two fists, with a snout two feet and a half [0.75 m] long, and a double row of very sharp, dangerous teeth . . . . When the birds come and light on its snout, mistaking it for a stump of wood, the fish is so cunning, that shutting its half-open mouth, it pulls them by their feet under the water. The natives gave me the head of one of them, a thing they prize highly, saying that when they have a headache, they bleed themselves with the teeth of this fish at the spot where the pain is and it eases them at once . . . . The picture of the fish is on the great lake [Huron] on my map [of] 1612 (II:91-92)(fig. 29).

Throughout all of Champlain's journals, this was the only specific reference to an illustration of wildlife that he ever made.

As the two sides neared each other, "troops of scouts reconnoitre[d] along the rivers [to] see whether there is any mark or sign to show where their enemies or friends have gone" (II:85).

Champlain, who had been in many battles, noted the strategic flaws that he believed would govern events. He noted many: delays, the wasted rituals of shamans, the negligence of the enemy in failing to guard their camp at night. But the greatest flaw that he noted was the loss of the advantage of surprise, as the stillness of the night was interrupted by the bellowing boasts hurled by the vanguards of both sides. Even so, Champlain offered an inconsistent observation — not his first or last — that, "stealthily by night," the one hundred and twenty-five miles (200 km) of Lake Champlain were crossed to bring Champlain and his allies to the Iroquois fortress. Champlain's composure seemed disturbed as he reported a last-minute conference between the Iroquois and the Montagnais to determine whether or not to fight at all.

But then it was decided. Champlain and his two companions concealed themselves in preparation for their moment of glory. Their muskets were their secret weapons. The story must be told by Champlain alone:

I saw the enemy come out of their barricade to the number of two hundred, in appearance strong, robust men. They came slowly to meet us with a gravity and calm which I admired; and at their head were three chiefs. Our Indians likewise advanced . . . . As soon as we landed our Indians began to run . . . towards their enemies . . . who had not yet noticed my white companions . . . off [in] the woods. Our Indians began . . . to make way for me . . . and put me ahead some twenty yards [18 m] and I marched on until I was within some thirty yards [27 m] of the enemy . . . who halted and gazed at me and I at them. When I saw them make a move to draw their bows . . . I shot straight at one of the three chiefs, and with this shot two fell to the ground and one of their companions was wounded . . . . I had put four bullets into my arquebus (IV:96).

There must have been terror among the Iroquois as they found that their wood and hemp shields were useless.

Then from the woods, the two other Frenchmen joined in and fired more volleys. The skirmish was over in seconds, and within three hours the warriors were headed home. But they did not leave until the Indian rituals of victory had been indulged in to the fullest.

What followed was a barbaric celebration designed not only to enforce victory, but to drive home the extent of the defeat. Champlain could not have been a stranger to the "spoils of war," nor to the idea of brutal vengeance taken out on the vanquished. Europe in this century knew its own barbarism. Nonetheless, Champlain tried to intercede, but could not stop the killing and torture.

Meanwhile our Indians kindled a fire, and when it was well lighted, each took a brand and burned this poor wretch a little at a time in order to make him suffer the greater torment. Sometimes they would leave off, throwing water on his back. They tore out his nails and applied fire to the ends of his fingers and to his *membrum virile*. Afterwards they scalped him and caused a certain kind of gum to drip very hot upon the crown of his head . . . . When he was dead, they were not satisfied; they opened his body and threw his bowels into the lake . . . . They . . . cut his heart into several pieces . . . to give to a brother of the dead man to eat and to others of his companions who were prisoners. They took it and put it into their mouths, but would not swallow it . . . . When this execution was over, we set out upon our return with the rest of our prisoners, who went along continually singing, without other expectation than to be tortured (II:101).

The battle between the Iroquois and the French and their Indian allies was a terrible price to pay for one good report to de Monts. But worse, it placed the powerful Iroquois Confederacy on the warpath. Hernán Cortés had frightened the Indians of Mexico into submission with his horses — animals that they had never seen before. Champlain, however, had only temporarily stunned the Iroquois with his weaponry. They would recover all too soon.

Never again would a battle in America be so easily won by the French. For one hundred and fifty years the Iroquois would fight their new enemy, proving that the four musket balls from Champlain's arquebus were the most expensive metal in the early history of this continent.

But unable to see into the future, and having misjudged the strength of the Iroquois Confederacy, Champlain returned to Tadoussac to witness even more ghoulish orgies. Gifts were brought to him and there were apologies by those who had not joined in the battle. To celebrate, "each took a stick, on the end of which they hung the scalps of their slain enemies . . . ; the women stripped themselves quite naked, and jumped into the water to receive the scalps" (II:106).

On the way back to Québec, the warriors stopped over during the long portage on the Richelieu River where the shallop had to be sent back. Here, they reviewed their battle. The Indian allies were pleased with the outcome, and the Hurons and Algonquins left to return home, while the Montagnais returned to the settlement at Tadoussac.

On September 5, 1609, Champlain left for France from Tadoussac. He had a victory of which he could boast, but little else to show for the season. To obtain a new license, funds, supplies, and commitments for the future, Champlain realized that he now faced a "selling" job.

Unknown to him at the time, international competition for French initiatives in the New World were rapidly gaining ground. On September 3, two days before Champlain left New France, Henry Hudson, who sailed for the Dutch, had arrived in New York harbor to begin his exploration of the river that would bear his name and take him to within eighty miles of Lake Champlain (fig. 26).

26 LAKE CHAMPLAIN, NEW YORK AND VERMONT STATES:
THE BATTLE AGAINST THE IROQUOIS, JULY 1609
Deffaîte des Yroquois au Lac de Champlain

This battle illustration is the most frequently reproduced work of all
Champlain's graphics. The focal point, of course, is the self-portrait of
the commander at center stage during the battle. This is the best
extant portrait of Champlain, although it reveals little of him beyond
his armor. Aside from two other similar sketches at Sorel and
Syracuse (figs. 27 and 34), all others are fakes.

   The graphic details conform exactly to the text of the journals. The
two fallen Iroquois chiefs are shown lying on the ground in front of
Champlain near a third Indian who is wounded (D and E). Firing
shots from the protected cover of the forest are Champlain's two
compatriots. In this first illustration of three battles between the
French and the Iroquois, there was only a small shower of arrows
discharged in reply to Champlain's initial murderous volley. A year
later at Sorel, the story would be different. In a way, this bizarre battle
at Lake Champlain turned out to be little more than a continuation
of the weapons demonstration held earlier at Québec.

CHAPTER TWELVE

The Second Battle Against the Iroquois: Sorel, Québec: 1610

"And on the highest throne in the world, we still sit only on our own bottom."

Michel de Montaigne (1553–1592), French essayist

SAMUEL DE CHAMPLAIN ARRIVED BACK IN Honfleur, France, on October 13, 1609. He went directly to the beautiful sand-colored chateau at Fontainebleau in order to meet with de Monts and King Henry IV:

> I at once waited upon His Majesty, to whom I told the story of my expedition, wherein he took great pleasure and satisfaction. I had a belt of porcupine quills, very well woven, according to the fashion of the country, which His Majesty deigned to accept, along with two small birds the size of blackbirds and of a scarlet colour. I also had the head of a certain fish [garfish] which was caught in the great Iroquois lake, having a very long snout with two or three rows of very sharp teeth (II:110).

Champlain had also been given the scalp and the arms of one of the dead Iroquois by the Indians to deliver to the King of France, but he stopped short of making this gift to his monarch.

Champlain recorded that the King was delighted with the story of the expedition as well as with his gifts, but history records that this delight did not translate into a promise of renewed support.

One historian has suggested that the King was maneuvering behind the scenes to secure the services of Henry Hudson; although this cannot be substantiated, one matter seemed certain: de Monts appeared to have lost royal support. Eventually reimbursed with only 6,000 livres from the royal treasury for his personal loss of 100,000 livres in the Acadian voyages, de Monts likely concluded that there was no incentive for further risk.

King Henry had inherited a government that had been spending more than twice the tax revenue it gathered, and for more than a decade, first minister Sully had struggled with fiscal insolvency. Years later, Champlain would write that de Monts's "requests and proposals were just and reasonable" (I:111). But Champlain had a vested interest in exploration and, in the early years, it would certainly have been difficult to justify royal funds on the basis of returns.

For Champlain, de Monts, and the other backers, the lack of a legal license and backing created uncertainty. But even without the license to show the competitors in the coastal ports, Champlain and Pont-gravé launched out again for New France, leaving Honfleur on March 7, 1610, with "a certain number of artisans" (II:115).

This voyage was plagued with trouble from the moment it began. Bad weather in the channel drove the voyageurs to Weymouth, England, for several days. On setting sail again, they found themselves fog-bound and blown back to France. Then, for the first time, Champlain was taken ill and for one month was "attacked by a very serious illness which gave [him] . . . no hope of making the voyage". After more than a month, however, "although [he was still] somewhat weak and debilitated," the voyage began (II:116).

The spell of bad luck was broken on arrival at Tadoussac (fig. 23) when on May 26, 1610, it was learned that the other ships due had made the crossing in one month — the fastest in sixty years. Further good news was received when it was learned that the winter had been mild for the settlers. "Their greatest trouble had been to amuse themselves" (II:118).

Champlain plotted two courses of action on his return to New France. First, if the Montagnais were willing to assist, Champlain wanted to press northward on the St. Maurice River from Trois-Rivières, and then search for the "great inland sea" (Hudson Bay). Second, he wanted to be "escorted" to the great lake (Huron) to see "some copper mines and other things which they [the Indians] had mentioned to me" (II:119). This latter "escorted" tour had been offered to him by the Indians when he defeated the Iroquois. But the Indians were wily when it came to negotiations: Champlain's weaponry was

requested again for a repeat performance against the Iroquois, and Champlain was urged to assist them.

The Indians also tempted Champlain westward by showing him a strip of copper one foot (30 cm) long that "was taken out in pieces, and when melted was made into sheets and smoothed out with stones" (II:123). Proof that New France held valuable copper ore would most certainly revive interest in France, and support for the fledgling colony would be forthcoming. The Indians would lead him to the "mines" and he, in turn, would help them defeat their enemies.

On his way to a meeting with the Montagnais at Trois-Rivières (fig. 40), Champlain learned that at the mouth of the Richelieu River, which led into Iroquoia, some two hundred Huron and Algonquin allies had gathered and were ready to do battle. On his arrival at Trois-Rivières, he discovered that the Montagnais had also committed themselves to fight. Further, he learned that Iroquet (fl. 1609–15), the Algonquin Chief, intended to follow up his vanguard force with still another two hundred braves.

The plan seems to have been that Champlain would help the

---

27 SOREL, QUÉBEC: A SECOND BATTLE AGAINST THE IROQUOIS, JUNE 1610
Fort des Yroquois

In Champlain's illustration of the battle near Sorel, all the major events are all crowded into the design in much the same manner as were the battle scenes at Stage Harbor and Lake Champlain (figs. 20 and 26). There is also the second of the artist's self-portraits here. Champlain (D) fires his arquebus, while other Frenchmen flee into the water in the chase following the major battle (B). Those drowning are also illustrated, shown at the same time that the alliance Indians are attacking the fortress aided by those ten or more French comrades in plumed helmets (D and F). The work is almost a comic strip.

In comparison to the first French encounter with the Iroquois a year earlier, there are far greater difficulties illustrated and much more action documented. More than sixty arrows have been discharged in this scene, and the carnage totals more than a dozen wounded or killed.

The illustration also suggests how the Iroquois were eventually overwhelmed. Although never mentioned in the journal, the drawing shows a large tree which has crashed across the barricade (F), felled by one of the attacking Indians, likely providing the access for victory.

As at Lake Champlain (fig. 26), the Iroquois at Sorel have learned some lessons in fighting the French and their Indian allies.

Indians do battle, the Iroquois would be defeated, and he would be escorted westward by his grateful Indian allies. For further transportation westward, Champlain settled for only one of the four pinnaces moored for trade at Trois-Rivières. Thus he set forth with his Montagnais allies.

His overconfidence caused a strategic mistake: they underestimated the enemy. The Iroquois had profited from the battle of the previous year. This time, they intended to stop their enemies at the mouth of the Richelieu River on the St. Lawrence waterway — long before the allies could penetrate their territory.

Ready for battle, Champlain and his Montagnais allies arrived at the mouth of the Richelieu only to find the area deserted. The Algonquins and Hurons who had been there before were nowhere to be found.

As the Montagnais and Champlain prepared for the arrival of the Algonquin Chief and the "reserve" warriors he had committed to battle, Champlain learned what had happened: the "missing" Algonquins and Hurons had already attacked the Iroquois, the Iroquois had repelled them, and now some one hundred Iroquois were barricaded in their fortress.

For Champlain, a man used to the regimentation of European warfare, this development represented nothing less than military chaos. He and the Montagnais were without guides to locate the Hurons and Algonquins who had rushed into battle; leaving them to trek for more than a mile (1.6 km) "through thick woods, among swamp and marsh, with water up to our knees, each loaded with a pikeman's corselet, which bothered us greatly, as did the hosts of mosquitoes, a strange sight, which were so thick that they hardly allowed us to draw our breath and so greatly and severely did they persecute us, we should not have known where we were" (II:127).

At last Champlain and the Montagnais were discovered by their anxious allies and guided toward the enemy. As they came within earshot, there was a huge uproar of shouts and insults.

The performance this year was no simple demonstration of firearms. This time, the Iroquois were better protected behind a well-made wooden bastille. From the cover of trees, Champlain directed the opening gunfire. Less confident for this contest, he concluded that the kind of situation that would allow him to demonstrate the frightening superiority of French weapons was unlikely to develop. Last year, he had faced, in single combat, two armed enemies. He had shot them before they could fire their arrows and thus frightened the others; this year such a show of strength seemed impossible.

On both sides many Indians were killed, and Champlain himself came close to being killed: "As I was firing my first shot close to their barricade, I was wounded with an arrow which split the tip of my ear and pierced my neck. I seized the arrow which was still in my neck and pulled it out . . . . One of my companions was also wounded in the arm by another arrow, which I pulled out for him" (II:129). With ammunition running out, Champlain ordered the storming of the barricade. It worked but only after he was reinforced by some of his personal complement of troops, who had been waiting at the pinnace.

When the fortess was finally taken, the scene was less than gratifying. There was blood everywhere, and many who tried to escape by water were drowned. Champlain was disgusted when another shallop of "our companions" arrived only to scrounge for the spoils of some personal effects and a few beaver skins. In the end, with contempt, the whole business of warfare was dismissed as "such a nasty occupation" (II:133).

CHAPTER THIRTEEN

The Aftermath of War and Return to France: an Interlude and Marriage: 1610–1611

"In love, it's not a bad idea to have
the consent of the person concerned."

Voltaire (1694–1778), *L'Ingénu* (The hero, the Huron native,
speaks of love.)

CHAMPLAIN'S ACCOUNT OF THE BATTLE AT
Sorel (fig. 27) and its aftermath is both gruesome and unique.
He outlines in graphic detail the brutality visited upon the vanquished
as the victors celebrate and perform the rituals of conquest.

According to Champlain, for several days following the defeat at
the fortress, Iroquois prisoners were subjected to a variety of cruelties.
Fingernails were pulled out, and fingers were cut off as the victors
indulged in all conceivable forms of butchery. He described how
prisoners were taunted, tested, and castigated before being staked on
poles at the water's edge. While they were impaled, white birch-bark
torches were ignited and applied to their bodies where the effect would
be the most painful. Champlain related that to lengthen the victim's
agony, the seared skin was drenched with cold water and then, finally,
the captive was clubbed to death. Champlain went on to describe
mutilation, cannibalism, and the feeding of human carrion to the
dogs. At Sorel, Champlain found the atmosphere polluted with the
odor of burning flesh, and the greenery of the earth drenched in
blood.

According to tradition, most prisoners were dispatched in the
manner described. It was, after all, risky to transport angry captives
across hundreds of miles of wilderness. But in spite of the danger, the

victors reserved some of the unlucky captives for further trials, though most did not survive the trek back to the victor's camp, where they "were reserved to be put to death at the hands of the wives and daughters . . . who . . . show themselves no less inhuman than the men; in fact they greatly surpass the men in cruelty; for by their cunning they invent more cruel torments, and take delight in them" (II:137).

During the torture of one Iroquois victim, Champlain intervened and, by bargaining, managed to secure control of the prisoner in the hope of setting an example. While he won this lone battle for one prisoner, Champlain also jeopardized the future of the alliance. His reward for this act of charity was mistrust; the confused wretch managed to escape Champlain's custody and in the months to come proved a surprisingly persuasive malcontent who successfully undermined Champlain's hard-won reputation amongst his Indian allies.

At length, the victory orgy subsided. Then, too late for the battle, or even the grand victory celebration, the two allied Indian Chiefs, Iroquet of the Algonquins and Outchetaguin of the Hurons, arrived with eighty men. This, apparently, was all of the grand reserve contingent of the "extra" two hundred originally promised for the battle weeks earlier. In total, less than one half of those committed to do battle ever showed up. This was the second time in two years that the Algonquins had failed to meet their commitments. This was to be the pattern in the future as well. Neither the French nor the Indians ever lived up to, or even came close to, fulfilling their pre-war manpower commitments to each other.

With everyone now present, including the new arrivals, there was a powwow on Île de Saint-Ignace in the St. Lawrence River, just off the mouth of the Richelieu River. For Champlain, the gathering presented an opportunity to cement French–Indian relations for the future. Certainly he had his plan for westward expansion in mind. He began negotiating the traditional cultural exchange so that several young Indian men might go to France and a young Frenchman might live among the Indians in order to learn their language. Outchetaguin, the Chief of the Hurons, was the liaison, and, in this first step of the post-war process, Champlain offered the Indians a young man who had wintered twice at Québec. Champlain did not record the name of the French candidate; even though there were others, Étienne Brûlé was most likely the choice. He would go forth "to learn the language . . . , to see the great lake [Huron] . . . , explore the mines

... so that ... we might be informed of the truth" (II:138). In exchange, Outchetaguin offered a young Huron named Savignon. Champlain readily agreed, and decided that the young Huron would accompany him to France.

These negotiations were a brilliant stroke. The personal connection with the Hurons meant that the French no longer had to depend on the Algonquin to act as "information intermediaries." Champlain hoped to learn more of the Nipissings, or "Sorcerers," whose lands were between the Ottawa Algonquins and the Hurons. These arrangements at Sorel laid the groundwork for the first feasibility study for the westward expansion of New France.

Feeling confident about the future, Champlain returned to Québec as the first stop on his way back to France. But when he arrived at the settlement, he learned shocking news. Great King Henry of those "happy memories" had been assassinated, and there were rumors of other atrocities. Champlain's gift of the great garfish skeleton evidently had not proven a good luck charm for the monarch. Champlain felt an urgent need to return to France immediately. He wasted no time.

On August 8, 1610, war-weary and still recovering from mental and physical wounds, Champlain sailed to his troubled homeland. Once at sea, he was obviously more relaxed in his favored role of geographer and navigator. He also found time to reflect on the report that he would have to make to de Monts and the new royal authority, Marie de Médicis, who was acting as Regent for the nine-year-old Dauphin who would one day be crowned King Louis XIII (1601–1643).

Champlain realized that he faced a difficult task on his return to France. Apart from some slim signs of progress toward capitalizing on the original agreement with the allied Indians made in 1603, by 1610 the French had achieved only marginal success. They had accomplished little beyond Jacques Cartier's explorations; there had been no great discoveries, charts, or even one mining bonanza unearthed. In all, only a cultural exchange held out a thread of promise for the future. Thus far, the Indians were in complete control. As far as the financial backers were concerned, the bottom line remained negative — the cash profits were far below expectation.

Shortly after his arrival in France, Champlain discovered the magnitude of the problem he faced. With King Henry's widow as Regent, young Louis was shackled with personal problems as well as with the constraints legally applied to a royal minor. For Champlain, who was now without royal support, a new era had begun, one which would require modifications in logistics and strategy. There was no reason for optimism when his patron, the Sieur de Monts was declared by the Regent to be no longer a "member of our chamber" at Fontainebleau. With nothing further to record for the season, Champlain closed his journal on September 27, 1610.

For the next five months, Champlain recorded nothing, nor did he refer later to this pause in his adventurous life. The historian must rely on only a few sketchy documents, and be content with sparse information on life in France during these months. Nonetheless, from what facts are available, we do know that there was a startling turn of events.

On Monday, December 27, 1610, three days before the actual wedding, Samuel de Champlain entered into an elaborate marriage contract with Hélène Boullé (1598–1654), the twelve-year-old daughter of Nicolas Boullé, "Secretary of the King's Chamber, residing at Paris." The contract was signed at the home of Nicolas and Margueritte, the parents of the bride-to-be, and two "notaries and notary-record-keepers of the King our sovereign Lord [King Louis XIII] in this his Chatelet of Paris," were witness to the covenant (II:315).

The contract stipulated matters sexual, spiritual, and secular. Champlain was to receive a total of six thousand livres as a dowry, and the contract was to come into effect within two days with an advance payment of four thousand five hundred livres. "In consideration of the tender age" of the bride, it was agreed that the marriage would not be consummated "until two years elapsed . . . unless it is deemed advisable and be decided between them, their relations and friends" (II:317-18).

On December 30, 1610, Samuel de Champlain of Brouage and Hélène Boullé of Paris were wed at L'Église Saint-Germain-l'Auxerrois, the parish church of notables and Kings in Paris. Located in an enclave of royal buildings and upstream on the Seine opposite the Louvre, Saint-Germain-l'Auxerrois was an imposing sand-colored structure of cathedral archways, elaborate wood carvings, and subdued light.

From the marriage contract of December 27 and the additional covenant of December 29, it was not clear who was present for the actual wedding ceremony on December 30. The two legal documents available set out the terms of the forthcoming marriage, and many names were enumerated as being involved. It seems likely that most of those mentioned in the document attended the wedding. Champlain's continuing proximity to the source of power is the most important point to note. Even the name of the King's horse doctor was to be found in the marriage contract, along with Champlain's faithful supporter, the Sieur de Monts. Anthoine de Murat, a King's Councilor, was one of those mentioned, as was the most popular barber surgeon of Paris, Anthoine Marye. Yet, aside from a cousin and Champlain's parents — only one of whom could have attended the actual nuptials — none of the groom's other relatives were mentioned. It was, however, the December 27 contract that confirmed the fact that Champlain's father was dead and that this parent had been "in his lifetime Captain in the Navy" (II:315). (See Appendix IV for comments concerning Champlain's marriage.)

After five months of marriage and coming to terms with the new political reality, Champlain prepared for another departure despite the fact that there was no improvement in his commercial arrangements. Although de Monts was still relatively secure as a participant shareholder, there was still no new commission granted, and this uncertainty would continue. For this, the second year in the free-trade environment, and in the continued absence of a partnership with the Crown, Champlain seemed to have opted for building political alliances. But colonial development would demand more, and Champlain's difficulties were far from over.

CHAPTER FOURTEEN

The Return to Québec and Westward to Montréal: 1611

"Glorious Champlain with his high objectives and burning soul."

Pierre Motin (c. 1566–1610), French cabaret poet

ON MARCH 1, 1611, CHAMPLAIN, AGAIN WITHOUT a Royal Commission, left France and headed back to the tenuous little colony in New France. His young wife remained in Paris, but Pontgravé was once again with him, acting as second in command. The young Huron Indian, Savignon, was also on board. He was to return to Huronia where he would tell wondrous tales of Paris and manage to express a good measure of contempt for the French.

This voyage proved to be another fight for survival: the Atlantic crossing was the worst that Champlain recalled. As in 1606 when Champlain and his companions had hurried to explore the Massachusetts coastline, the vessels left France too early in the season. This time, Champlain notes for the first time that supplies were lost en route: "Still, with much difficulty and labour by dint of going on one tack and then on the other," they reached the Grand Banks. "Here we met with icebergs thirty [55 m] or even forty fathoms [73 m] high; . . . we feared lest we might meet with them during the night . . . . About eleven o'clock at night the sailors noticed more icebergs, which frightened us . . . but we made such efforts, . . . that we avoided them . . . . Although we were out of danger, yet each one's blood cooled down slowly from the fright." On the next day, "the cold was so great that all the ship's running rigging was so frozen and covered with big icicles that we could not work it or stand on the vessel's deck" (II:157-61).

Late in the season on May 13, after seventy-five days at sea, the shivering seamen reached Tadoussac (fig. 23). To their surprise, they found that the whole country "was still almost covered with snow" (II:171). Worse yet, the Indians were starving, and all the signs pointed to a repetition of the devastating winters at Île Sainte-Croix and at Port-Royal. There was little Champlain could do, though he did offer some emergency aid before moving on. He felt that his first priority was up-river. After all, if Tadoussac downstream were in trouble, how had the habitation at Québec fared? And what of the year's proposed mission to venture beyond the Grand Rapid at Montréal (fig. 28) and reach Huronia? In this instance, Champlain's anxiety was unwarranted: at Québec, the settlers had wintered well.

In this little colony, good hunting and a bountiful harvest from the previous year had prevented hardship. Happily, Champlain found everything ready for the start of the season's explorations. At Trois-Rivières, west of Québec (fig. 40), Champlain was distracted from his initial plan to move west to Huronia. The tantalizing vision of the inland sea to the north intrigued him. He proposed that one of the French explorers, assisted by an Indian guide, should follow the St. Maurice River northward in search of this prize. But Algonquin Chief Batiscan (fl. 1610-29), refused. The Algonquins resided on lands less arable and harder to traverse than other lands in the territory now being explored by the French. Their land, between the St. Maurice River on the east through to the Ottawa River on the west, afforded them only a meager existence; but this was, at the same time, the gateway to the next area of exploration as well as its being located on the migration route of other tribes. In order to meet their needs, the Algonquins had become gate-keepers; they had learned to barter goods and services for passage through their territory, and to provide information about what lay beyond it. To open their lands to the French, without reservation, would lower their prestige and place their trade with both the French and other tribes at risk. Thus, they answered Champlain's questions vaguely, offered tidbits of tantalizing information, but continued to refuse absolute cooperation in the matter of discovery.

Undaunted by the Chief's refusal, Champlain made another proposal. He requested only a single canoe for a northbound survey. This too was rejected. Batiscan was unwilling to part with it "on any account whatever" (II:174). Without transportation, and facing an Indian blockade to the north, Champlain was reduced to a westward survey on the St. Lawrence River. But even this cutback mission proved difficult to achieve as there was only one damaged pinnace that could be freed from trading duties at Trois-Rivières.

Anxious for any success, on May 28, Champlain left Québec and, on the same day, arrived at the Grand Rapid (fig. 28), or Lachine, as it had been named by Jacques Cartier. The landing site was named Place Royale, and Champlain referred to the nearby mountain as Mount Royal (Montréal), the same name as had been bestowed by Cartier.

At this point, Champlain had knowledge of Cartier's voyages, and in all likelihood he had read Lescarbot's *History of New France*, published in 1609. But regardless of Lescarbot's insults to Champlain, or Lescarbot's allegation that Champlain tried to take credit for Cartier's exploration, Champlain left his own mark on this future site of Montréal: "In the middle of the river is an island which we named St. Hélène's Island, . . . where there is room to build a good strong town" (II:178). His young wife, now aged thirteen, took her place in the geographic history of Canada.

By May 20, the Hurons who had promised to be on hand for a mid-month meeting had not appeared — or Champlain, who arrived a few days late, had missed them. Champlain did not wait long. He reconnoitered the surrounding area using the "poor canoe with the Indian whom I had taken to France [Savignon] and one of our men" (II:175). He proceeded to skirt the Grand Rapid through "thin woods," and reached the lake waters which form where the St. Lawrence and Ottawa rivers meet. For the first time, Champlain had gone farther than Cartier. But this was not the year for further investigation. To go on, canoes in good condition were needed, and so was more information.

Trapped for the moment, they confined their observations to the Montréal region, and the great island in the St. Lawrence was immediately identified as ideal for settlement. There were "fine meadows which would feed as many cattle as one could wish and there are all varieties of wood which we have in our forest." He listed many edibles of wild fruit — including cherries and strawberries, and a bountiful inventory of large and small game. The site was an immediate invitation to start settlement construction as Champlain noted that there was "good rich potter's clay suitable for brickmaking." Place Royale was cleared of trees at the shoreline, and Champlain experimented by building a wall "four feet [1.2 m] thick, three or four feet [1 to 1.2 m] high and ten yards [9 m] long, to see how it would survive during the winter when the waters came down." On the agricultural frontier, soil tests were undertaken and seeds planted "which all came up quickly and in perfect condition" (II:176-79). Poutrincourt would have reveled in the sight.

On June 2, irritated at the failure of the Hurons to rendezvous with him, Champlain sent Savignon and another ahead "to meet those of his tribe" to tell them to come quickly. The voyageurs then struck out again in the poor canoe in search of the missing emissaries. Finding no one, the search party returned. But now others wanted to try; this time, Savignon and the Montagnais Chief, Outetoucos, "a very agreeable person," who had traveled before with Champlain, along with a young Frenchman, Louis, "a great lover of hunting," to try their luck (II:179, 181). Taking the faulty canoe, these three headed out into the rapids.

The journey started off well enough; taking a moment for relaxation, the volunteers hunted for herons on an island, which they named "Heron," in the middle of the torrent. At first, Savignon balked at the risk of going farther to the west in the raging waters; but then he relented, and soon all three — Louis, Outetoucos, and Savignon — straddled the cedar thwarts in the unstable craft and eased out into the whitecaps. "They let themselves drift with the current; but when they were on the brink of the rapid, they tried to get out of it by throwing over their load. It was . . . too late, for the swift water had them completely in its power. And their canoe filled quickly in the whirling waters which tossed them up and down in all sorts of ways. They clung to it for a long time. At length the strength of the current wore them out . . . . Poor Louis who was quite unable to swim, lost his [grip] completely and [with] the canoe going under, he was forced to abandon it . . . . In this miserable manner did the poor fellow die. Outetoucos, who was naked, and trusted his ability to swim, abandoned it, thinking he could reach the shore although the water was still running very swiftly. But he was drowned, for he was so exceedingly worn out by his exertions." Savignon, "being more prudent, continued to hold firmly to the canoe, until it reached an eddy, to which the current carried it. Here he managed, in spite of the labour and fatigue he had undergone, to reach shore easily" (II:183-84).

Savignon alone escaped to tell the tale, and Champlain, who forever sought firsthand confirmation, went to the site to see for himself: "And I assure you that when he showed me the spot my hair stood on end to see such an awful place and I was astonished that the victims had been so lacking in judgement" (I:184). He shuddered with

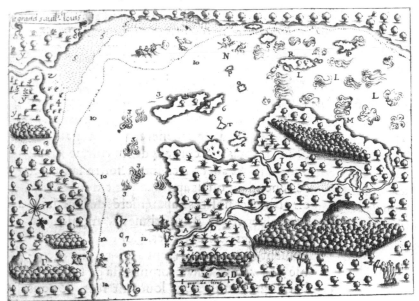

28 MONTRÉAL AND THE LACHINE RAPIDS, QUÉBEC,
MAY 1611
le grand sautl st Louis

good reason. Like poor Louis, Champlain couldn't swim.

Having lost their only canoe, Champlain and his party were now
marooned until June 13 when, more than three weeks late, Chief
Outchetaguin arrived with two hundred Hurons and Chief Iroquet of
the Algonquins. Both chiefs were veterans of the battle at Sorel (fig.
27). As the Indian fleet of canoes approached Place Royale "slowly and
in order," Champlain and his men "received them with a salute of
arquebuses, muskets and small pieces" (II:186). Then, suddenly the
reader of the journal is told that there was a full French flotilla
assembled at Place Royale, which included thirteen pinnaces. It was a
small armada — the largest regatta ever reported in New France.
However, these pinnaces were only practical for the season's trade east
of the Grand Rapid; none of them could be used for westward exploration duty because they were too large to take on the river above the
rapids. For lack of the right kind of transportation, the year's mission
remained at a standstill.

In accordance with the arrangements made the previous year at
Sorel, Savignon was returned to the Hurons, and the young French
exchange student (Étienne Brûlé?), who had spent the winter in Huronia with Outchetaguin, was returned to the service of Champlain.

Among the Indians was Savignon's brother Tregouaroti, who had come down to the Grand Rapid to see the sights.

Champlain was clearly looking forward to further alliances and agreements with the Indians — agreements that would allow him to penetrate the river and assist him in finding minerals. But two difficulties had developed. First, the Iroquois prisoner that Champlain had rescued from torture at Sorel had convinced the Huron chief that Champlain was really an ally of the Iroquois. Acting as interpreter, Savignon was at last able to convince the Chief that Champlain was not an ally of the Iroquois and explain why he had requested the release of the prisoner. But even with competent interpreters, the Indians still did not entirely trust the French.

The second problem raised by the Indians was one that concerned Champlain as well. It was a problem that could be traced directly back to the difficulties he had experienced in France. According to Champlain, there were complaints from the Indian allies concerning the number of traders from France — a number that had not existed two years before: "So many Frenchmen . . . not very friendly towards one another." As Champlain and the company of investors led by de Monts had wanted exclusive license to trade, and as the Crown had not granted it, this report might well have been self-serving. Whether it was or not, this complaint provided the perfect leverage for de Monts to regain his trade monopoly, and Champlain relished the chance to clarify the complaint: "I was to bring as many people as I liked, provided they were under the leadership of one chief." Champlain went on to promise to furnish settlements, and to petition "His Majesty to assist us, to the extent of forty or fifty men . . . with arms and implements" (II:193-95). The reader is assured that the Indians have made their views concerning the French extremely clear: they may come and they may settle, but they must be led by one man, and his journal makes it very clear that Champlain is the Frenchman whom they trust.

Great as was the benefit of these complaints to Champlain's case, however, they were also a masterful ploy by the Algonquins and the Hurons. French exploration was now stalled over matters of trust. Champlain was forced to renegotiate the previous year's commitment that he be taken west. All that he had gained this year was another promise in exchange for an even greater commitment from the French. The Indians had again won, and the cost to Champlain would be the discovery of Hudson Bay.

Before leaving, the Hurons recovered the drowned body of Out-etoucos for a secret burial on Île Sainte-Hélène. Then, in an amazing farewell gesture, Champlain boldly took the initiative and demonstrated that quality that he knew would be most admired by the Indians: raw courage. The non-swimmer lashed himself alone in a canoe and shot the Lachine Rapids: "I assure you that even the bravest people in the world . . . could not do so without great apprehension . . . . But these tribes are so clever at shooting rapids that it is easy for them. I ran this one with them, a thing I had never done before, nor had any other Christian, except my young man [Louis]" (III:204). This was Champlain the Ulyssean, making a grand physical gesture at great personal risk. This was no ordinary forty-four-year-old husband with family responsibilities on his mind, and, as at Lake Champlain, he deservedly won the admiration of all present.

In spite of disappointment, it was not a year of no progress. Prior to their departure from Place Royale, the Indians provided cartography of the interior for the first time: "I had much conversation with them regarding the source of the great river and about their country . . . as to which they gave me many particulars as well of the rivers, falls, lakes and lands . . . taking pleasure in telling me about all these things." Champlain now had further evidence of Niagara Falls and the Great Lakes. He also reported from the Indians: "Four of them assured me they had seen a sea [Lake Huron] from their country, but that the way to it was difficult" (IV:140-41). This was the third time that Champlain had heard about the great inland sea (Hudson Bay), and these revelations are documented on his 1612 map (fig. 29), which is fully discussed in the next chapter.

In the history of the exploration of New France, this was the year of the great information breakthrough. Champlain now had evidence that a continental empire lay in wait, and that, through him, the French were on the leading edge for control of the interior. The real question was, could the French now muster the resources for the largest land grab in discovery history? Speed was essential. The international race for all of America north of Mexico was on.

On July 18, Champlain left Place Royale for Trois-Rivières and arrived at Québec the next day with the promise of a grand future and the recent memory of a milder winter. All the residents agreed to hang on till next spring. Roses were planted and a sample of oak wood was trimmed to take to France to test for wainscoting and window-frames. The first modest economic plans were afoot.

Champlain spent only two days in Québec before pushing eastward to Tadoussac, where routine departure matters were summarily settled. Samuel de Champlain was in a great hurry. For the first time, he had enough evidence to justify nearly a decade of effort; at last there were now enough details to enable a comprehensive study to prove the case for further exploration and investment. It was time to clean the slate of past failures and to move on to new horizons; time to hustle — and that meant politics. Accordingly Champlain made a prudent and timely departure for France on August 11 during the "safe" sailing season.

CHAPTER FIFTEEN

Back to France: from a Dream to a Nightmare: 1611-1612

"[The Indians] draw the most exact maps imaginable
to the countries they are acquainted with."

Baron Armand-Louis de Lahontan (1666–1715), French
explorer

CHAMPLAIN ARRIVED AT HIS HACIENDA, REAL DEL
Rey Nuestro Señor, at La Rochelle on September 10, and from
there he went directly to see de Monts in neighbouring Pons. He was
enthusiastic about the Indian maps, the progress made in the colony,
and, of course, there was the matter of the complaint: the Indians
themselves wanted the trade and the number of traders controlled.
But as enthusiastic as he was, Champlain found the meeting a disappointment. Despite all the opportunities that Champlain's report
offered, de Monts's financial situation was desperate. He had long
endured the expense of frustratingly slow progress in the colony's
development; the entrepreneurial traders of the coastal areas had
gained the upper hand, and now his partners wanted out.

At this point, Champlain was seeking new backing, while de
Monts sought only to stabilize his fortunes. It seemed clear that the
two might not be able to continue down the same road. Both desperate in their own ways, they decided on one last duel with the Crown to
win back their exclusive trading privileges and to attract new partners.
They agreed they should go to Paris together to bargain for a new
arrangement.

Despite the maps of the interior provided by the Indians, the future
of the colony depended on two commitments: the French must

engage in a third battle with the Iroquois in the coming summer of 1612 to regain the complete confidence of their allies. And there could be only one authority in New France and that must be the Champlain/de Monts partnership.

De Monts and Champlain headed to Paris. As if fate had ordained that the two of them should fail, Champlain suffered an accident: "I started off ahead to go there . . . but on the way was held up by a wretched horse which fell upon me and nearly killed me. This fall delayed me a long time; but as soon as I was in fit condition, I set out to complete my journey and meet the Sieur de Monts at Fontainebleau" (II:215-16).

The timing could not have been worse. The enterprise's momentum had been lost and, during the interruption, the competition had been able again to cashier de Monts' plans for a renewed monopoly. Whether or not Champlain and de Monts eventually met in Fontainebleau or ever followed through with a royal interview is not known; but eventually they learned that their plea for an exclusive license had failed. No reasons were given; depressed, beaten, and burdened with other priorities, de Monts retired from the business of colonizing.

The Sieur de Monts, the financial hero of the exploration and development of New France, faded into the background while Champlain became the only visible promoter. For the first time the "soldier of fortune" was without a champion in high places. He was also left with "the task of finding ways and means" to carry on (I:216). There was much to be done.

During this lengthy period of reorganization, which lasted more than a year, Champlain wrote nothing in the journals. The single bit of information he provided about these times came years later when he read a report sent from Québec. Referring to it, he noted that in the summer of 1612 two hundred Hurons and Algonquins had showed up at the Montréal Rapids where "I had agreed to meet them . . . ; [but] When they saw that I had not kept my promise, they were much annoyed. However, apologies, which they accepted as real, were made by our men" (II:217). It is typical of Champlain's writing that the reader is notified years later, with no explanation, that, while others went, Champlain himself did not voyage to New France in 1612.

It is now evident that during the years 1611 and 1612, Champlain was totally pre-occupied in the preparation of his greatest work: *Les Voyages de Sieur de Champlain* (1613). Preparing this monumental work for publication must have demanded considerable solitude.

Much of the writing was likely done at the estate in La Rochelle. The result was one of the most important historic documents of the seventeenth century.

Champlain divided his new work into two books, his original intention having probably been to publish them separately. The first covers the voyages to Acadia (1604–1607) and the second the return voyages to the St. Lawrence River (1608–1612), published in 1614. The one-volume set, *Les Voyages*, was Champlain's second publication, and his third written work of record, taking into account the unpublished *Brief Narrative*. It was an astonishing achievement for the period. *Les Voyages — 1613* has no less than twenty-six charts and illustrations offered in support of the author's many methodical firsthand observations (figs. 5 to 32, and excluding the two maps by Lescarbot and Hudson). (The last ten chapters of this book — chapters 6 through 15 — have drawn heavily on this triumph.) The two great summary charts from the unabridged edition of Champlain's 1613 publication reveal the state of his knowledge during this interlude while he was in seclusion in France (fig. 29).

At last, a new Royal Commission was granted to de Monts's replacement, "The Lord the Prince Charles de Bourbon" (1566–1612), an uncle of young King Louis. For Champlain, it was a moment of rejoicing when on October 15, 1612, in a letter, the new Viceroy showed a heartening idealism and shared high expectations for the fledgling colony. Champlain was appointed Lieutenant for the first time, and had the "entire trust" of his superiors although he was only a "Captain in ordinary for the King." It seemed as if there would be a promising future for this officer of "good sense, competence, practical knowledge and experience in nautical matters" (IV:209-10).

Just as this license, which was for a period of twelve years — the longest ever to be considered — was on the verge of publication, Charles de Bourbon died of smallpox. As a result, that authority was automatically transferred to a less desirable recipient of royal patronage, the twenty-four-year-old Henri II (1588-1646), "Prince de Condé, First Prince of the Blood, First Peer of France, His Majesty's Governor and Lieutenant in Guyenne" (II:239). De Condé was also a manipulator, and his appointment signaled future difficulties.

At first the new appointment yielded some positive results. With a new license in hand, issued on November 22, 1612, Champlain could now form a broader restructured corporation to include interested merchants from Rouen and La Rochelle. With the union of those who had formerly been fiercely competing for a slice of the same trade, he

29 CHAMPLAIN'S GRAND SURVEY OF 1612
Carte Geographique De La Nouvelle France . . .

Although Champlain commented that he had "drawn the large map in this way, for the satisfaction of the majority of the pilots and navigators to the coasts of New France" (II: 224), this cartographic extravaganza is really an advertisement. This map reveals Champlain at his best as illustrator and chart-maker: here he laid out the possibilities and promise of America all in one copper engraving.

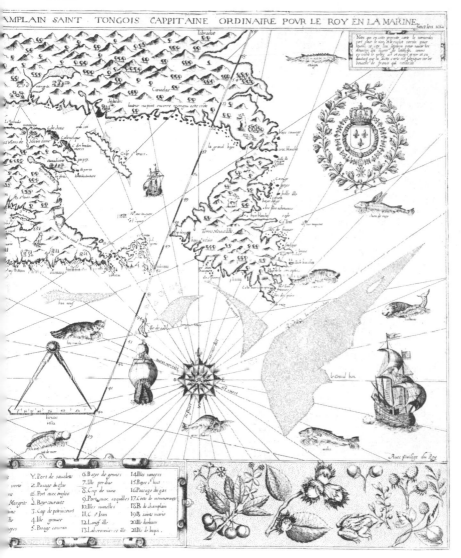

Those who expect scientific accuracy in the piece will miss Champlain's point in drawing it. A deliberate mixture of fact, fiction, and promise for the future, the map was drawn to attract attention and inspire economic investment in colonizing New France. The survey is a summary of contemporary knowledge of French discovery as well as a document to aid registration of land claims, as was the 1607 summary survey (fig. 21). For information provided about the lands to the north and west, credit must be given to the Hurons.

The map can be divided into eastern and western sections: the eastern section shows those lands discovered primarily by first-hand exploration; the western section is drawn from information provided by the Indians and represents future possibilities. The dividing line between the two sections is at approximately the middle of the map. For easy reference, the farthest point to which Champlain had explored in 1611 was the Grand Rapid at Montréal located just north of Lake Champlain (fig. 28). From this demarcation line westward to the Great Lakes and northward lay the promise of the future.

Champlain's political message is found in his imaginative and varied illustration of the land west of Île d'Orléans and Québec. Its agricultural and settlement value was indicated by minute illustrations of forests, lakes, and wildlife. By this time Acadia's importance was minimized while that of Huronia and other western lands not yet seen was heightened. Perhaps the only remaining whiff of nostalgia for Acadia is seen in the inclusion of the "beautiful harbour," at Gloucester, Massachusetts (fig. 18), which hitherto had been neatly excluded from the 1607 summary survey map (fig. 21). On this 1612 update, any area that held promise and might attract funding was included.

The main feature of the survey, however, is Champlain's depiction of the lands and lakes to the west. Here is the first illustration of Niagara Falls, which can barely be detected at the narrows separating the Great Lakes of Ontario and Erie. Lake Huron at the western extremity of the map was drawn as a giant body of water. By leaving the western boundary open, Champlain initiated a cartographic practice that lasted for almost a century. He was suggesting here that the route to Mare Pacifica and on to China might be found through the waterways in the center of the continent.

Champlain's optimism extended to the easterly section of the map, where he exaggerated the size of the St. Maurice River north from Trois-Rivières. Perhaps he still thought it could be a possible route to Hudson Bay (fig. 30). To the northwest, there was a number of mysterious watercourses which formed the speculative cartography of the known, but as yet unsurveyed, Ottawa river.

In places the viewer is often blindfolded and unable to see many major features of the continent such as Lakes Michigan, Superior and Erie. To the extreme west where Champlain depicted a fox standing on its hind legs, it's not clear whether the intention was to show Lake Nipissing or Lake Superior.

In political terms, the map was also an important document. At the outset, the Indians that were allied to the French were correctly located north of the St. Lawrence, and Iroquoia, the home of the enemy, was shown south of the river. It is unlikely that there were no more Iroquois settlements around Lake Champlain as implied here. Within three years of the drawing of this map, Champlain would have vivid memories of Lake Onandaga in the upper New York State area (fig. 34).

For many viewers, the tiny illustrations are the most captivating features of the whole map and some of these, in contrast with the dour text of the journals, are refreshingly comical. For example, just off the coast of Labrador, Champlain fits in a sturgeon. His beloved Chaousarou, the crocodile-like garfish he found at Lake Champlain, is with some difficulty squeezed into Lake Huron. In this same punchy artistic style first revealed in the *Brief Narrative*, Champlain includes a few of his old favorites: the Cape Cod wonder, the Siguenoc, the horseshoe crab he discovered at Nauset Harbor (fig. 15), which is not found on Champlain's 1607 summary survey of Acadia (fig. 21), where it should be. And, of course, he included a whale, one of the many he depicted over the years in his regional charts. For Champlain, however, this magnificent mammal was a symbol of wealth to be plundered, not a creature to be preserved.

The illustrations inserted under the portraits of the Indians seem to be attributed to the engraver David Pelletier. Without evidence, it's difficult to credit these excellent renderings to anyone other than Champlain. This is especially the case considering the detail in the text. And Champlain described himself as an illustrator. Indeed his competitors complained that he was a preoccupied artist, apparently to a degree that was seen as detrimental to his scientific observations.

In this artistry, the Indians that Champlain first met on the north shore of the St. Lawrence, the Montagnais, are prominently shown as well as the more lightly clothed Almouchiquois Indians of Massachusetts, the wily warriors that defeated the French at Port Fortuné (fig. 20). These illustrations are not, as has been suggested, fanciful European stylized representations of the "noble savage." Champlain is a geographer and ethnographer presenting life as he saw it.

The vegetation section of the map is also worthy of close study. Some historians have scoffed at the idea that Champlain was interested in agriculture, yet he repeatedly mentioned farming and agricultural self-sufficiency as requisite to long-term colonization. Here he tempts Europeans with illustrations of strawberries, beans, roots, nuts and, for the graphically vulnerable French gourmet, a finely detailed frog.

Despite its wealth of detail, the grand graphic omits one important piece of geography. Since 1603 Champlain has heard much of the great inland sea jutting into the continent from the north, but he has not shown it here. Unknown to him at the time of drawing, Henry Hudson had sailed in search of the Northwest passage on April 17, 1610, and, during the winter of 1610–1611, had unwittingly seized that body of water of which Champlain dreamed — "Hudson's Bay."

Champlain learned of Hudson's discovery while he was in France, likely in the fall of 1612 and after the sailing season. One source of information was Nicolas de Vignau, who claimed to have taken an expedition to this "sea". Some time during this period, Champlain evidently had an opportunity to view the Hudson map published in Holland in 1612 by Hessel Gerritz (fig. 30).

For Champlain personally, Hudson's discovery was heartbreaking news. After all those years and so much effort to gain accurate information about it, co-operation from the Indians, and support from the home government, he's in second place. Moreover, his 1612 map, still unpublished when he heard the news, lacked a major piece of information.

And for France and particularly for Champlain, de Vignau's news had other serious implications. In recounting the tale of his visit to the inland "sea which is salt" (I: 124), de Vignau had effectively suggested the possibility of a third access route to the Arctic Ocean down the Ottawa River. This was reason for optimism and excitement, but there was now also the threat that the English would shortly move to solidify their gain, just as they had already undertaken in Acadia and New England. The French had to move with speed now to take possession of the territory they claimed.

At this point Champlain had to decide between several options: he could ignore Hudson's map and, if later proven wrong, be himself ridiculed for his omission, or he could gamble and publish with his current information, adding another map including Hudson's chart, but without the Ottawa river network in place; or he could postpone publication until he had verified the discovery himself hoping to find the route in the coming season perhaps with the help of Nicolas de Vignau. There was no 'best' choice.

Troubled, and perhaps aware of potential ridicule from Marc Lescarbot (Ch. 9), Champlain covered all three options over the next two years. First he published his manuscript with the great graphic chart as it was; second, he added another chart (fig. 31) to the first revised edition prior to his own exploration. In this later case, he simply plunked Hudson Bay onto the survey, but without its relationship to the Ottawa River route implied by Hudson's Mare Magnum. Later, he followed his third option, after his own voyage.

---

hoped that the same merchants would now support the development of the colony in their forged partnership, rather than sabotage it.

Champlain would now be able to concentrate on the love of his life: geography. This was to be a year of discovery and verification, and his priority tabled to de Condé in writing was "to prosecute with more care and diligence . . . the search for the northern sea" (II:239). The key was the report from a newcomer, one Nicolas de Vignau (fl. 1603-13), who claimed that he had seen the sea himself and, furthermore, that it only took seventeen days to get there from the Grand Rapid at Place Royale (fig. 28). Even more astonishing, de Vignau claimed to have seen "pieces of a wreck of an English ship which had been lost on that coast, on which were eighty men who had escaped to land. These the Indians killed because these Englishmen tried to take from them by force their Indian corn and other supplies. He said, too, that he had seen the scalps of the men which these Indians according to their custom had cut off. These, they would show me and would also give me an English boy whom they were keeping for me" (II:256).

For months, Champlain was shaken by the news that English explorers had already discovered the inland sea. Yet he remained suspicious, and because of this, de Vignau's alleged journey was not recorded in the body of the journals even though Champlain knew of it at the time of publication. Only the beginning of the tale is found in a letter that Champlain wrote to the Viceroy de Condé, which was then published by Champlain as a supplement to his record of events.

To this date, it is not known whether or not de Vignau's mission was a part of an agreement made with the Hurons and Algonquins in 1611 as an exchange mission hitherto unmentioned, or, which seems more likely, that de Vignau went out to New France with Pontgravé in 1612, the year that Champlain was forced by economic circumstances and politics to stay in France. The record is vague and, in view of how it turned out, perhaps some of this obfuscation was intended by the writer (fig. 30).

Regardless of exactly when and how de Vignau obtained his information, Champlain reacted to it like a well-trained public servant. He wrote a report on the matter, which is no longer extant. Then, in a second step, he reported going over the options with the nation's chancellor, marshal, and president, and with Chief Justice Jeannin, the most respected jurist in France, who had served three monarchs. (Lescarbot had dedicated his *L'histoire* to Jeannin.) And Champlain carefully co-opted others of noble rank into a supportive position for the gamble to check out the evidence firsthand. Champlain also warned Nicolas de Vignau that if he was "telling a lie, he was putting a rope around his neck" (II:256) (fig. 31).

Provided Vignau joined the expedition to point the way, Champlain was finally persuaded of his story based on "this self-assurance, the honesty of which I judged him to be possessed . . . [all of which] had a great show of truth" (II:257). But to avoid running any more of a risk than necessary, and in keeping with a love of the law typical of the time, de Vignau was forced to swear out two separate affidavits in the presence of notaries. In these, he swore to the truth of his tale.

30 HENRY HUDSON'S CHART OF 1612 (date of publication)
Tabula Nautica

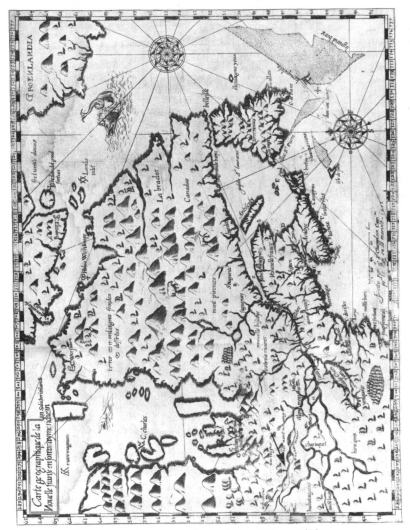

31 CHAMPLAIN'S CHART OF NEW FRANCE, c. 1612
(EXCLUDING THE OTTAWA RIVER)
Carte geographique de la Nouvelle Franse . . .

With all the consultations, reports, and legalities completed, an anxious Champlain, tired of playing the bureaucrat, set an early sail for Tadoussac on March 6, 1613, with Pontgravé. Pontgravé would brief his friend on the colony's progress; de Vignau's passage was arranged on another vessel.

CHAPTER SIXTEEN

The Push for the Ottawa River and Hudson Bay: 1613

"God appears to have been pleased to give
this frightful and abandoned region some things
in their season for the refreshment of man."

Champlain, *Les Voyages*, 1613 (on the Ottawa River)

THE VOYAGEURS REACHED TADOUSSAC NEAR THE end of April 1613 when it was still early in the season. Everyone was in good spirits — especially perhaps Captain Pontgravé. According to Champlain, the Captain had given Madame Pontgravé power of attorney prior to departure, and this, he hoped, would free him from having to deal with certain "tiresome domestic" affairs in France.

Whenever a ship anchored offshore at Tadoussac, curious Indians would board it, bringing with them items to trade with the seamen. Anchored offshore — and perhaps to celebrate the season's good start — Champlain indulged in some minor mischief by masquerading as an ordinary seaman while greeting the welcoming band of traders. The seaman himself told the Indians that the great commander had again not returned this year. However, one of the older warriors recognized him by the battle scars on his neck and ear — scars inflected at Sorel three years earlier. The recognition resulted in appropriate greetings.

The situation at the trading post was far less pleasant. Previously, it had been the Basques who had traded despite the King's monopoly license. But this year, it was renegade traders from France who mocked the King's latest commission. Unknown to Champlain at the time was the fact that the Viceroy himself, the Prince de Condé, was by far his

largest obstacle. Later, Champlain learned the details and even supplied some of them. De Condé's claim to fame was greed, and to
cement the original deal for his support in 1612, the partners were
forced to pay an annual bribe. This year, although an agreement had
been reached to stop the infighting among the traders, de Condé
undermined the arrangement by negotiating a separate contract with
the merchants of La Rochelle, who in the end gained nothing and
then wheedled their way out of the deal. Many years later, Cardinal
Richelieu (1585–1642) tallied the six-year price of de Condé's ravages
of the treasury. It was an enormous sum — 3,660,000 livres! But at the
time, all Champlain knew was that he had renegade traders operating
illegally.

And there was more trouble as well. Of those Indians who had
survived the winter, many were starving, and the most desperate were
found devouring animal entrails and eating the tallow used for caulking the ships. With such strong evidence of a bad winter, Champlain
became more anxious about the settlement upriver at Québec. In
order to achieve a successful exploration this year, he knew that he
had to move quickly on to the settlement that was to be his spring-
board for the year's thrust — the westward expansion of the empire.

On arrival, Champlain found the settlement had weathered the
season well, and this happy discovery prompted a rare aesthetic observation: "The trees also were beginning to put forth their leaves again,
and the fields to become bright with flowers" (II:252).

But he did not linger. He pushed westward to the Grand Rapid at
Place Royale (Montréal). There, he had expected the Indian allies to
meet and greet him on his arrival. But two years of broken French
promises had not sat well with them. The French had failed to show
up in 1612 with the forty or fifty men promised, and though Champlain had previously reported that apologies were sent and accepted, it
was clear on his arrival that this was not the case. Furthermore,
Champlain learned that some twelve hundred Hurons and Algonquins had gone on the warpath on their own against the Iroquois the
previous year. This year, Champlain had brought only five men and,
although the Indians seemed to expect nothing of the French this
time, neither were they trustful or cooperative. Broken promises
resulted in half-hearted support.

The small band of explorers bundled into two canoes regardless
and the north-westward journey into the wilderness began. Nicolas de
Vignau, the catalyst for the exploration, was to show the way. Years

later in his journal of 1632, Champlain, with the benefit of hindsight, informs the reader again that all were in the company of "the most impudent liar that has been seen for a long time" (II:255).

On May 29, the voyageurs reached the mouth of the Ottawa River (fig. 33), the presumed gateway west to the inland sea. This was also the location of the Algonquin base camp of Chief Tessouat (Besouat) (fl. 1603-13).

This journey was certainly no easy undertaking, and Champlain reported that he was nearly killed when his canoe was bashed into the rocks: "I could not quickly enough loosen the rope which was twisted around my hand, which hurt me very much, and nearly cut it off " (II:263). As he had at the Grand Rapid in 1611, Champlain, the non-swimmer, was white-water canoeing at tremendous risk, and he was warned by the Indians that conditions were worse upstream.

Continuing to cut the current westward, in a brief interlude, there was a midstream powwow with a party of Algonquins headed down to the Grand Rapid at Place Royale. For the French headed into the unknown on uncharted waters, this was their last opportunity to touch base with civilization. It was arranged that one member of Champlain's party would return with the eastbound Indian escort and, on arrival, make a progress report on paper.

Although hoping to discourage further French travel into the interior, the Algonquins reluctantly provided a guide when Champlain requested one. No doubt, they had decided in the end that it was better to send a guide and know what the French were doing rather than allow them to continue alone. The sudden request for a guide, however, reveals Champlain's suspicion that de Vignau's credibility deserved closer scrutiny. De Vignau was supposed to have known the way to Tessouat's headquarters as well as the route all the way to the inland sea. Continuing west on June 4, Champlain noted the mouth of the Gatineau and Rideau rivers, and the environs that were to become the future capital of Canada. There were "all sorts of game, . . . so that the Indians like to make a halt here. The Iroquois also come here sometimes and surprise them as they pass." Two days later, the voyageurs reached another milestone as they entered what is now Ontario: "We crossed to the west bank of the river . . . . We had much trouble in taking this route overland, being laden for my part alone with three arquebuses, an equal number of paddles, my cloak and some small articles" (II:267-68, 273). (It was in this same region that the most famous heritage artifact of New France was found in 1867. This was the so-called Champlain Astrolabe. See Appendix VI regarding the discovery of the Astrolabe. From this point on, Champlain's every word on this passage in 1613 takes on a special significance.)

By the time the explorers reached what is now the vicinity of present-day Cobden, Ontario, it is evident that de Vignau was confused about routing and directions. Here, Champlain met a lesser sagamore, Nibachis of the Algonquin River Chiefs. Nibachis arranged for two canoes to be fitted out for the final lap to a meeting with Tessouat, the elder Chief of the Algonquin nation, with whom Champlain hoped to sort out de Vignau's account of his alleged previous journey. Before leaving, however, Champlain observed the sandy soil and the sparsely planted corn, and — in an astonishing revelation — the agricultural practices of this region were compared with those of the Indians in Florida. This flourish of detail adds support to the view that Champlain had visited the Florida region during his voyage to the West Indies: "When the trees have been burned, they turn up the ground a little, and plant their maize, grain by grain, as do those in Florida" (II:276).

The last lap of the journey was made without incident, and, after half a day's paddle, Champlain and his fellow adventurers arrived at Allumette Island (opposite present-day Pembroke). Here, Champlain would meet with one of the toughest of Indian leaders, the one-eyed old chief, Tessouat. This wily survivor is believed to have been known to Champlain from earlier days, and was probably that warrior who led the very first reported attack against the Iroquois in 1603 — long before the idea of aid from French muskets had occurred to Indian minds. This was the Algonquin leader who had for years successfully managed a continental "tollgate" to all the western lands, including the adjacent country of the Nipissings and the vast agricultural tract immediately south of Georgian Bay, known as Huronia. These gate-keepers had most likely been forced by the circumstances of war to settle here by the Iroquois long ago, and they now manipulated the river geography to advantage by holding all passers-by to ransom: either those who sought wealth from the western lands of the Nipissing and Huron country or those who portaged south to trade at the Grand Rapid, Trois-Rivières, or Tadoussac. Of these Indians Champlain asked in amazement: "How could they waste their time cultivating such a poor region?" The answer was simply that agriculture was not their main economic livelihood.

Tessouat was astonished at the sight of Champlain: "He thought I was a ghost . . . and that he could not believe his eyes [one eye?]." At first, with the advantage of surprise, all seemed to go well. Champlain was allowed to tour about freely; he quickly noted their "badly-made bark wigwams." Noting their cemeteries, he was

> filled with wonder at the sight of the tombs — in the form of shrines — made of pieces of wood, crossed at the top, and fixed upright in the ground . . . . They place a large piece of wood . . . on which is carved rudely (as one might expect) the face of him or her who is there buried. If it is a man they put up a shield, a sword with a handle such as they use, a club, a bow and arrows; if it is a chief, he will have a bunch of feathers on his head and some other ornament or embellishment; if a child, they give him a bow and arrow; . . . if a woman or girl, a kettle, an earthen pot, a wooden spoon, and a paddle" (II:278-80).

The interest in Indian culture apparent here in Champlain's writings for the first time marked the beginning of yet another career change.

Over-confident, Champlain revealed to Tessouat the initial phase of the French plan: to build a settlement and fortress in the following year at Place Royale, and also to protect the Algonquins from the Iroquois by making much war against the enemy in the future. Tessouat listened politely; then all assembled were promptly ordered to a great feast, "each with his wooden bowl and spoon." Champlain noted that for drink there was "fine clean water," and that one dish was "a sort of hasty pudding, made of maize crushed between two stones, mixed with meat and fish" (II:282).

Then, after a rare, reported half-hour of meditation, it was Champlain's turn to convince the Indians of the desirability of the ongoing partnership with the French. With his guard completely down, Champlain revealed too much: his desire to make allies of the Nipissings "six days' march from them" (II:283); and he also let slip his fervent ambition to explore those western lands that he had first learned about three years ago at Sorel in 1610. In his confession, he reserved only one piece of information: he made no mention of the main reason for this years' coming — the quest for the inland sea. But when Tessouat saw Nicolas de Vignau, who had spent the previous winter at his base camp, the old Chief realized immediately that Champlain intended to find that sea, and the old warrior was angry.

He immediately claimed that he and the Algonquins had been

betrayed. He had showed up at the Grand Rapid the previous year exactly as promised with some two thousand braves and then he and his allies had gone on the warpath to fight the Iroquois alone. On their discovery of de Vignau's and Champlain's current mission, the Indians threatened de Vignau physically; even Champlain was harassed, and his integrity further questioned. Soon the psychological warfare took its toll. Finally even Champlain turned on the terrorized Nicolas de Vignau, while the Indians railed at both of them.

Intimidated and threatened from both sides, poor de Vignau caved in and confessed that he had fabricated the entire story about the inland sea.

At last Tessouat warned of the dangers of even going as far west as the adjacent Nipissing country (Nipissing means sorcery), describing it as a wicked land filled with difficult portages and numerous rapids. The Chief apparently went back on his initial commitment to give the French the four promised canoes to go at least that far. To make sure of the blockade, Tessouat sent emissaries ahead to warn the Nipissings of Champlain's coming.

De Vignau's role in the incident is a puzzle. If he were simply a liar for profit, as some scholars have suggested, then what had he to gain? And why would he have carried on the charade to this point in the face of such personal risk to himself at the hands of his employer? None of this has ever been explained.

Champlain was himself of a divided mind as to whether or not to continue. At one point he confessed that "there was little likelihood of this youth having invented all this and of his not having made the journey. It was more likely that he had seen these things, but that his ignorance did not allow him to reply to the questions of the Indians" (II:292). Even years later, still agonizing over the incident in his final journal of 1632, Champlain admitted to having a "mind wavering in uncertainty" (IV:191). Totally frustrated at the time, Champlain pardoned poor de Vignau on certain conditions: some unspecified penalties and public confessions. (See Notes.)

For the French, the de Vignau affair must have been déjà vu: the bewitching promise of another great copper bonanza. Now the Mare Magnum of Henry Hudson had also proven elusive; but perhaps the homeward journey from Tessouat's camp was the right tonic for Champlain. En route to the Grand Rapid after courtesies had been exchanged with Tessouat, now described as "the kind old chief," Champlain set off on June 10 with Tessouat's son and an escort of 40

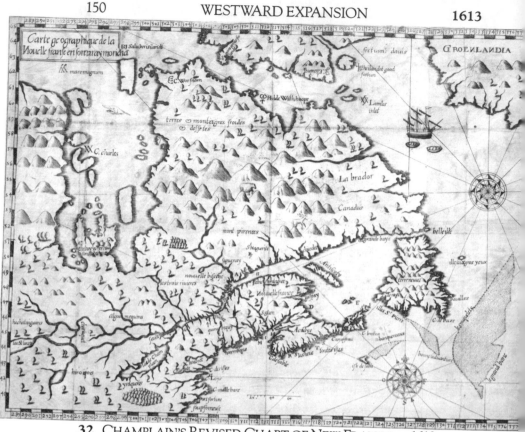

32 CHAMPLAIN'S REVISED CHART OF NEW FRANCE, c. 1613 (INCLUDING THE OTTAWA RIVER)
Carte geographique de la Nouvelle franse . . .

The work on *Les Voyages* was well advanced and some copies were already in circulation before Champlain was able to add the details of the Ottawa River. As a result the unabridged edition contains a chart of New France without the river of the Algonquins in it (fig. 31). Somehow, Champlain interrupted the publishing and distribution process and added a revised chart which included a crude survey of the Ottawa river and its connection to Lake Nipissing (fig. 32). To mark the difference between the two editions of the map he removed the illustration of the ship in the upper right hand corner (fig. 31) and replaced it with a whale (fig. 32).

canoes, joined by another 20 as they proceeded, all loaded with "a good deal of merchandise." Their first night out was a disturbed one:

> An hour before daybreak, an Indian, dreaming that the enemy were attacking him, started up, and in order to escape took to flight towards the water, screaming out "They are killing me." The rest of his party awoke quite bewildered, and thinking they were pursued by their enemies, jumped into the water, as did one of our Frenchmen, who thought he was being toma-hawked . . . ; we . . . were also at once aroused . . . and rushed towards them: but seeing them moving here and there in the water, were much astonished; for we perceived no enemy in pursuit of them, nor indeed, had there been any . . . . Having in this way realized what happened, the whole thing passed off as a joke (II:298-301).

On reaching the Chaudière Falls in the Ottawa region, Champlain told of the "usual ceremony" of the Algonquins, whereby they assembled at the foot of the cataract, took up a collection of tobacco, put it on a plate, and danced around, and the "orator takes the plate and throws the tobacco into the middle of the boiling water, and all together utter a loud whoop" (II:302). The dream/joke and jovial tobacco ceremony were to prove the only joys of a short and unproductive season (fig. 32).

It was, however, on this first journey westward on the Ottawa River in 1613, that Champlain noted great quantities of a "small fruit very good to eat." He named this now famous sustenance of many voyageurs and campers in Canada the "bluët," or blueberry (III:38).

So, beaten for yet another season, Champlain quickly departed New France: "Seeing I had no further business in this country, I decided to sail home in the first ship that was returning to France" (II:307). In an uncaring muddle of diary dates that make no sense, Champlain terminated the year's journal record. Only one task for 1613 remained, and that was to update his information for the publication of *Les Voyages*.

CHAPTER SEVENTEEN

The Return to France and a Change of Strategy: 1613-1615

"I am fond of the French
when they do not ask too many questions."

Voltaire (1694–1778), *L'Ingénu* (The hero, the Huron native, speaks out in France.)

IN THE AUTUMN OF 1613, CHAMPLAIN RETURNED TO France prepared to meet his critics. Over his years of exploration and attempted development, he had failed to establish a colony along the New England coast (called the Acadian coast by the French during Champlain's time), failed to establish a viable settlement in Florida, and most recently failed to discover the land route to Hudson Bay.

On the positive side, he had enabled the trading post at Tadoussac to continue functioning, had built a small settlement at Québec, and there was now constructed a well-stocked storage and naval outpost at the Gaspé. These few outposts that marked the French presence in America were, alas, small, vulnerable, and dependent. After all these years, there were less than one hundred souls in all of New France, and worse, there were only a few months in each year when these small islands of French habitation could be supplied for the long winter and fortified against piracy. Champlain's latest promise to the Indians to build another post at Place Royale at the Grand Rapid was not the kind of development that appealed to investors at home. Champlain's enemies could easily argue that all there was to show for six overseas missions so far was evidence of marginal military success against the Iroquois at Lake Champlain and Sorel. These victories were certainly positive, but their value was diminished by the fact that Champlain had failed to rendezvous with the Indians in 1612, and his failure to do so had created mistrust between the French and the two larger nations of the alliance, the Algonquin and the Huron. All these factors created a negative environment in France within which Champlain would argue the cause of continued funding for the young colony.

Further colonial development was thus threatened from inside France, just as another threat to it was growing outside France. By 1613, the English had established a productive colony in Virginia, where tobacco produced a lucrative cash crop to feed further development. And, although the first settlement in Massachusetts would not take place until 1620 — and the Dutch would not settle until 1624 — both countries were now launching regular trading expeditions into New England and upper New York State. Both the British and the Dutch would soon prove a real threat to further French settlement in North America.

But in 1613, when Champlain returned to France to garner more support, France's competition for the northern part of the continent was only beginning. The Dutch had staked discovery claims along the Hudson River, discovered by the Englishman Henry Hudson, who in 1609 had worked for the Netherlands prior to his epic journey to the inland sea. The Dutch were now ready to commence fur trading on the Hudson River route into Iroquoia, and already the seeds of a Dutch-Iroquois alliance were germinating.

As if commerce was not enough to cause trouble between nations, religious issues also assumed tremendous importance. Although Maryland and Rhode Island would eventually receive Catholic settlers, the early Virginia colonizers were Protestants, and in 1613 religious differences were still cause for war in both Europe and the New World.

In 1613, while Champlain was in France, the Jesuits attempted to establish a mission on the Penobscot River (in Maine). Captain Samuel Argall of the Virginia colony captured disembarking Frenchmen at Île des Monts Déserts (Mount Desert Island) (fig. 21) and the French surrendered. All claims to the land once known as the Acadian Coast were lost in an English court of law.

Pushing their claim still farther, Argall set the torch to Poutrincourt's re-established habitation at Port-Royal in November of the same year. For some time the English had laid claim to all the lands south of the 49th parallel. At this point, the French regarded Argall's action as a mere title dispute to be resolved in the courts of London and Paris. This marked the beginning of a continuing pattern of French retreat on the continent — they gradually moved inland and northward.

Given the circumstances of 1613, Champlain would have to maneuver skillfully and quickly to salvage his own plans for New France. His new vision called for an intercontinental strategy: the development of a second front that would place the French in a position — from behind — to commercially and militarily squeeze the Dutch and English towards the sea. Some new strategy was needed, and to win, he felt the initiative must be recaptured. The old game of persuasively prodding and pushing here and there, of toying with cultural exchanges with the Indians to gain language proficiency, and of gaining geographic knowledge to charm the rulers at home was over.

From September 26, 1613, to April 24, 1615, Champlain toured France for his cause; he was putting together a new promotional package. It was a difficult task, and at this late stage he had neither the time, nor even the moral support in evidence for such an undertaking. Still, every avenue was now examined. Champlain moved to alter the direction of his colonial efforts in three different areas. First, with information about the Ottawa River now in hand, he put the finishing touches on his 1613 journal, which was to be published the following year. Next, he worked on the creation of a new venture-capital corporation, which was formed on November 20, 1613, *La Compagnie de Canada*. Finally, and suddenly, Champlain switched his own career from that of navigator, surveyor, and explorer to that of crusading missionary and ethnographic geographer. He followed his own advice to others for such occasions, and tried new "ruses, strategems and inventions" (V:296).

Inherent in the new plan was the revitalization of those ideals enunciated in the first commission granted to de Monts in 1604 by King Henry IV. There would be a return to a strong moral foundation with some added twists. With religion as his battering ram, Champlain was now campaigning in France to muster support for the first religious conversion and settlement of America. He outlined his plan in a letter that he wrote to King Louis XIII, as the introduction to his third work, another *Les Voyages*, which was published in 1619: "Sire, . . . in this volume you will be able to note more particularly the manners and mode of life of these peoples . . . . In time and through intercourse with a civilized nation, they may be refined . . . in order to plant in this country the standard of the cross" (III:4-5).

Recommending to the King a method to ensure unwavering religious and political allegiance, Champlain outlined an extensive bilingual thrust into the

> yonder communities and colonies to teach those peoples, along with the knowledge of God, the glory and triumphs of Your Majesty, so that with the French speech they may also acquire a French heart and spirit, which, next to the fear of God, shall breathe nothing but the desire to serve you (III:6).

It was the seed of a mandate on the French language that was to culturally thrive in North America for centuries. (See Appendix I.)

By 1614, the prospect for progress on new funding was almost hopeless. In France, de Condé's army was on the move, and his conduct was the subject of court action and military intervention.

The Regent, Queen Marie, was threatened, and she took action; but not until the fall of 1614 and the spring of 1615 was de Condé brought temporarily into line. He made peace with the royal family and promised the court to behave. The Queen was lenient with him and he was let off. After all, this powerful Bourbon Prince was a young man, aged twenty-six.

In the meantime, Champlain had missed another year. He struggled on alone, making inroads where he could. Then he returned to his birthplace, Brouage, where he was on "terms of ordinary acquaintance" with the Sieur Louis Houel, the King's secretary and the controller-general of the Brouage salt works. According to Champlain, this well-placed contact was "a man of pious habits, and inspired with a great zeal and love for the honour of God and for the extension of His religion, who gave me some information which was very acceptable to me, to wit, that he knew some good fathers of the Récollet order" who could be "induced . . . to undertake" the voyage (III:17). But Champlain did not give the reasons for this choice and substantial change of missionary direction.

The reason why the Récollets were chosen, however, probably had nothing to do with financing. Indeed, as an order, the Jesuits were probably better off financially at the time. The reason may have had to do with the differences between the two orders. The Jesuits were close to the source of power in the Church and were strict in the extreme. The Récollets, although equally disciplined and intellectually respected, may have been more concerned with social service. Known as the "Grey Friars" for their robes of undyed sheep's wool, they had established a reputation for working to improve the lot of the lower classes, for tending the sick, and for embracing poverty. Moreover, they already had a long-established record of colonial missionary work in Spanish America: by Champlain's time, there were already five hundred Franciscan convents and seminaries.

Houel recommended to Champlain that the Franciscan Order Récollets be taken to New France rather than the Jesuits. In retrospect, we know that the Franciscans were supplied with a considerable amount of money for their new missionary undertaking. For the expedition to New France with 1,500 livres provided to defray expenses, the missionary zeal of these clergymen was reinforced in a practical manner.

For Champlain's purpose, these spiritual legionnaires were an ideal choice and, as proof, they eagerly met the challenge. Four were chosen to launch the crusade, "moved by holy zeal" as they "burned to make the voyage" (III:22). The four were: Father Denis Jamet (d. 1625), the administrator who was to take charge as the first Superior of the mission in New France; Father Jean Dolbeau (1586-1652), a twenty-nine-year-old student of philosophy and theology; Father Joseph Le Caron (c. 1586-1632), a twenty-seven-year-old who was the former tutor of the duc d'Orléans, brother of Louis XIII, and the keenest of the four; and Brother Pacifique Duplessis (d. 1619), a lay brother who had been an apothecary merchant. They were a diverse and talented group.

Like an archbishop in charge of a new diocese, Champlain also had his own specific mission, and he stated his motives in the preface to his 1619 journal. While others, he pointed out, have been out to "gain praise and reputation, together with some profit . . . , I have made the choice of the most vexatious and painful course, which is the perilous navigation of the seas, to the end however not to gain wealth so much as honour and the glory of God, on behalf of my King and country, and by my labours to contribute to the public weal something of utility. And I solemnly declare that I have not been tempted by any other ambition, as may be clearly perceived both by my behaviour in the past and the narratives of my voyages made to New France at His Majesty's command" (III:9).

In high spirits and filled with optimism, Champlain left Paris at the end of February and, at Rouen on March 20, 1615, the four Récollet fathers joined him for one month of planning and weather-watching prior to moving on to Honfleur for their departure on April 24. Once again, Champlain was to travel in the old seaworthy friend from bygone days in Acadia, the 350-ton *Saint-Étienne*. Then there was a moment of great solemnity as each voyageur undertook to examine "himself and be cleansed from his sins by repenting and confessing" (III:24). Champlain now had a new trinity of endeavors: geography, ethnography, and religion.

CHAPTER EIGHTEEN

A Journey to the Nipissing Country and Huronia: 1615

"My task will be to prepare the way for those who, after me,
desire to engage in this enterprise."

Champlain, *Les Voyages*, 1632

ON APRIL 24, 1615, CHAMPLAIN LEFT FRANCE with the four missionaries who were fired up for the conquest of souls. It was a voyage that, "fanned by a very favourable wind . . . and without encountering ice or other dangers," reached Tadoussac a month later (III:24-25). Within a week, the complete party left for Québec where they would ready themselves for their crusade westward — first to the Grand Rapid, then onward to the Ottawa River. The expedition's goal was to penetrate the Nipissing country and Huronia in force.

Anxious to save time, Champlain divided the early season duties among the participants, while at the same time trying to control the exuberance of the missionaries who were excited at the prospect of so many potential converts. Denis Jamet, the Father Superior whose background was in administration, remained with Champlain, and Father Jean Dolbeau, the philosopher, and Brother Pacifique Duplessis, the apothecary, were assigned the task of preparing a chapel at Québec. Father Le Caron, the former tutor of nobles, was the most anxious to be gone so that he might ply his craft in the pastures of Huronia. But concerned for the priests' safety, Champlain persuaded him to be patient. At this point, Étienne Brûlé, the interpreter, joined the group, and Champlain informed the reader that Brûlé had been on previous westward excursions.

To set the stage for the westward journey, Champlain and Pont-gravé hastened ahead to Place Royale (fig. 28) for the yearly meeting with the Algonquins and Hurons. But, just as in 1612, Champlain had not shown up during the summer of 1614, and the Indians were clearly put out. In response to Champlain's absence the previous year, few Indians showed up this year, and those who did were mistrustful of their French allies. Broken promises were not taken lightly. In addition to mistrust, there seemed to be subtle changes in Indian policy. Unlike the disdain expressed in 1613, the Indians returned to the traditional terms of the alliance "because the Iroquois, their ancient foes, were continually along the route and preventing them from passing; that moreover I had always promised to help them in their wars" (III:31). Champlain now realized that the war party from the alliance that went to battle without him in 1614 had accomplished little. The Iroquois were still a menace.

For the right to preach and proceed, Champlain adjusted quickly to the new priorities set forth by the Indians. The Hurons and Algonquins were to "furnish us with two thousand five hundred warriors, [and] with the same object I on my side should bring as many men as I could. This I promised them to do being well content to see them so firmly resolved." And Champlain quickly added, to justify the war and bloodshed ahead, "this [the war] to them would be a kind of pathway for embracing Christianity" (III:32).

With this change of focus, the meeting at Grand Rapid was cut short; it did not, however, end before the celebration — on June 24 — of the first mass ever held in New France. The service was held on the north shore of the Île de Montréal. Father Jamet celebrated the mass, and Father Le Caron assisted. Le Caron had already been back to Québec, had packed his bags, and was now poised to venture forth as the first priest to be sent to Huronia. The summer weeks quickly passed with more planning — a year's expedition was in the making. This year, there would be no return at season's end.

Ever since his arrival in New France, Father Le Caron had been fidgeting to get on with the missionary plan to bring Christianity to Huronia. He planned to go ahead and spend the winter in this "parish" west of the Ottawa River; but Champlain preferred that Le Caron make only a summer sortie and then winter safely at Québec. On this point they could not agree. Le Caron, "confident of overcoming" adversity and "of adapting himself very well and cheerfully to their foods and to the absence of comforts, through the Grace of

God," was in no way discouraged. For Father Le Caron, "as regards to temporal goods, very little was necessary to satisfy a man who only professes perpetual poverty and who seeks nothing but heaven not only for himself, but also for his brethren" (III:29, 32).

After much debate, in midsummer — with Champlain's reluctant blessing — Le Caron departed. But there were anxious moments, and Champlain was concerned on at least two counts. First, he noted that in the Le Caron party "not more than four or five knew how to handle fire-arms . . . , [and] in such an undertaking the best are none too good." And second, he recorded that had he had the chance to intervene before their hasty departure, he would have "ordered many [other] things for the journey" (III:35).

But if Le Caron departed in haste without the necessary food, clothing, and tools to face the harsh winter, Champlain himself took the time to prepare. On July 9, two weeks after the priest's departure, Champlain left with two French comrades and ten Indians. They headed for the Ottawa River in two canoes loaded to the gunwales with supplies. Between the two parties were some sixteen Frenchmen heading into the Nipissing country and Huronia. This was not the company of forty or fifty soldiers promised in 1612; but, it was by far the largest force of Europeans ever sent into the interior of the continent. And what faced them? After years of what amounted to propaganda and opposition from the Algonquins, could the French penetrate the western lands? What of the Nipissings and their alleged sorcery?

At last Champlain was moving westward up the Ottawa River. This year, he passed by Nibachis's scrimpy corn fields and Chief Tessouat's Algonquin cemetery stronghold without incident. The silence from the Algonquins was deafening, and Champlain did not comment on the whereabouts of "the gatekeepers" who had warned so strongly about the dangers in the west.

Farther up the Ottawa River, Champlain and his party entered the Mattawa River system, and from there continued westward upstream into the Nipissing country of what is today northern Ontario. Portaging through brushland and paddling through some of the most treacherous waterways in the entire linkage system on the way to the Great Lakes and western plains, Champlain offered no observations. The trip was a relentless drive through a string of rivers and lakes (fig. 40) until they reached the "Lake of the Nipissings." Here they encountered none of the predicted sorcerers or the anticipated hostility.

In fact, to everyone's delight, they receive a warm reception from "quite seven or eight hundred souls" ready with greetings (IV:232).

Champlain's westward exploration in 1615 into the Nipissing country and Huronia was accounted for in the third of his published journals, *Les Voyages*, which was released in 1619, and, as he noted in the introduction, geography, exploration and cartography were secondary to the crusade for the minds and souls of wilderness man. As a result of this emphasis, large parcels of real estate were passed over without reference. For all of Lake Nipissing, there was only one brief comment that there was a "great number of very pretty islands . . . on which there are three of four fine ponds and a number of beautiful meadows . . . and the lake is very abundant in many kinds of fish; among others a very good one, which is a foot in length . . . . It is a country stocked with great numbers both of animals, birds and fish." For Champlain, who was in a rush to reach Huronia, the fact that the "Nipissings cultivate the soil very little" was enough to dismiss all the surroundings in favor of his new thrust: Indian culture, religion and economics. Instead of regional charts, sweeping surveys and crude cartoon-like illustrations to back up the text, there was now a substitute bonus of elaborate artwork to be viewed as a complement to the cultural discussions in the text (III:40).

Champlain maintained a hectic pace in order to catch up to Le Caron, and he was greatly aided en route by Indians who had developed basic skills of map-making "with charcoal on a piece of treebark." The party navigated Lake Nipissing and the French River system which drains Lake Nipissing westerly into Georgian Bay on Lake Huron. Here they entered the Thirty Thousand Islands, and were met by another branch of the Algonquins, the Ottawas. Champlain named this huge gathering of Indians "the High Hairs" because of their magnificent coiffures "elevated and arranged very high and better combed than our courtiers." Their bodies he described as "much carved . . . in divisions of various patterns. They paint their faces with different colours and have their nostrils pierced and their ears fringed with beads" (III:43-44).

In his ethnographic treatise on Huronia, he depicts the Indian as a warrior in these newly discovered lands, making reference to his previous illustration of the Algonquin and the Montagnais (A and C, fig. 33), "which shows the manner of their equipment when they go on the war-path. For arms they have only the bow and arrow, but made in the manner you see in the picture; these they carry as a rule, and a

33 THE INDIANS OF LAKE NIPISSING AND LAKE HURON,
ONTARIO, JULY 1615
(Untitled)

Champlain explains that A in this illustration "shows you the dress of
these people when they go to war," and another, B, shows an example
of one "of the women which is in no way different from that of the
Montagnais and Algonquins." These illustrations have been
presented before on Champlain's great map of 1612 (fig. 29), but in
practice the change of method is a reversion to the artistic style of the
Brief Narrative, the sketchbook of the West Indies (e.g. fig. 4), where
the human figures are full-bodied and posed.

round buckler of tanned leather which comes from an animal like the buffalo" (III:44-45).

After meeting the "high hairs," the voyageurs canoed on to catch up with Le Caron in Huronia. Given the territory, the pace Champlain and his compatriots maintained was truly impressive. From the Grand Rapid to the shores of Huronia in southern Georgian Bay, they averaged about 25 miles (40 km) a day; and one estimate remarks that the route included as many as 58 portages. For the student of geography, however, the 1619 journal is disappointing. Champlain's lightning passage through Georgian Bay, for example, makes only one geographic observation about this recreation paradise — a fish story about the trout, "which are of enormous size; I have seen some that were as much as four and a half feet long [1.37 m], and the smallest one sees are two and a half feet [0.75 m] in length" (III:45). Champlain was the first to tell whoppers about fishing in Ontario!

Weaving through wooded islands and barren outcroppings of richly colored granite and treacherous shoals, Champlain reached Huronia at the southern end of Georgian Bay on August 1. He landed at Otouacha. (See Notes.)

Champlain offered this anecdote about the evening delights, after his arrival in Huronia: "having gone outside the lodge to escape the fleas which were very numerous and a great pest to us, a shameless girl came boldly up to me, offering to keep me company, which I declined with thanks, sending her away with gentle remonstrances" (III:47). At long last, we have Champlain involved in a sexual encounter that goes beyond a description of the Indians and what they do about their "privities." The insight is only of interest because *he* thought it worth including. With thousands of souls and much sin in evidence in Huronia, the Récollets had their work cut out for them.

On August 12, Champlain caught up with Le Caron. Their meeting place was the village of Carhagouha (present-day Midland, Ontario). (This spot is one that has been identified on the basis of archaeology and remaining markers.) To celebrate their successful rendezvous, the reunited French celebrated mass just as they had at the Rivières des Prairies (fig. 28) near the Grand Rapid a few weeks earlier. To mark the occasion this time, a cross was erected near the village. Carhagouha, however, was no small collection of wigwams and huts. It was a well-made fortress for protection against a full-scale Iroquois attack with a "triple wooden palisade, thirty-five feet [10.7 m] high" (III:48). This construction, of course, was the forerunner of the famous mission to follow: Ste. Marie Among the Hurons.

In spite of the long trek, Champlain was anxious to get on with the year's work. But first he had to fulfill his promise to the Indians by engaging the Iroquois in battle. The Indian allies, however, were not to be rushed. They displayed the same indecision they had shown before the attack at Lake Champlain in 1609. They made excuses and delayed preparations, and even expressed their surprise to see Champlain, whom they thought had been taken by the Iroquois. Their procrastination dragged on: "I was staying there [Carhagouha] and waiting for our Indians to get ready and prepare to go on the war-path, which took them a very long time" (III:49).

To ensure a massive gathering of the clans for battle, Champlain took the initiative — but this time without a weapons demonstration prior to the battle as in 1609. He moved instead to propagandize "by small stages from village to village" eastward through Huronia as far as Cahiagué, near present-day Orillia, Ontario, "where the whole army was to rendezvous" (III:49).

Champlain arrived at Cahiagué on August 17, and there found a heartening sight for a commander trying to rouse warriors for a battle: a huge Indian settlement, the largest he had ever seen, "which contains two hundred fairly large lodges where all the warriors were to assemble" (III:49).

Even with these impressive numbers, the battle plans were still only firmed on the basis of flimsy promises and rumors; but then news came of another hitherto uncontacted Indian nation that was anxious to join forces for the attack. There was much excitement as Champlain and the Huron Chief, Darontal (fl. 1615), considered how the potential new allies altered their position. The newcomers were the Susquehannas, a maverick Iroquois grouping, who were situated just south of Iroquoia, roughly at the border of New York State and Pennsylvania, likely in the vicinity of present-day Waverly, New York.

Strategically, the Susquehannas were in a perfect position to attack the Iroquois from the south. This was every field commander's dream — the ability at a limited cost to drag an enemy into a war on two fronts. Moreover, the French would have a strong ally in readiness to thwart and eventually to eliminate English and Dutch interests to the east — should it all work out. With such possibilities in mind, Champlain and his allies had to hone their plans to perfection, coordination and timing providing the twin keys to success.

Kawartha Country and a Third Battle Against the Iroquois: the Defeat at Syracuse, New York: 1615

"God is usually on the side of the big squadrons
and against the small ones."

Roger de Bussy-Rabutin (1618–1693)

ON SEPTEMBER 1, WITH THEIR PLANS ALMOST COM-
pleted, an attack force of some five hundred Indians and French
moved eastward from Cahiagué to the narrows at Lake Couchiching
near present-day Orillia, just north of Lake Simcoe. Here they paused
for another week of preparations, and then, on September 8, Étienne
Brûlé set out with an advance party of twelve Indian warriors in two
large canoes. His orders were to travel south of Iroquoia and make
contact with the Susquehanna Indians. He was then to arrange a
synchronized pincer assault against the Iroquois by moving up from
the south with the new allies. To be effective, Brûlé had to be at the
battle site on the eve of October 10 as the attack of all forces was
planned for the following day, October 11.

Étienne Brûlé was not seen again by Champlain until they met at
Trois-Rivières in July 1618 — more than three years after he was
charged by Champlain to journey south to the Susquehanna. The
question of what happened to Brûlé over that time has made for one of
the great controversies in the Champlain epic. In spite of searching
analysis since, there is no real certainty as to what happened to him
during those years; for many reasons, Brûlé's account, as relayed by
Champlain later, remains less than satisfactory.

By mid-September, the fully mobilized, unruly mass of invaders
had pushed their way from the Couchiching narrows and turned

southeastward along the shores of Lake Simcoe. Their objective, after weaving eastward through the Kawartha Lakes country, was to exit near the eastern extremity of the lake of the Onandagas (Lake Ontario. This is not to be confused with Lake Onandaga, New York, the location of the Iroquois fortress where they were headed.) Again their exact route is unknown because Champlain provided no regional maps or charts for this trip.

In the absence of hard information, many have guessed at Champlain's route, and historian G. H. Needler suggests that the large war party of Hurons, Algonquins, and French picked a spot somewhere on the northeastern shores of Lake Simcoe and then made a lengthy portage of about twenty-five miles (40 km) directly to Sturgeon Lake. Champlain himself was only clear about one matter: the first leg of the journey from Lake Simcoe was a long overland portage, "and thence the Indians carried their canoes overland about ten leagues [c. 30 miles or 48 km], and we came upon another lake" (III:58). From here it is surmised the entourage entered Sturgeon Lake and navigated through lakes Pigeon, Buckhorn (which adjoins Upper Chemung), and then onward into Clear Lake which, at its southern end, drains into the Otonabee River and into Rice Lake. Then they are assumed to have exited through the Trent River into the Bay of Quinte at Trenton, Ontario.

It was a sight: five hundred warriors in full battle dress and more than a hundred painted paper birch canoes moving across the orange and gold autumn landscape. For his part, Champlain was ecstatic about the "several lakes of very considerable size," and where "one would think the trees had been planted for ornament in most places" (III:59). As in the case of the journey to his first battle with the Iroquois, Champlain again found moments for leisure and sport, and this time he made a study of bear and deer hunting. In a few weeks' time, when the fighting was over, the information he gathered would prove useful on the homeward journey (fig. 35).

The war party exited the Trent River system into the waters of Lake Ontario in the first week of October, and proceeded from the northeastern shore to leap-frog "five very large islands" (III:62) in order to reach the south shore of the lake at Stoney Point in the heartland of Iroquoia — present-day New York state.

Once in the land of the Iroquois, the carnival atmosphere of the trek ended. In order to ensure a safe return later, the company hid their canoes. Now the troops moved stealthily according to Champlain's European battle plan, which called for a synchronized surprise attack. For four days, the strategy worked as the Indian-French forces moved southward from Lake Ontario toward their objective — in the vicinity of what is today Syracuse, New York. To reach this battle site, the warriors proceeded inland to present-day Henderson, New York. Then they turned southward and crossed the Salmon River and the present-day Selkirk Shores State Park. The attack force then moved on to what is now Brewerton on the eastern perimenter of Oneida Lake, just north of Syracuse.

On October 9, while sneaking into the enemy territory some ten miles (16 km) from the Iroquois fortress, the Hurons and Algonquins captured eleven Iroquois and began the usual ceremonial tortures. "One of the chiefs, on seeing these prisoners, cut off a finger of one of these poor women for a beginning of their usual torture, whereupon I came up at once and reprimanded the chief, Yroquet [Iroquet]" (III:64-65). As at Sorel, the Indians took their revenge; but as the war-whooping warriors blundered onward to the Iroquois fortress (fig. 34), and the troops became more and more excited, the element of surprise was lost.

Champlain stood before the enemy fort around 3:00 p.m. on the afternoon of October 11. He was one critical day late for his rendez-vous with Brûlé, and the rest of his plans were also in a shambles: "we arrived before the enemy's fort where the savages did some skirmishing against each other, although our [revised] plan was not to disclose ourselves until the next day; but our savages' impatience would not permit this" (III:66). Champlain's inability to control the Indians was not as large a problem as the non-appearance of Brûlé. Neither he nor the Susquehannas were anywhere in sight. Either Champlain was late, his dates were mixed up, or there are dating mistakes in the journal. All these explanations are possible.

Regardless of the reason for the confusion, Champlain and his Huron and Algonquin allies ended up fighting the Iroquois without the support of the Susquehannas. Surely Champlain was aware of the odds against his forces as he surveyed the Iroquois stronghold. It was the most impressive Indian fortress he had ever seen; and it must have been obvious to him that the Iroquois had learned a great deal from the two previous battles. This ready adaptability became a hallmark of the Iroquois: they learned quickly and profited from their past experiences.

Right from its beginning, the battle at Syracuse was a disaster. In the first round, Champlain and his men fired at the Iroquois who rushed to take cover inside their fortress; but, the enemy arrows still found their mark and, within seconds, half the French were wounded, one fatally. Now the Hurons, Algonquins, and the French were on the defensive. At this crucial point in the proceedings, the attackers' only chance for victory lay in recovering the lost initiative. Momentarily secure in the cover of the surrounding forest the alliance forces regrouped.

Champlain was livid at the lack of discipline, and the noise and chaos around him, and he raged at his Indian allies with "some very hard and unpleasant words . . . for I foresaw that if everything went according to their caprice and under the guidance of their counsels, evil alone could result, to their loss and destruction" (III:67).

They needed a new strategy to win. This Iroquois fortress was unlike the others at Lake Champlain and Sorel (figs. 26 and 27). "Their village was enclosed by four stout palisades, made of large timbers, thirty feet [9 m] in height, interlaced together with not more than half a foot [15 cm] between them, and galleries like a parapet which they had fitted with double timbers, proof against our shots; and they were near a pond where there was no lack of water" (III:70). This was more of a bastille than a wilderness stockade (fig. 34).

The French and their allies retreated into the forest for the night to see to the wounded and plan for the morning. Duly impressed with the fort, Champlain, the old-world warrior, ordered the construction of a medieval cavalier — a movable tower to hold men who could then fire directly into the fortress. He also had shields of thick wood made to protect the attackers and the porters of armaments. As Champlain discovered, leading Indians into battle was considerably different from leading a French army. The Hurons, in the mood for retreat, resorted to hurling insults at their foes, and, while two hundred of their strongest dragged the tower up to the fortress walls, they dropped their newly made mantelets. At the same time, their compatriots indiscriminately volleyed arrows toward the inside of the fortress, where the Iroquois were easily able to dodge them by taking cover in the more than fifty shelters within and around the walls.

Frustrated in their purpose, four of Champlain's marksmen mounted the cavalier and then only with repeated musket fire were able to clear the enemy off the fortress ramparts; but these same musketeers were then repelled by a stream of arrows and rocks projected from inside the palisade.

Toward the end — in a desperate and last-minute effort — Cham-

34 THE IROQUOIS FORTRESS, SYRACUSE, NEW YORK,
OCTOBER 1615
(Untitled)

Champlain's illustration of the Iroquois fortress on Lake Onandaga
was the most carefully crafted of all his battle scenes, but like the three
others of Stage Harbor, Lake Champlain, and Sorel (figs. 20, 26 and
27), this design presented several events. On this occasion, even
though the Iroquois were well protected, one can pick out seven or
eight vulnerable French arquebusiers, loading and firing their rifles.
One musketeer, completely exposed, was even shown using a tripod
to support the heavy obsolete weaponry that Champlain had brought
from France. Since the allies had lost the battle this time, Champlain
gave no credit for any effort made by the Huron and Algonquin
participants. Of the hundreds who came, only a dozen of the five
hundred main contingent were even portrayed. The artist squarely
laid the blame for placing the fire upwind on the lone Indian in the
foreground.

For the historian, the great unknown is how much Champlain
knew of the Iroquois stronghold in advance, but one thing is certain.
He knew enough to attack it with a large war party. Oddly, this is the
only major illustration in his published works for which Champlain
provides no legend. *(See the Notes for chapter 19 for more information
on the fortress.)*

plain ordered the barricade torched; but even this task was bungled: the fire was set in the wrong place and the wind blew the flames away from the walls. In the end, there was so much shouting and noise that the allied troops could not hear commands. The Iroquois seized the opportunity to sneak outside and douse the fire.

The attack was a rout and, while taking cover, Champlain was badly wounded: "we withdrew into our fort, I having received two arrow wounds, one in the leg, the other in the knee, which gave me great trouble, besides considerable and extreme pain, and when we were all assembled I addressed several complaints to them for the confusion that had occurred, but all my discourses availed as little as [if] I had been silent, and moved them in no way; for they said that many of their people had also been wounded" (III:75).

This second battle on the second day lasted only three hours, but the defeat affected the colonial history of America for years afterward. The conflict is considered by many as the opening battle in the Indian wars of America; it was here that the Indian, both ally and enemy, learned that the white intruder with his wiles and weapons was no longer invincible. For the Indian, Champlain was now not only unreliable for failing periodically to show up for battle, but he was also a deficient medicine man, discredited because he was vulnerable. The French were to pay a great price for their exposure at Syracuse.

Defeat was not unknown to Champlain; but this disgrace was much more painful than the humiliation suffered at Cape Cod nine years earlier. Perhaps trying to regain his lost position, Champlain pleaded for a renewed attack against the fortress. But his army of Indians was bent on a full retreat. The gloom of failure was well rooted, and with each day, the Hurons and Algonquins were more certain that Étienne Brûlé and the Susquehannas were not coming. Writing of the occasion and subtly shifting some of the blame from himself, Champlain underscores his loss of power: "They decided to depart and beat a retreat as soon as possible" (IV:264).

In spite of the terrible defeat, he recorded no recriminations against Brûlé or even a note about his absence. Champlain was diplomatic — even in his retelling of the story. In a confusing explanation given three years later, in 1618, Champlain revised the record of the battle preparations at Cahiagué and at the Couchiching narrows at Orillia. He alleged that Brûlé struck out for Iroquoia directly from Midland in Huronia and not, as earlier indicated, from Orillia. This is unlikely as it contradicts the sense of Champlain's fresher and more detailed account; but, if it is correct, then there was a greater possibility of problems in timing and in communications as the two lead players would have been separated during the final stages of the strategic planning. Given the chance to explain the missed battle, Brûlé only reported the end result, i.e., that he journeyed through Iroquoia to the Susquehanna country (in Pennsylvania) in a struggle that included a trek through swamps and "frightful and unfrequented places and wastes." On arrival at the Susquehanna River, the Susquehanna Indi-ans greeted the proposed pincer attack with great enthusiasm, but they "were a very long time in getting ready." Brûlé then claimed that he and the "reinforcements" arrived at the barricade just two days after Champlain's departure (III:215, 217).

Brûlé's account as relayed by Champlain is suspect. Brûlé had left with a smaller party and well in advance of the battle. He had consid-erable lead time to cover the short distance, and, in view of the slow pace of the battle, he should have had time to send a runner ahead to warn of his delay. He did, after all, have twelve friendly guides with him, and surely one of these could have been used as a courier. And what happened when Brûlé did arrive with his five hundred Sus-quehannas? There is no historic evidence of a single contact, let alone a skirmish or battle. And most perplexing, why did it take Brûlé three years to contact Champlain, especially as he had returned from Huro-nia long before 1618? Then too, Brûlé claimed that he was pursuing discoveries as far south as the outlet of the Susquehanna on Chesa-peake Bay — were such explorations part of his assignment? Perhaps, when all is considered, both men had miscalculated the length of time needed to travel to the Susquehanna country. Champlain's ready forgiveness seems to indicate that he was satisfied with Brûlé's explana-tion. But we have not heard the end of Étienne Brûlé, or an end to the historic debates that surround his name.

The retreat from Iroquoia began as the beaten and broken contin-gent withdrew northward to where the canoes were hidden. On the way, there were numerous scuffles with the enemy as the defeated army cocooned their disabled and dying. Champlain, wounded and powerless, noted the kindness that he personally received:

> They [the Indians] began to make certain panniers for carrying
> the wounded, who were put into them piled on top of each
> other and doubled up and bound in such a manner that it was
> impossible to move any more than a little child in its swaddling
> clothes, and this causes the wounded great and extreme pain. I

> can say this indeed with truth from my own case, having been
> carried for several days because I was unable to stand, chiefly
> on account of the arrow-wound I had received in my knee, for
> never did I find myself in such a hell as during this time; for the
> pain I suffered from the wound in my knee was nothing in com-
> parison with what I endured tied and bound on the back of
> one of our savages. This made me lose patience, and as soon as
> I gained strength to stand, I got out of that prison, or rather
> hell (III:77-78).

There can be little doubt that those who bore this vocal burden must
have suffered great discomfort.

The array of attendants, medicine men, arguing chiefs, and warrior
patients took a full month to retreat to the safely hidden canoes at
Stoney Point. These were found in good condition, so the defeated
French and Indians were assured transportation.

Champlain was not satisfied with the plans that the Indians had
made. He argued against returning to Québec by the grand circle route
(Huronia, Georgian Bay, Lake Nipissing, and the Ottawa River), and
instead begged to be taken via the shorter route on the St. Lawrence
River. For health reasons alone, he wanted to avoid a winter at
Cahiagué: "I begged them to take me back to our settlement." At first
his hopes were raised, but in the end his preferences were passed over.
The comment that he and his comrades were "very badly equipped for
spending the winter with them, or otherwise I should not have
minded" was as much an indication of the state of his injuries as a
comment about inadequate clothing and provisions. This was a commander who had only planned for victory and, without this, Champlain had lost his clout and his power to persuade: "I had to resign
myself to be patient" (III:80-81). For the time being, Samuel de Champlain, explorer and commander extraordinaire, was resigned to more
than patience. He was in effect a hostage of the Hurons, faced with a
long road back to health and power.

CHAPTER TWENTY

The Retreat and Winter in Huronia: 1615-1616

"Doubts are more cruel than the worst of truths."

Jean de La Fontaine (1621–1695)

SKULKING OUT OF IROQUOIA, THE DEFEATED BANDS of the once proud alliance headed homeward. Their immediate target was the northeastern end of Lake Ontario, and with winter setting in, there was no time to waste as the retreating army would have to deal with sheer survival once the weather turned cold.

Champlain, more witness than participant, was taken in hand by the Huron Chief, Darontal, with whom he reported being "on terms of some intimacy." With the battle done, Champlain could now focus on his original priority for the year's work: a cultural study of Huronia. His first initiative was an illustration and description of a game hunt in Ontario (fig. 35): "They made a triangular enclosure, closed on two sides, open on one . . . made of great wooden stakes eight or nine feet [2.4 to 2.7 m] in height . . . . Each side was nearly fifteen hundred paces [c. 1,300 m] . . . . They set out half an hour before daybreak to go into the woods . . . keeping about eighty paces [33 m] apart, each having two sticks which they strike together . . . . The deer, hearing this, flee . . . until they reach the enclosure . . . . In the thirty-eight days, they captured one hundred and twenty deer" (III:81, 83). In passing, Champlain claimed that there were buffalo in the region as well.

On one of these outings, Champlain got lost — and made a bizarre observation: "When we first went out hunting, I penetrated so far into

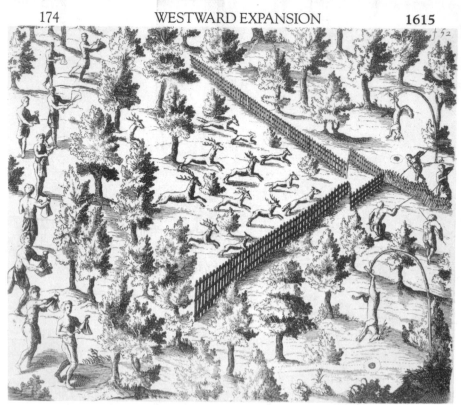

35 DEER HUNT, NEAR KINGSTON, ONTARIO, OCTOBER 1615
(*Untitled*)

the woods in pursuit of a certain bird which seemed peculiar, with a beak almost like a parrot, as big as a hen, yellow all over, except for its red head and blue wings, which made short successive flights like a partridge, that my desire to kill it made me chase it from tree to tree for a very long time, until it flew away in good earnest" (III:86).

Champlain was lost for four days; he spent one night under a large tree and two others in an open meadow. He was well armed; but on this foray into the forest, the naturalist forgot to bring along the tool of his other occupation – his astrolabe.

Perhaps while lost he thought about the trials of poor Master Aubry lost for seventeen days in Acadia. With equally good fortune, and having kept his head, Champlain picked his way back to Darontal's camp. Fearful of French reprisals if Champlain should again become lost, or worse, suffer some accident while wandering, Chief Darontal decided to keep a closer eye on his guest. The new proximity of the two resulted in a warm relationship that proved advantageous to both in the future.

The final lap of the journey back through the Kawartha country to the base camp at Cahiagué in Huronia began on December 4, 1615, as they

> [walked] on the frozen river and on the ice-covered lakes and ponds . . . . This was not done without much labour and toil, both for the savages who were loaded with a hundred pounds' [45 kg] weight and also for myself with a burden of twenty pounds [9 kg] which in the long run wearied me greatly. It is quite true that sometimes I was relieved by our savages, but in spite of that I did not escape discomfort. On their part, in order to cross the ice more easily, they are in the habit of making a kind of wooden sledge, . . . and they go along very quickly. But a few days later came a thaw which caused us much trouble and discomfort; for we had to pass through fir woods full of streams, ponds, marshes and swamps, with many fallen trees lying one upon another, giving us a thousand troubles . . . on account of being always wet, even above the knee" (III:92-93).

The cold, struggling return through Kawartha was exploration in the raw, and in no way did it resemble the confident march of the five hundred in their war paint four months earlier.

After nineteen days of tough trekking on fields of ice and snow, Darontal and Champlain arrived back at Cahiagué only two days before Christmas. On arrival, they learned that Chief Iroquet's son had been killed by a rampaging bear. The news cast a pall over their homecoming.

For most of January and half of February, Champlain recuperated. He had ample time to meditate in the smoke-filled longhouses and to begin work on his overdue cultural appraisal of the Indians. In mid-February, after a quick conference with Father Le Caron, the two set out to explore the Indian populations. The census that they took was the most extensive taken in America to date; but in the absence of Champlain's splendid regional maps, the formal record of words is a chaotic jumble of names, locations, and customs.

On the first stop, the two visited the tribe of Indians known today as the Tobacco nation; Champlain reported that these tribes were noted for planting "Turkey corn." Next, they were conducted south-westerly to meet a third branch of the Hurons, the Bears, who were not warriors but farmers. Somewhere in the vicinity of the shores of

Lake Huron, Champlain learned that nearby there were four thousand "warriors" of a nation now called the Neutrals; but he also writes that *these* Indians were the ones noted for planting tobacco! Soon after this, the reader is trapped in a whirlpool of erratic data. At some point in all these travels through the spring and summer months, Champlain met up with his old friends the Sorcerers (fig. 33) from the Nipissing country. In spite of Algonquin warnings back in 1613, the Nipissings turned out to be no more threatening than any other tribe. And once again Champlain encountered his old friends, the "High Hairs," the Ottawa Indians (Algonquins) whom he had met the previous summer much farther up, west of the Ottawa River at the mouth of the French River in northern Georgian Bay. These "courtiers" of the forest with their lofty coiffures may well have been from the Ottawa River. According to Champlain, they were busily promoting a war against the "fire people," who supposedly lived west of the Great Lakes region.

Champlain investigated the boundaries of Huronia and the surrounding country in this manner for weeks; but he was dissuaded from going farther west by his Indian guides. The Hurons, like the Algonquins of the Ottawa River, protected their own territories from uncontrolled intrusion.

During this period of research and review, Champlain recovered his reputation as the wise and trusted arbitrator who could wade through many seemingly trivial but potentially explosive problems. This period marked the emergence of a more mature commander at the helm of French interests in the North American continent.

Champlain's personal timetable and work plan for the cultural mission was set forth in his 1619 journal: "During the winter season, which lasted four months, I had leisure enough to study their country, their manners, customs, modes of life, the form of their assemblies, and other things" (III:114). From Acadia to Huronia, Champlain constructed the most complete geographic primer written in the period. The result was an ethnographic study that covered the entire geography of the Great Lakes region. He began to sketch the panorama in words:

> Their life is wretched by comparison with ours, but happy for
> them since they have not tasted a better and believe that none
> more excellent can be found . . . . Their lodges are fashioned
> like bowers or arbours, covered with tree-bark, [and inside] on
> both sides there is a sort of platform, four feet [1.2 m] in height,

on which they sleep in summer to escape the annoyance of
fleas of which they have many . . . . At the end of these cabins
is a space where they keep their Indian corn, which they put in
great casks, made of tree-bark . . . . Pieces of wood are sus-
pended on which they put their clothes, provisions and other
things for fear of mice which are in great numbers. In one such
cabin there will be twelve fires which make twenty-four house-
holds, and there is smoke in good earnest, causing many to
have great eye troubles, to which they are subject, even towards
the end of their lives losing their sight; for there is no window
or opening except in the roof (III:122-25).

The long houses were constructed as high as thirty feet (9 m) and as
long as 150 feet (46 m). With as many as twenty-four families and a
dozen fires in each, Indian-style living in the winter was a grim business that shortened one's life span in the wilderness. Champlain knew
that vermin and disease spread easily in close quarters.

For today's taste, however, perhaps the Indian diet would be a little
easier to stomach: "Their principal food and usual sustenance is
Indian corn and red beans, which they prepare in several ways. They
pound them in wooden mortars and reduce them to flour from which
they take the hull by means of certain fans made of tree-bark, and of
this flour they make a bread with beans which they first boil, as they
do Indian corn for soup . . . . Sometimes they put in blueberries or
dried raspberries" (III:125-26). A good many canoeists would readily
accept such a recipe for survival.

For the more venturesome, there was bouillabaisse: "Migan . . . is
the best to my taste . . . . In figure H [fig. 36], . . . you will see how the
women pound their Indian corn. And to prepare it they cook a
quantity of fish and meat . . . put it into large kettles, letting it boil
well. After this they skim with a spoon the fat . . . then add this
roasted meal, stirring it constantly until the said Migan is cooked and
becomes thick like soup" (III:128).

But if Migan seems mouth-watering, the historic gourmet should
be cautioned that there were many ghastly concoctions as well. Sometimes the Indian dishes were "bad-smelling" and often there was little
care taken to remove "bones, scales or entrails." He noted, too, that
"dogs are in demand at their banquets . . . . And . . . they have
another way of eating corn . . . — they take it in the ear and put it in
the water under the mud, leaving it two or three months in that state
until they judge that it is putrid . . . . I assure you that nothing smells

so bad as this corn when it comes out of the water all covered with mud" (IV:305-08; III:129).

Champlain wrote of Indian artistry and craftsmanship with admiration:

> As to their clothing, they have several kinds and styles and varieties of wild beasts' skins . . . . They dress and prepare the skins very well, making their breeches of a moderately large deer-skin, and of another their leggings which reach as high as the waist, with many folds . . . . Further they have a robe of the same fur, shaped like a cloak, which they wear in the Irish or Egyptian fashion, and sleeves which are tied behind by a cord. That is how they dressed during the winter as is seen in figure D [fig. 33] . . . . Among these tribes are some more skilful than others in preparing skins and clever in inventing patterns to put upon their clothes. Above all others our Montagnais [Québec] and Algonquins [Ottawa River] are those that take the most trouble with it; for they put on their robes strips of porcupine-quill which they dye a very beautiful scarlet colour (III:131-32).

As at Saco, Maine, years ago, he makes guarded observations about the Indian women: "In this manner, gaily dressed and adorned, they like to show themselves at dances, where their fathers and mothers send them, forgetting no device . . . to bedeck and bedizen." Champlain illustrated the style of female clothing (F & G, fig. 36), and then concluded with a glowing account of the Amazon qualities observed: "Their breasts hang down very little except when they are old. Among these tribes are found powerful women of extraordinary stature" (III:135-36). On the subject of sex and marriage, Champlain allows ample space in this journal.

> They have a kind of marriage among them, which is this, that when a girl is eleven, twelve, thirteen, fourteen or fifteen years of age, she will have suitors, and many whom she will get according to her attractions will woo her for some time: after that the consent of the parents will be asked, although often they do not seek their consent except those girls that are best behaved and the most sensible, who submit to the will of their parents. The lover or suitor will give the girl a present . . . . If the girl finds this suitor to her taste she accepts his present, whereupon the lover will come and sleep with her three or four

36 THE INDIANS OF NIPISSING AND HURONIA, 1616
(Untitled)

In the history of the art world, many of Champlain's full-bodied
illustrations of the Indian men and women are treasures of American
realism. These are the pencil-strokes of the artist on site and each
detail is confirmed in the text. As in the case of the *Brief Narrative*,
Champlain now has time to fully flesh out the human form. It's
interesting to compare these careful drawings of the human form with
the hastily recorded cartoon-like caricatures, drawn for the battle
scenes (figs. 20, 26, 27, and 34).

nights without saying a word to her during that time, and there they will gather the fruit of their love. Next, it usually happens that, after a week or a fortnight, if they cannot agree, she will leave her suitor . . . . Afterwards, being disappointed in his hopes, he will seek out another girl, and she another suitor, if they see fit. Thus they continue this plan of action until [there is] a satisfactory union. Some girls spend their youth this way, having had more than twenty husbands, and these twenty husbands are not the only ones who enjoy the creature (III:137-39).

As to the nurture and bringing up of their children, they place the child in the daytime on a little wooden board; and clothe and wrap it in furs or skins and tie it to the board which they stand upright, leaving a little opening by which the child does its little business. [If the baby were a girl, Champlain reported that nature had already provided a ready-made diaper:] they put a leaf of corn between its thighs which presses against its privates and they turn the end of the said leaf and bring it outside, and by this means the child's water runs off (III:141).

Throughout the treatise there are also pages devoted to more serious cultural differences: "As for their laws I did not see that they have any, nor anything approaching them; as indeed is the case, inasmuch as there is with them no correction, punishment or censure of evildoers except by revenge, rendering evil for evil, not as a matter of law but through passion" (III:142-43). Thus at times, with little more than a glimmer of understanding, Champlain boldly tried to penetrate the world of the Indians as he struggled with their actions and reactions.

As the account progresses, it becomes clear that, despite faith and commitment, the chronicler was neither a linguist nor a theologian. He failed to appreciate the extent of influence nature had on Indian legends, as well as their mysticism and anthropomorphic pantheism. He could see Indian spiritual values only simply, in black-and-white frames of reference. Good was perceived only in terms of European Christian ethics. The Indian without Christianity could not be saved, and his afterlife would be spent neither in hell nor in paradise. Simply, "Des Sauvages" were not outcasts, but those yet to be called to God's purpose: "They recognize no divinity, they adore and believe in no God nor in anything whatsoever, but live like brute beasts. They have indeed some regard for the Devil, or a similar name, although this is a

matter of doubt" (III:143). In Champlain's view, poverty and ignorance were the works of Lucifer, often brought to the surface by his
agents on earth, the Indian medicine man who is called an "Oqui" or
"Manitou."

Thus, in the scheme of God's favor on earth, the French saw the
Indian as a tragic victim, captured and exploited by evil, and as
Champlain phrased it, this was the reason that the Indian had "filthy
habits, looseness of . . . morals and . . . rude license" (III:145). Tar-
nished forever was the romantic notion that there existed between
Christianity and the belief of the Indians some common threads, as
hinted in Champlain's first discussion over the loss of paradise with
Grand Sagamore Anadabijou at Tadoussac. Cynicism had taken root
in Champlain's outlook. Undoubtedly, it was nurtured by the defeat
at Syracuse, and by the atrocities he had observed over the years of
battle in Acadia and Iroquoia. This was no longer the conciliator bent
solely on the creation of some benevolent bilingual state, but the
crusader bent on the conquest of souls. As the Indian was not an
outcast of heaven, but some lost bystander, there was hope for his
rescue. This perception eventually developed into a philosophical
stance that would be elevated within a hundred and fifty years by
Rousseau to the doctrine of the "noble savage." There was also a
stream of Calvinism sewn into Champlain's Catholic fabric in that he
saw the world as being made up of God's elect. Under these conditions, while the Indian remained as an innocent victim in a state of
demoniac possession, the cathedral of the body corporate was now
without original sin. In searching his own soul, Champlain rational-
ized their conduct as that of the willing learner fully prepared and
open to Christian proselytizing. Ironically, however, in response to
this crusade, the Indian called for proof by way of example. It was as
Christian as "Go and do ye likewise."

This cultural tome is not without its lighter moments: some Indians
were

> beside themselves, like lunatics and madmen, throwing fire
> about the cabin from one side to the other, swallowing red-hot
> coals, holding them for a time in their hands, also throwing
> red-hot cinders into the eyes of the onlookers; . . . on seeing
> them in this state, one would say that the Devil, Oqui, or
> Manitou, if such we must call him, possesses them and tor-
> ments them in that manner . . . (III:151-52). [The cure was an
> Indian sauna; the one possessed would] fall into a rage in which

37 INDIAN CUSTOMS: THE DANCE OF THE WOMEN TO
HEAL THE SICK, HURONIA, 1616
(Untitled)

In his journal, Champlain records that the Oqui, or Manitou, studied
the illness of the patient and then gathered

a great number of men, women and girls, with three or four old
women . . . and these enter the cabin dancing, each with a

he summons several of his friends to sweat with him, which is a remedy that serves them best for keeping well, and while they sweat, the kettle works hard to satisfy their hunger. They remain sometimes two or three hours enclosed with big pieces of tree-bark, covered with their robes, and having in their midst a great number of stones which have been heated red-hot in the fire. They sing all the time they are in the rage, and sometimes they stop to take [a] breath. Many jugfuls of water are given them to drink, since they are very thirsty, and after this the demoniac or devil-possessed madman becomes sober . . . . For two who get cured ten others die from the noise and great din and the blowings they make (III:152-53) (fig. 37).

In a fitting finale towards the end of the treatise, Champlain provides a description of Indian burial customs and for this too he draws a tidy supportive illustration (fig. 38): "They take the body of the deceased, wrap it in furs, cover it very neatly with tree-bark, then lift it up on four posts . . . . Others they put into the ground." This first resting place is temporary and after "about eight or ten years" there is a festival to celebrate a relocation of the bones "which they cleanse and make quite clean . . . although they smell like bodies newly buried."

---

bearskin . . .
He described one particular episode concerning an ill woman:
   there will be two or three other old women near the sick person
   or patient, who most frequently is feigning or imagining
   sickness . . . Having danced for an hour or two, the old women
   take hold of the sick woman to make her dance and she
   pretends to get up sadly, then begins to dance . . . and enjoy
   herself as much as the others. You can imagine how sick she
   must be . . . The medicine-man thereby gains honour and
   reputation at the sight of his patient being so soon cured. (III:
   148-50).
Champlain described the ritual as a "ballet or masquerade," and one of the steps reminded him of a dance he had seen in Brittany. On a more sober note, however, he remarked that in the case of a genuine ailment, "this kind of medicine gives them death." For the ceremony the women are "decked out and painted as I have represented in Figure G" (fig. 36) (III: 151,155). Here, the patient is barely visible on the other side of the lead woman, who recites the incantation while she carries a "dry tortoise-shell filled with little pebbles which they rattle in the ears of the sick woman."

This final funeral is a grand and costly undertaking. A huge pit is dug and the bones of relatives and friends are mingled with a large inventory of "necklaces, wampum chains, tomahawks, kettles, sword-blades, knives and other trifles, which however are of no small value . . . . This is the method they employ for the dead; it is their greatest ceremony" (III:160-63).

Insofar as he was capable, Champlain assessed the religious perspective: "Some of them believe in the immortality of souls, others doubt it, but nevertheless do not wander too far from it, saying after death they go to a place where they sing like crows, but this song is quite different from that of angels" (III:163).

At the close of this alluring information on Indian life, Champlain includes an account of the journey homeward to Québec. Just prior to the departure from Cahiagué, onApril 22, 1616, however, Champlain learned of Étienne Brûlé's return to the Midland area. No mention was made as to where Brûlé had been these long months, nor were the reasons why he did not show up at Syracuse mentioned. Indeed, they were not to meet again until 1618.

On July 8, 1616, after having followed the same route that he took in coming to Huronia in the spring of 1615, Champlain arrived home at Québec with his close friend, the Huron Chief, Darontal, at his side. By bringing the Chief to Québec, Champlain had hoped to cement relations with the Indians that would endure over the long months of his absence in France. As with the visit of Chief Iroquet of the Algonquins in 1609, Champlain designed events to impress the powerful Indian leader. One such event was a grand performance with drums, musket fire, and volumes of cannonade.

And after more than a year's absence, there was much work to be done on the habitation, especially now that new deposits of sand and lime had been discovered. This year, everything had to be in order before his return to France. Champlain, knowing that there would be trouble ahead in the homeland, had to somehow turn the news of defeat in Iroquoia into a marketable package for a French audience long tired of dreary tales.

There were at least five accomplishments to boast about and to offset the losses. There was an alliance with the Hurons that, despite the defeat at Syracuse, was still intact; a firsthand knowledge of Indian living conditions and customs; a safer and more solidly constructed Québec fortress; some evidence of the colony's greater degree of self-sufficiency, with transplanted vegetation taking hold; and finally,

38 INDIAN CUSTOMS: THE INDIAN BURIAL CEREMONY,
     HURONIA, 1616
     (Untitled)

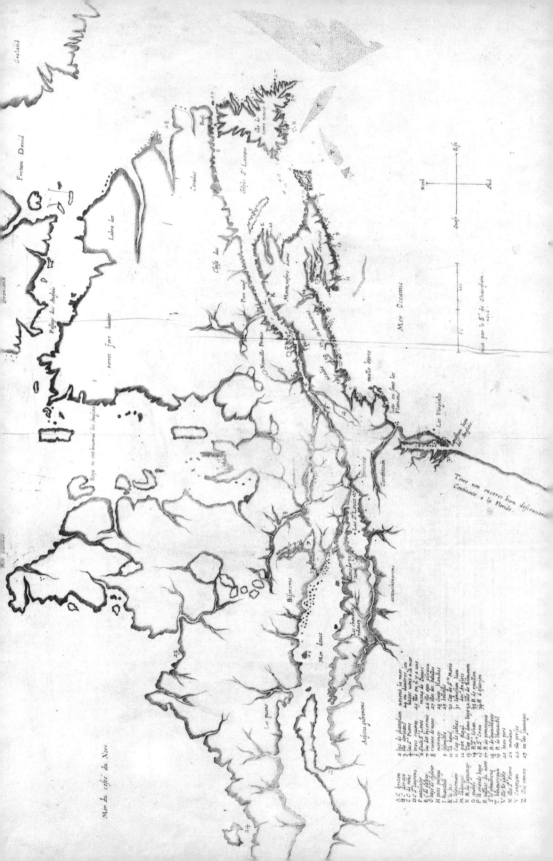

39 CHAMPLAIN'S GRAND SURVEY OF 1616
(date of publication) (a proof print)
(Untitled) [La Nouvelle France]

Champlain's 1616 summary survey reveals for the first time his
knowledge gained from the war in Iroquoia and during the cultural
expedition during the fall, winter, and spring of 1615–1616. The chart
is an unexpected bonus from a period in his life when it was thought
that he had entirely abandoned map-making. More importantly, it is
the first survey of America to show any of the Great Lakes based on
exploration contact.

Most of the map is a reworking of Champlain's charts of 1612 and
1613 (figs. 29 and 31). However, his most important contribution to
this map was the addition of sites discovered in the years 1615 and
1616. Included are the village of Carhagouha, the first Midland,
Ontario, and Carantouen, the Susquehanna village in the
Pennsylvania region, where Étienne Brûlé claims to have sojourned
during 1615–1616 (ch. 18). This map is the first ethnographic chart of
America and it was only published by the cartographer Pierre Du Val
in 1653 after Champlain's death and only after being up-dated.

Although the 1616 survey has no title or cartouche or even the
name of the engraver, experts are in agreement that it is the work of
Champlain. As in the case of the grand survey of 1612 (fig. 29), much
credit is due to the Indians and, here, to the chief of the "High Hairs"
(the Ottawa) who personally drew a map for Champlain as he
watched, likely near Georgian Bay on the way to Huronia: "I asked
him about his country, which he drew for me with charcoal on a piece
of tree-bark" (II: 44). (For more details about this unique Champlain
map, see Notes, chapter 20.)

there was a mountain of evidence of many new lands and Indian nations (fig. 39).

Leaving with Champlain were two of the clerical contingent. The two more junior, Pacifique Duplessis and Jean Dolbeau, were to remain at Québec. The Superior, Father Denis Jamet, and Father Joseph Le Caron were to return to France to promote support of the holy crusade.

With this departure, Champlain's own exploration voyages were at an end, and he sailed for France from Tadoussac on August 3, 1616. After years as an explorer, navigator, cartographer, warrior, illustrator, and, of late, missionary crusader and ethnographer, the chameleon was once again on the verge of another career change. Champlain's upcoming role, however, was to be the toughest of all, and it was one that he would play for the rest of his life. To salvage New France, Champlain had to become a political activist battling a sea of indifference. By now he was nearly fifty years of age and, after a life of strenuous physical exertion and at least five serious wounds, he had to ration his dwindling energy more carefully.

In his new role, Champlain would return five more times and rescue the tiny colony more than once. This proud son of Apollo — the colonizer of classical times — had much work ahead. For more than a decade and a half, Champlain had concentrated his energies on the exploration of early America. Now he was committed to fight to keep that which he had founded.

PART II

✦

THE FIGHT
FOR THE
FOUNDATION:
1616 - 1635

CHAPTER TWENTY-ONE

From France to New France: Politics, Intrigue, and Murder: 1616-1619

"They take revenge on their enemies,
but at least they never oppress their friends."

Voltaire (1694–1778), *L'Ingénu*
(The hero, the Huron native, speaks of his people.)

CHAMPLAIN ARRIVED IN FRANCE ON SEPTEMBER 10, 1616, only to learn that Viceroy de Condé had been imprisoned for sedition just nine days earlier. Stunned, but perhaps by this time used to unpleasant welcomes, Champlain commented "that our enviers would not be very slow in spewing out their venom . . . for when the head is sick, the members cannot be in good health" (IV:339).

Marie de Médicis, still acting as regent for young Louis, immediately named the Marquis de Thémines Maréchal de France, as well as viceroy of New France. But de Thémines quickly proved little better than de Condé. He had been personally responsible for de Condé's arrest and, in addition to being rewarded with the aforementioned titles, he also managed for himself a one-third increase in the "annual fee for a horse." Not surprisingly, the matter ended up before the courts and, only moments before Champlain's next planned sailing for Québec, the court ruling revoked de Thémines's long-term license, stripped him of his title, and left Champlain in limbo for the season of 1617.

Disgusted, Champlain moved on: "Let us leave them to their pleadings and go and make ready our ships, which lost no time in proceeding to the succour of those who had passed the winter at the settlement . . . . Here was my reward from these gentlemen the partners . . . . So I embarked for the voyage of the year 1617, on which nothing happened worthy of note" (IV:342-44).

This cryptic note is the basis of another controversy surrounding the voyages. Historians are divided as to whether or not Champlain ever undertook a voyage in 1617; but it seems that the negative argument rests largely on evidence that places him in Paris on July 22 of this same year, implying that such a short journey was unlikely. On the other hand, there are even greater problems posed when this account is challenged. Writing in 1618, and making reference to the past in a passage that seems to have been overlooked by academics, Champlain corroborated his earlier reference to the 1617 voyage, and explained the circumstances that "prevented me from assisting [the Indians] was that last year [1617] when the chance and opportunity presented itself, they failed me at need, in that they promised me to return with a good number of warriors but had not done so, which was the cause of withdrawing without producing much result" (III:209-10). Clearly, Champlain made a voyage to New France in 1617.

There were good reasons for such a short voyage. With matters going so badly in France, a quick trip to protect the assets abroad would have been a sensible move. Just as important, there was ample reason for a speedy return. At home, Champlain was besieged with publishing problems, and there were squabbles over the accounts with many merchants, who were at each other's throats. The business quagmire alone was a lawyer's delight that dragged on for more than a year. In the end, only as the volcano was about to erupt was there royal intervention to prevent "a multitude of disputes and suits [which] would have arisen both in New France and before His Majesty's council!" It was a weary Champlain who stated: "But I was well aware they were afraid of something more serious, that if the country [New France] became inhabited their power would wane, since they would not be doing just as they like in those parts." Slickly covering up the loss of Acadia, he sloughed off the entire blame to those self-serving merchant interests without which "the English would never have been there, as he is, by means of French rebels" (IV:349, 351-52).

He was personally buoyed by the arrival on January 14 of the remaining dowry funds due from his marriage. By the start of the new year (1618), though, his fight for concrete support was in full swing. He was fed up with more than a year of carping and, with no clear direction in sight, retaliated with a fusillade of paper missives to the power-ful. In the first discharge, he fired a factum to the "Gentlemen of the Chamber of Commerce" in which he "humbly begs to be heard." For any who care to study it, it includes a snappy cost benefit review setting out the handsome reward for prospective investors. Each resource was carefully tallied and priced: there were salmon for the general market and sea sturgeon, a favorite delicacy in Germany; eel and sardines, relished throughout France; in the more exotic category, whale oils, whalebone, and walrus tusks that are "better than ele-phants' teeth"; and "forests, which are of marvellous height." The prospectus was designed to intoxicate those with a nose for profit (II:339-41).

In his second round of letters, Champlain wrote to the King and to the nobility advising of his overture to the Chamber of Commerce as well. In these letters, he pontificated that the accounts from the Indians were now so reliable "that one cannot doubt . . . the means of reaching easily to the Kingdom of China and the East Indies, whence great riches can be drawn" (II:326). This was an old dream culled from the first de Monts contracts for Acadia. To flatter the monarch, Champlain spoke of a new town to be constructed near the habita-tion, named Ludovica (Louis); he also mentioned another fort equal in size to the present habitation, but this time to be built directly opposite the Québec settlement on the south shore of the St. Lawrence River (fig. 24).

To ensure the success of these grand undertakings, Champlain promised "to conduct thither three hundred families, composed each of four persons" (II:334). This represented a monumental change of expectations — 1,200 colonists. This was the grand sales come-on; fat profits, empire, and glory all dressed in godly purpose.

The sales pitch worked; but, in terms of Champlain's long-term credibility, it proved a costly overstatement. In the interim, however, things began to pick up when, on February 9, the Chamber of Com-merce took up Champlain's gauntlet with a written plea to the King asking him to accept the project and to grant the monopoly that would enable the funding he had so long sought.

With reservations, the Crown accepted the grand design; on March 12, 1618, King Louis signed an extraordinary "To Whom It May Concern" letter, addressed generally to the "Dearly Beloved." This dispatch, the first of several directly from the King, entrusted the authority to Champlain for him to use as he saw fit, entreated every-one to co-operate in support of the plan for "exploring, inhabiting, clearing, cultivating and planting the land, and to carry on all the work he shall judge necessary for establishing the colonies we wish to found in the said country." But in spite of these lines, the royal entreaty included an escape clause for anyone with a flimsy excuse. Support was only commanded "in so far as one conveniently can . . . without allowing the said exploration and colonization to disturb or hinder your factors, clerks and agents and in the matter of the fur-trade in any manner and fashion whatsoever" (IV:365). From this, the monarch's priority was clear: seasonal commerce ranked well ahead of colonial development and the spiritual crusade was a secondary concern.

So, armed with little more than moral suasion, Champlain left Paris on March 22 for Honfleur, the "usual place of embarkation"; having now earned his place as a permanent colonial fixture. Pontgravé was waiting to command the larger of the two vessels that were to set out on the year's journey. Joining the venture this time were the Sieur des Chesne and the Sieur de La Mothe. The latter "had formerly made the voyage with the Jesuits to Acadia, where he was captured by the English and taken by them . . . back to England and thence to France" (III:177-78). La Mothe had a great deal of information to impart about Acadia and the growing English threat to New France. Bad weather delayed the departure till the last week in May; but, once at sea, the accumulated frustration after months of preparation and a late start were happily relieved by an ideal crossing. This year, to offset the hardship of ocean travel, there was time for sport: some of the passengers cast fishing lines to catch the gulls following the vessel for scraps. These were rare moments of pleasure that would not last.

On arrival at Tadoussac on June 24, Champlain and his compatriots discovered that a new and dangerous situation had developed in Cap Tourmente, near Québec. Two French settlers who had been missing for months were found to have been murdered by two Indians seeking revenge. Those left at the post were in a state of terror, and with each moment that the crime was left unresolved, the security of all was threatened.

The business had to be settled with speed. This was the third time that Champlain had arrived at the colony and immediately been forced to establish law and order; but this time, the issues involved were more complex. These murders represented a cultural confrontation, and a direct challenge to the Crown and colonial survival.

Champlain presented only a fuzzy account of the case in his journal: "It is almost impossible to extract the truth, both because of the scantiness of the evidence that could be obtained, and of the discrepancy in the accounts that were given, most of them being by way of presumption; but at least I will here relate it, according to the story of the greatest number" (III:182).

Champlain states that the murders took place in the farming meadows at Cap Tourmente, a few miles (c. 4 km) east of the settlement at Québec, just after his departure in 1616. The gist of the story was as follows: Two Indians successfully secured favors from the interim commander of the settlement, the Sieur de Parc. This triggered a jealous retaliation from one French settler, "a locksmith by trade," who took it upon himself to "beat the said savage so soundly that he gave this one reason to remember it; and not content with having beaten and insulted him, he incited his companions to do the like; which the more swelled the hatred and animosity of the said savage . . . and prompted him to seek occasion for revenge . . . behaving himself discreetly and as usual without showing signs of any resentment . . . . Some time afterwards the said locksmith and a sailor named Charles Pillet . . . decided to go out hunting and to sleep out for three or four nights" (II:183).

The two unsuspecting Frenchmen embarked by canoe to Cap Tourmente, just east of Québec on the north shore of the St. Lawrence River near the easterly end of Champlain's favorite place, Île d'Orléans. They were followed by two Indians, and attacked on arrival. The first victim, the locksmith, was bludgeoned with a club, and then — for the coup de grâce — knifed with "three or four stabs in the belly" (III:185). The second victim, the sailor Pillet, was brought down by a shower of arrows and also finished off with a knife attack.

Concluding this grisly business of two years earlier, the "murderers carried this body to the other, and tied them together so tight they could not be separated; then they fastened a quantity of stones and pebbles to them along with their arms and clothes, in order not to leave evidence whereby they could be found out, and carrying them to the middle of the river, threw them in and sank them to the bottom" (III:186).

The account of the murder has all the elements of a modern gangland killing, complete with weights to sink the incriminating remains. But in this case the bodies showed up — "cast upon shore and marvellously far from the water, all to serve as prosecutors and irreproachable witnesses against these two cruel and treacherous assassins. For these two bodies were found far from the water, more than twenty paces [18 m] in the woods, still tied and bound together, being no more than fleshless bones, like skeletons" (III:187). No more explanation was offered. Were the skeletons recovered downstream and then carried back to the scene for a dramatic trial of justice? Perhaps, but Champlain only teases on the matter.

For the French, the resolution of the two-year-old issue was considered routine; there had been a premeditated murder and, under the law, death was the only penalty. But as far as the Indians were concerned, the murders had been provoked and the remedy was not further bloodshed, but compensation for the families of those murdered.

To restore law and order, a preliminary hearing at the Québec settlement was arranged; but the Indians "found this procedure and mode of justice very strange and difficult, inasmuch as they had no established judicial procedure among them, but only vengeance or compensation by gifts." As a lure, the French promised that if the two accused would come to the settlement "they should receive no harm; that the French were gentle and inclined to forgiveness . . . on condition that they would return no more to such evil ways" (III:191-93).

The trial proceeding was partially accepted, and "these two criminals being convicted in their own conscience submitted to the proposal . . . that is, one of them, made ready and attired himself with all the garments and ornaments possible, as if he had been invited to a wedding or to some solemn festival . . . . As for the other murderer, he excused himself from this journey for fear of some punishment" (III:193). For the one accused who did come, the trial was a solemn occasion of ceremonial bravado. (The identity of the two murderers has been a perplexing problem for readers of the Champlain journals for decades. For some insight into this extremely complex case, see the Notes for this chapter.)

A multitude of Indians gathered at the fifteen-foot (4.6 m) ditch surrounding the habitation; the drawbridge was raised and, while the settlers were fully armed and at the ready, the Indians gingerly entered the fortified enclosure, but believing all along "that it was intended actually to do justice on the culprit who had put himself so freely at our mercy, and not only on him but also on those who had accompanied him inside, who were likewise not too sure . . . " (III:194).

For stage manager Champlain — just as at Port-Royal — it was an occasion "very well contrived, arranged and executed, to make them feel the enormity of that offence and to be afraid in future; . . . otherwise there would be . . . perpetual distrust" (III:194). The French, however, were not the only ones in charge of the production. Manipulating the scene with equal competence, the Indians also presented an awesome spectacle of color and legal theatrics.

First, the Récollets offered the prosecution arguments in a series of sermons. The Indians were reminded of the "friendship . . . borne them for the past ten or twelve years," and how Champlain had "personally aided them in their wars against their enemies . . . impelled to this merely by friendship and goodwill" (III:195). It was a stirring recall to the original terms of the alliance.

The next speaker was the father of the accused, who was acting as defense council. After being verbally assailed with the merits of French law and censured for keeping the murder a secret, he pleaded for compassion with "tears in his eyes": "Here is my son who has committed the supposed crime, he is no good, but take into consideration that he is a foolish and thoughtless youth who did this deed rather in a fit of madness, impelled by some feeling of revenge, [rather] than by premeditation" (III:197-98).

Numbed by this brilliant response, the French onlookers were amazed. The defense was worthy of any in the courts of France, and it constituted an immediate and appealing psychological victory. In one shot, he had pleaded that the accused was only a minor and that the whole incident was really one of justifiable homicide on grounds of temporary insanity! It was a standoff, and the French were stalled for three reasons: "First we were weak, considering the numbers; . . . secondly there would be no more security . . . and we should live in perpetual mistrust. Thirdly, trade might be injured and the king's service impeded." Even so, the accused was judged guilty, but then in a face-saving maneuver the court decided that "henceforth he [the accused] should work for the French; and his [the accused's] life was granted to him [his father] in order that he and all the savages might remain friends and servants of the French" (III:199, 201).

For Champlain, this resolution was not a solution because the penalty was insufficient and further, it established a dangerous precedent. The dilemma gnawed at his mind: "And meanwhile on our side we consulted together to determine what we should do in the matter of the murder of those two poor men, so that justice might be done and that way they [the accused] should be taught to do nothing [like it] in the future" (III:209). Ultimately, it was decided to wait "for the return of the vessels from France in order, according to the opinion of the captains and others, to reach a final and more authoritative decision, promising them [the accused and his family] always every mark of favour and the preservation of their lives" (III:201). As with the mutiny in 1608, Champlain opted for deferring the affair to overseas authority; in terms of the young colony's ever winning self-sufficiency in administrative matters — if indeed, this was ever a concern for the long term — such a decision sent the wrong message to France.

The French were thoroughly frustrated. Until the ships arrived, their only revenge was "postponing any assistance to them [the Indians] till another time, and requiring them to come down to us again next year with a good number of men" (III:210). This handling of the situation was vintage Champlain. Gradually he was turning the business to advantage; "we decided to settle this matter amicably, and to pass things over quietly, letting them trade in peace" (III:213). The years had brought wisdom and lessons learned to Champlain; but even though no strangulation orgy followed the proceedings as it had at Cape Cod, the French continued to feel the sting of injustice.

As the journal *Les Voyages - 1619* winds to a conclusion, the account deals briefly with the long-overdue reunion between Champlain and Étienne Brûlé. The two men met in mid-July, 1618, during the annual trading fête at Trois-Rivières. Champlain apparently accepted the explanation offered by Brûlé without a murmur and, after "he had told me his story I gave him hopes that his services would be recognized." Champlain promised to return to New France next year "with a good number of men, both to reward him for his labours and also to assist the Indians, his friends, in their wars as in the past .... I begged him to continue" (III:225-26). Yet, for some reason, none of these promises made to Brûlé were kept and, years later, Champlain could speculate on the implications of this failure.

To close his cultural treatise, Champlain summarized his ethnographic efforts: "It is to be noted that in my last and preceding travels and explorations I had passed through several different tribes of savages not known to the French . . . Several newly described tribes . . . came down [the Ottawa and St. Lawrence rivers to Québec], some to barter their peltry, others to see the French . . . . The sight of this encouraged everybody" (III:226-27). Brûlé's information about the Susquehannas was also added to complete the picture. With the 1618 season at an end, the voyageurs embarked on a late sailing for France on August 28 and, for record purposes, the closing events of the year 1618 and the years following were not published until the final published journal of 1632. Although for Champlain the geographer much had been achieved, the account was less impressive for the investors. They had to accept that there were only some 80 settlers throughout the colony, not the 1,200 promised, and that there had been no further progress on the route to China which was supposed to be so easily identifiable, according to the Indians. Nor had a new city or fortress been built opposite the settlement at Québec. On balance, there was little to justify an early return in the spring.

When Champlain arrived back in France in the fall of 1618, even with nothing significant to report, he immediately set to work to regroup his finances and plans for his next thrust in the spring of 1619. In a formal statement issued by the partners of the company, he set forth revised commitments for the coming year, with all the original objectives scaled downward. For a start, the plan for immigration was reduced from 1,200 to the more realistic goal of a doubling of the present population. A list of the provisions necessary set the tone for reduced expansion: "For every two persons there will be a mattress, a straw bed, two blankets, three pairs of new sheets, two coats apiece, six shirts, four pairs of shoes, and a cloak" (IV:353). This is the stuff of bare survival, not the building of empires. This time, there were no prefabricated settlements and warrior weapons to expand the French horizon.

Champlain dismissed the entire period between the recent voyage to the colony and the next: "The year [1618] slipped by, and nothing was done, nor yet in the following year, when new outcry and complaint began to be raised against this Company, which made promises but gave no performance. This is how the business went on, and it seemed as if all kinds of obstacles put themselves in the way" (IV:357). Only on rare occasions was there a complaint from Champlain; but perhaps at this time there were other reasons for his apparently reduced level of energy to fight. At fifty-one Champlain was getting on in years and had by this time suffered five physical injuries including the wounding of his hand at Cape Cod in 1605, injuries to his ear and neck in 1610 during the battle at Sorel and, more recently, the injuries to his knee and leg during the battle at Syracuse.

In his writings, he laid some of the blame squarely on the religious conflict between the Catholics and the Huguenots: "And it was partly this that brought about so many divisions and controversies . . . . They lived in such mistrust that each man had his own clerk to watch everything that took place, and this merely added to the cost . . . .

And besides what a host of suits they instituted" (IV:358). Here again, the lawyers were the winners.

During this trying period for Champlain, the larger obstacles to colonial development arose from the twisting ways of the commercial world. In spite of meticulous planning for the next expedition, the partners threw a torch at the next venture. Perhaps perplexed by Champlain's stated intention to move his family to the habitation, or fearful at the prospect of the commander who had already abandoned exploration activities in favor of administrative ones, they made a decision to award the colonial command to his junior comrade, Captain François Pontgravé, now in his mid-sixties. It was an insult, and Champlain's temper boiled:

> In a word, they thought they had the administration in their own hands, and were setting up a sort of republic there according to their own notions, and making use of His Majesty's authorizations to gratify their own impulses . . . . As for the Sieur du Pont-Gravé, I was his friend, and his years would lead me to respect him as I would my father; but to consent to the assignment to him of what belonged to me by right and reason, . . . I would by no means suffer. The Sieur de Pontgravé and I had lived as good friends in the past, and wish to continue in that relation (IV:361-63).

In the end, angered by his adversaries, but to no avail, Champlain sported the wimpish letter from King Louis XIII of March 12, 1618, calling for support only "in so far as you conveniently can" (IV:364). One merchant and jealous partner in particular, Daniel Boyer, a "pettifogger" said to have no rival for such mischief, was blamed for many of the problems.

Years later in the 1632 journal, his final record, Champlain lectured on the broader economics needed to solidify the colony: "Welfare [prosperity] increases to an infinite extent by increase of population, and the more who are industrious, the more commodities may be looked for; for when they have secured their food and lodging, they take pleasure in to turning to account the products which are there, and the sale of them can only take place by the ships which bring them goods . . . . By dint of trading and bartering, if the trade is made free to them [the colonists], they will gain the courage to work, and to go to the various regions for the purpose of this trade" (IV:361). For Champlain, free enterprise was the economic engine of wealth, and immigration was the fuel to ignite the process.

With all the problems, Champlain scrapped his departure plans for the 1619 season at the last minute and sought legal redress for losses that he had suffered: "They made the voyage . . . while I was pleading my case before His Majesty's Council." This time the plaintiff won, however, and there was a provision for a "penalty of paying all costs, damages and losses, and a special fine besides the costs" (IV:366).

And there was another hopeful sign — or at least Champlain seemed to think so. At the end of the voyage season, on October 20, 1619, the "Lord the Prince de Condé" was freed from prison; but the former Viceroy, just as suddenly, yielded to other priorities and relinquished any interest in colonial matters to his brother-in-law duc de Montmorency (1595–1632), cousin of the King and, in the family tradition, also an Admiral of France. With Champlain legally vindicated, the new Viceroy, Henri, duc de Montmorency, ordered there be a voyage in the coming spring of 1620. It was at least a signal for change, and hope was renewed as the Father of New France organized his return to Québec. This time, however, he was going, not as a warrior or as the gallivanting explorer, but as a family man, with Hélène at his side.

CHAPTER TWENTY-TWO

Hélène Champlain and the Return to Québec: 1620-1624

"They were made for mutual incomprehension."

Morris Bishop (1893–1973), *Champlain: A Life of Fortitude*

IN 1619, CHAMPLAIN ANNOUNCED HIS INTENTION TO move his family to Québec in the spring of 1620. This was a rare reference to his wife — and if there were other family members making this journey, they are not mentioned. The relationship between Champlain and his wife, Hélène, after ten years of marriage, remains a complete mystery. Indeed, what documentation does exist only serves to deepen the mystery.

If Champlain had entered into the marriage contract solely to gain power and/or financial backing, then the marriage would have to be judged a failure as the union had done nothing to alleviate either cash problems or a decade of undermining the colony politically. If, on the other hand, Champlain married for love, passion, or companionship or even in the hope of rearing future children, then he kept the secret well.

All that *is* known about this marriage indicates there was nothing between Madame and Monsieur Champlain save the chemistry of law and business. Agreements and documents pertaining to the marriage, agreements to hire a maid, and contracts to rent or purchase property are all that remain, and from them precious little is to be learned about the day-to-day life of these two historically important people.

There is, however, one set of documents that raises interesting questions because it hints at some sort of marriage breakdown early in the relationship. In a notarial affidavit complaint dated January 10, 1614, four years after the wedding, Hélène's parents, Nicolas and Marguerite Boullé, publicly disinherited their daughter Hélène at age fifteen. The severity of this measure seems to have been undertaken in anticipation of, or to head off, some kind of reprisal by Champlain.

Two years from the date of the marriage contract in 1610, and the ceremony thereafter at L'Église Saint-Germain l'Auxerrois in Paris, Champlain had conjugal rights, according to both secular and canon law, that is, the marriage could have been consummated any time after December 29, 1612. From the complaint of the Boullés in 1614, it is evident that Hélène had indeed taken up residence with her husband. This same affidavit, however, also revealed that after only a few months there was some great difficulty. According to the parental testimony, certain unspecified events took place, on October 1, 1613. These included Hélène's "unmentionable" crime, for which there was also no explanation. Flayed on paper, Hélène was accused of "scandalous" and "atrocious" remarks, and it was further "specifically" asserted that she was disobedient and uncontrollable. But the offense that raised tempers to such a fever pitch was the fact that Hélène had run away from her husband and gone into hiding.

The lively young woman, it appeared, could not abide the steady companionship of a husband who was twenty-eight years older than she. Unfortunately for poor Hélène, the seventeenth century did not abide such independence in women. Champlain roused the chief of police to trace his truant spouse and to "prove the evasion." Hélène, like all women of this period, was a mere chattel of her husband once she was married off by her parents. And of course there was still the matter of the balance owed on the dowry agreed to in the marriage contract. It was a cruel business without sense or feeling. But Champlain was not markedly different from other men of his time.

The eminent American cultural historian Natalie Zemon Davis offers this perspective on society's attitudes to women:

> As every physician knew in the sixteenth century, the female was composed of cold and wet humours [the male was hot and dry], and coldness and wetness meant a changeable, deceptive, and tricky temperament. Her womb was like a hungry animal; when not amply fed by sexual intercourse or reproduction, it was likely to wander about her body, overpowering her speech and senses.

In the end, some twenty-two years after Hélène was disinherited by her parents, and shortly after Champlain's death in 1635, the Boullé family formally revoked their original act of disinheritance in a final step, on May 23, 1636. In this second notarial document, it was revealed that Hélène had been forgiven by her parents years earlier on November 24, 1614, only three weeks after the original complaint. It seemed that with Champlain dead, the Boullés were easily able to shift the blame for their initial censure away from their daughter. More importantly, in the withdrawal document, the Boullés claimed that they were manipulated with lies and tricks into their action against Hélène in the first place. Champlain appears not to have known that there had been a "secret" recantation on the part of her parents. But there was no indication of who was responsible for all this manipulation and deceit, and the implication remains that the legal activity was only undertaken in the first place to placate an angry husband. The balance of the dowry money was paid in 1618, and this could indicate a reconciliation. But in truth, on this eve of Hélène's departure for Québec with her husband, we know nothing of the state of their marriage.

The account of the 1620 voyage to Québec is found in the fourth journal, which is Champlain's fifth complete work, *Les Voyages*, published in 1632. It was his last work and included a re-working of material previously published in *Des Sauvages* in 1603. This last publication, however, contains both mistakes and omissions. There are times when the aging warrior meanders from year to year in a narrative that seems aimless.

At the opening of the journal, for instance, there was for the first time neither a date nor a place of embarkation given. This is a small but nonetheless important signal to the reader. Champlain, previously much given to the details of navigation, seemed less concerned about such matters now.

Begun at the start of the new season, the new journal opens with Champlain and his family on the way to Québec. Unless informed by other sources, the reader has no idea what family Champlain is talking about.

Just prior to departure, Champlain received the second of the four letters from King Louis. Dated May 7, 1620, this letter acknowledged Champlain's appointment under Montmorency, and included a call to duty: "Champlain . . . I shall find acceptable the services you will render me on this occasion, especially if you keep the said country in obedience to me, making people who are there live as closely in conformity with the laws of my kingdom as you can, and having the needful care of the Catholic religion" (IV:370). There was no need for this royal reminder to this loyal servant of the Crown.

Champlain was happily away to sea in early May; but it was a frightful crossing with nearly two months of battering by rough weather during which the family "suffered much discomfort" before arriving at Tadoussac on July 7, 1620. Champlain's brother-in-law, Eustache Boullé, was the first to greet the commander and the newly arrived "first lady" of the colony. Having come out to the settlement earlier in 1618, Boullé was also Champlain's lieutenant, and Champlain reported that Eustache was "greatly surprised to see his sister and think that she could have made up her mind to cross so stormy a sea." This curious reference was the only one that verified a woman was indeed on board, let alone the fact that the woman was the wife of the lieutenant of the colony (V:2).

When Champlain arrived at Tadoussac, he found that the merchants of La Rochelle were ignoring the new Viceroy's monopoly and were stirring up trouble in the frontier by trading illegally on the St. Lawrence River and undermining Champlain's reputation with the Indians. This situation was not new; but if unattended, it had the potential to become more serious. Deserving of even more immediate attention, however, was the fact that these "rogue" traders had provided the Indians with a "large supply of firearms, powder, lead, and match," and Champlain was quick to say that this was a "most pernicious and mischievous thing to arm these infidels, who might on occasion use these weapons against us" (V:3).

When they reached Québec on July 11, there were more unpleasant tidings. The Louis Héberts, the first self-sufficient settlers of America, had lost a daughter in childbirth; also, an old friend, the Récollet friar Pacifique, one of the plucky four who had come out with Champlain in 1615, had died. But the biggest shock was the run-down condition of the settlement, which was in an "abandoned and ruinous condition, [a] very wretched state owing to the fact that the workmen had taken off to build a dwelling for the Récollet Fathers . . . ." The "rain was coming in everywhere; the wind blew through all crevices of the planks, which had shrunk . . . . The storehouse was on the point of tumbling down; the courtyard was in such a dirty and disgusting state, one of the buildings having fallen to pieces, that the whole looked like some poor abandoned tenement in the fields, which soldiers had occupied" (V:7). It seemed that the beautiful habitation that Champlain illustrated in 1608 (fig. 25) no longer existed. For the twenty-two-year-old Parisian-born Hélène, all this was a hardly an encouraging start to a new life.

Champlain had another concern: it was now evident that he was no longer completely trusted by the company. The voyage had included a "spy," Jean-Jacques, the Sieur Dolu, Grand Usher of the Kingdom of France, described by Champlain as "The Audiencer." He had a mandate to put "French society into a better condition of prosperity than it had been" (IV:368). This economic quartermaster could not have arrived at a more embarrassing moment for Champlain, and it was evident now that those many broken promises, such as the commitment in 1617 to settle 300 families, were being called to account.

Undaunted by Dolu's presence, Champlain waded into the task of problem solving. He noted the prospects for the future and the fact that work higher up on the escarpment had already begun on the construction of Fort St. Louis, named after the King. This huge and lofty enterprise became Champlain's priority for the year, and new buildings were erected using the "excellent limestone" discovered in the area. This was done to make certain that at least by the end of this season the Sieur Dolu could report that there had been significant progress. After Dolu had left at the end of the year, Champlain wrote a report noting that the early winter months had passed well, and that everyone was in good health, "save one man who was killed by the fall of a tree, which crushed his skull, so he died pitiably" (V:10). The only question was the matter of what the Sieur Dolu might report to his superiors.

Neither Champlain nor the colonists had to wait long for an answer. Early in the spring of 1621, while preparing for trade with the Indians, news from France reached Champlain at Québec. It was delivered with an advance party from a flotilla that had already landed at Tadoussac.

The duc de Montmorency, no doubt acting on the information provided by Sieur Dolu, had arbitrarily liquidated the Company of Canada without consulting overseas shareholder Champlain. To replace the Company, Montmorency had formed a new company with new participants. He gave no reasons for his decision but ordered that all company property, including all assets, be confiscated and handed over lock, stock, and barrel to the new directors, Guillaume de Caën and his nephew, Émery de Caën. This was clearly an insult to Champlain even though his salary was doubled and a letter from the King stated "not only do I feel thankful to you [Champlain] . . .

but it will give me pleasure to recognize it to your advantage when opportunity offers" (V:13).

The de Caëns arrived in the spring of 1621 and it soon became obvious that Champlain's position would be a difficult one from now on. In future his authority would be either divided or undermined. The machinations of change came quickly. In the following year, under the King's authority, there was a new company formed, the Montmorency Company, and this would last until after Champlain's death.

In the coming years, three de Caëns of note were to be involved with the fledgling colony: Ézéchiel, the architect of the de Caën merchant empire, his son, Émery, and Guillaume, Ézéchiel's nephew. The lives of the two cousins, Émery and Guillaume, would be the ones wrapped up with the affairs of New France. Guillaume was a Huguenot and Émery a Catholic. Their arrival marked the beginning of a new era in the development of the colony as well as the beginning of a new season.

The change of command meant that Champlain was expected to take instructions from the King, Viceroy Montmorency or the Sieur Dolu and there was therefore considerable room for intrigue. The confusion propelled Champlain into a struggle for position and, although ordered at Québec to seize the property of the "old company," his first move was to verify the authenticity of the license granted to Guillaume and Émery de Caën. As it turned out later in a dispute before the courts in France, there was something amiss: the de Caëns had deliberately disguised the limited scope of their mandate.

The de Caën conspiracy was intended to place Champlain in a secondary role, and to make him not only the victim of the takeover, but the executioner of it as well. The de Caëns moved quickly, utilizing their superior forces and a number of ruses. They had the good will of the King, 150 men, and three vessels, more than twice the population of the settlement. But before dealing directly with Champlain at Québec, they entrenched themselves at Tadoussac. In order to gain the compliance of the traders, they kidnapped the elder statesman of the colony and commander of the trading post, François Pontgravé, while he was making his annual trade preparations. Pontgravé was in possession of the company's only armed vessel; to intimidate him, the de Caëns told the old captain that he was technically guilty of failing to secure departure clearance in France. It was a minor infringement, but the perfect pretext for Champlain's intervention.

At this point, the de Caëns summoned Champlain from Québec to join in the mop-up operations against Pontgravé and the other traders of the old company. Champlain had to choose between royal disfavour in an undeclared war against these latest commercial opportunists or betrayal of his old friend. Typically, he played for time and advised that "it would be nine days at least before I should be at Tadoussac" (V:41). Unknown to him at the time, violence had already been forbidden by the King in writing.

Pontgravé made the next move. Under cover of night he sent a pinnace upriver to the habitation to pick up Champlain for a secret conference; the two met hours later at Tadoussac. In a touching scene, Champlain pleaded with his old friend to join him in a nostalgic chase of the Iroquois enemy, "not only in large vessels but in pinnaces, boats or canoes, and on land if necessary . . . . He cannot refuse this offer . . . and I pointed out that by so doing he will be serving the King and my said Lord" (V:45-46).

Cornered and vulnerable as the scapegoat, Pontgravé held fast to his territory and refused Champlain's invitation. But to save face, he surrendered his vessel to Champlain, who in turn abandoned it "so as not to be present when de Caën made the seizure" (V:47). Centuries later, some historians would accuse Champlain of cowardice; but such a judgment is too harsh. It was later proven that Champlain had in mind an alternative way to fight — to take the matter to court.

As one might expect under such conditions, Champlain was able to achieve nothing of consequence in 1621. The business affairs of the colony remained a whirlpool of politics, with much posturing and rearguard action. In practical terms, supplies were low and the situation was precarious; but Champlain struggled along through to year-end, found muttering, on the arrival of spring in 1622, "It is not a small matter to live in quiet and make a country secure by fortifying oneself in it" (V:57). For this uncertain chunk of the saga, Champlain went to ground like a wounded animal, and mulled over the melancholy times and the tasks ahead.

> I consider geographical discovery to be a matter of much
> importance; and yet it is something which cannot be accom-
> plished without great labour and fatigue . . . . An undertaking
> of this nature calls for mature consideration and it must be
> carried out with bold initiative and steady courage. But it is

also quite reasonable that the toilsome work of persons who take all this upon them should be recognized by certain honours and benefits, as such service is rewarded amongst other nations, in order to inspire them with more zeal and courage to do and dare. If such rewards are not bestowed, there is little chance of anything big being accomplished (V:58).

During 1622, only a few events were noteworthy and none of these were pleasant. On June 8, Champlain learned from France that the King's Council had only just approved the merger of the two companies that the King had been bullied into unifying the previous year. For all this force, it was not until July 15, 1622, when Champlain was at Québec that he received the third epistle from King Louis via Émery de Caën. Dated March 22, it clarified the situation, and revealed for the first time that a lawsuit had in fact been filed regarding the corporate hijacking of the previous company by the influential de Caëns in the previous year. The letter confirmed the settlement of litigation between the old company and the new firm, and the result was the coldest and most explicit correspondence ever sent by the Crown to Champlain. There was no flattery in this missive. Perhaps, in reading between the lines, one can detect royal rage. The King's unequivocal support for his cousin Viceroy Montmorency was very clear. "I desire and expect you to govern yourself in relation to the said new shareholders, maintaining the country in peace, and upholding my authority therein in all matters" (V:84). There was no love lost here between master and servant, and at this critical point in Champlain's career, it seemed that all hope for recognition and honor from France was lost. The shareholders of the old company were compensated for their losses, and for Champlain and Pontgravé, the injured parties, it was time to make the new arrangements work. Champlain, as the Lieutenant of the colony, a family man with a wife in Québec, had a larger stake than ever in peace, order, and good government. François Pontgravé was ill, getting on in years, and only wanted to be left alone.

Hungry for success on any front, Champlain again dedicated his efforts to helping the Indians, encouraging their agricultural efforts with a plan for a party of thirty to clear and cultivate the land near the Québec settlement. Using his charm as an arbitrator, Champlain nudged forward the communications another notch, and in another important step, he opened a channel for peace negotiations with the Iroquois nation by cultivating the good will of his old allies for two

Iroquois visitors as possible ambassadors. (Though he was often accused by historians of encouraging and fueling warfare against the Iroquois, the facts do not support this charge. This initiative toward improving French and allied Indian relations with the Iroquois is not an isolated instance in the journals.) The potential for unimpeded trade with all Indian nations along the St. Lawrence River was emphasized during this period. As the new twist developed, there were even some marginal successes to report and, when the time was ripe, Champlain ordered a great *Tabagie* to celebrate the occasion.

Just as some winnings appeared to be within reach, Champlain faced a renewed problem. In the middle of the celebration, "the murderer and his father came to the feast, although forbidden to do so, or even to come to our settlement; but the effrontery and audacity of these rascals was extreme." Unbelievably, four summers afterward, the issue of murder was still smouldering. In his journals, Champlain admitted that he hammed up this "little trouble" for effect on that occasion: "I pretended to be in a greater rage than I really was, springing up and asking for a weapon to go after the murderer." As usual, he had seized the right dramatic moment to stage-manage the scene. Still, the matter of the murder rankled the settlers, and by midsummer, Champlain's worst fears about this unpunished murderer were confirmed. Information was conveyed to him by the Montagnais Chief Erouachy (fl.1618–c.1836) from Tadoussac — the same Chief who back in 1618 negotiated over the first trial. He revealed that this one of the two murderers, although supposedly all this time laboring for the French under the watchful eye of his advocate father, had now secured support for a simultaneous attack against the French at Québec and Tadoussac (V:66-67). (For more information about this confusing case and the identity of Cherououny and the two murderers, see the Notes for this chapter.)

Although that particular plan was foiled, there was evident danger of another attack, and fear and dissension mounted throughout the colony. Moving fast, on July 30, Champlain held a quick conference to resolve the problem. Émery de Caën claimed to have the King's ear on the matter, and his instruction to grant a pardon to the Indian. It was done. But Champlain balked: "I could not agree, remembering the perfidy of which he had been guilty in the assassination of our men . . . . Nevertheless several considerations . . . caused me to give way, on the understanding that the assassin should render satisfaction before all the tribes, confessing that maliciously, perfidiously, and wickedly he had killed our companions" (V:103).

This time Champlain demanded a rerun of the drama to drive home some facts about French law to the Indians, and this was agreed; but once again the stage production had little to do with justice. With some changes of the props for the second rendition, the prosecutors forgot that there had originally been two murderers and the only one bearing the burden now was the one who had had the courage to attend the first hearing. Confession may be good for the soul, but for the single suspect on trial in New France, it was a different story.

There was another grand scene with the accused demonstrating a measure of contrition. Champlain as before was troubled with this smooth defence, and in an onslaught of moralizing and predictions, he rehashed old ground, concluding "these people do not care much whether it is through charity or otherwise that we act. Their belief is that his pardon was granted through lack of courage on our part" (V:107).

At year end, there was one sad signal: "Du Pont [Pontgravé] fell ill of the gout . . . and he was so disabled by it that he did not go outside the factory all winter." Pontgravé's attacks were chronic, and by the spring of 1623, he was in "such extreme pain that one could hardly venture to touch him, in spite of any remedies which the physician could employ" (V:91, 93). Champlain's grand companion was unable to leave his room until the month of May, and on August 23, 1623, unable to get proper treatment, he returned to France. It seemed doubtful that he would ever return.

During the summer of 1623, there was a happier note for the record. On June 28, the Récollet lay brother Gabriel Sagard (fl.1614–36) arrived at Québec. This friendly fellow, who tamed a muskrat as a sleeping companion and joked about his wooden clogs, wrote a superb journal about life in Huronia. Entitled *The Long Journey to the Country of the Hurons* — but not published until 1632 — it was written with warmth and a measure of humor. Sagard peeled away the cultural veneer of Indian life in Huronia for the reader. For the flicker of an eyelid during this small portion of the Champlain saga, there was some additional literary talent on board. Like Marc Lescarbot, Gabriel Sagard made a notable contribution.

The differences between the two men's writing styles are fascinating. Champlain, after years of writing about Tadoussac in his journal for 1619, wrote that its harbor was "the most disagreeable and barren in the whole country. There is nothing but pines, firs, birches, mountains and almost inaccessible rocks, and the soil very ill-adapted for any good tillage . . . " (III:308). Sagard, on the other hand, painted the same scenery as "high mountains, with little soil, mostly rock and sand covered with spruce and birch, then a little meadow with woods round it, just touching the little rocky island. On the right towards Québec was the beautiful Saguenay River, bounded on both sides by high barren mountains." Sagard compiled a dictionary of the Huron language, and he provided the first sheet of Indian music in America. He confirmed Champlain's observations of the great artistic skill of the Indians: "They are fond of painting, and practise it with considerable skill . . . . They make pictures of men, animals, birds and other things in caricature, both in perspective on stones, wood and other similar substances." Gentle Gabriel traveled Champlain's world of Huronia for only a short time from June of 1623 to the fall of 1624, enduring one winter as Champlain had at Cahiagué.

When Sagard returned to Québec in 1624, there was news that Étienne Brûlé had turned "native." This time, Champlain rendered a snap negative judgment on the spot: "And the influence was very bad in sending out such evil-livers, who ought instead to have been severely chastised; for this man was recognized as being very vicious in character, and much addicted to women. But what will not the expectation of gain make men do, a passion which tramples under foot all other considerations" (V:32). Any remaining friendship between Brûlé and Champlain was finished.

Like 1623, 1624 was an uneventful year, and Champlain, without any support from France, seemed ever more concerned with trivia according to his journals: "On the ninth, the raspberries began to bud . . . . On the tenth or eleventh the elder bush showed its leaves. On the fifteenth the trees were in bud" (V:121). After all the years of action and struggle, something was missing — the punch, the edge, the energy, and at the end of this lengthy sojourn in the colony, the reader is relieved when Champlain reports that he was at last "resolved to go back to France with my family, having now wintered in the country nearly five years, during which time we were but ill supplied with fresh provisions, and with other things very sparingly" (V:134). With little else to report after four years, the voyageurs set sail for home on August 21, 1624. When they arrived at Dieppe on October 1, Champlain proceeded immediately to Paris, where he found "the old and new shareholders involved in a lot of disputes arising out of the mismanagement of the expedition" (V:139). This amazed him. After nearly five years, the hagglers still hadn't resolved their difficulties; in the meantime, the English and Dutch had been busy — at the expense of the French. Champlain knew this and he was furious, but, there was perhaps one positive sign: Montmorency had resigned in the interim and there was a new Viceroy, the duc de Ventadour. At first glimpse, Ventadour seemed to have a higher moral purpose than his predecessor. One lives in hope. Ventadour was to be Champlain's sixth commander.

As for the return of New France's "first family" to Europe, Champlain himself offered no more information about them as husband and wife than the little already known. As to Hélène's years in the colony, all that remains after centuries is one quaint legend about her in New France. Its origins are uncertain. According to the story, Hélène owned a small mirrorlike object in her jewelry that reflected the face of anyone who looked on it up close. The Indians are said to have marveled at the trinket and yet were troubled by it. Hélène allegedly reassured them that in this manner *they* were "always" near her heart. It is a sweet and romantic tale.

CHAPTER TWENTY-THREE

In France and New France: the Colonial Retreat: 1625-1626

"The outcome of larger undertakings rarely conforms
with the orders initially given."

Cardinal Richelieu (1585–1642), First Minister of
Louis XIII, *Political Testament*

C HAMPLAIN HAD RETURNED FROM NEW FRANCE
with Hélène on October 1, 1624. From the time of his homecoming until April 15, 1626, the great journalist wrote nothing, and
only from other sources do we learn of his activities during this period.
The couple took up residence in a newly purchased house on the rue
Saintonge in Paris. They likely moved in to it during the autumn.
During this same period, records attest to the disposition of the
hacienda at La Rochelle. Clearly, Champlain felt it necessary to be
near the center of absolute power; so, he moved with his wife to the
French capital.

At this point, he was aware that with the success of the de Caën
takeover, and with de Monts in retirement — no longer jousting on his
behalf in the royal conclave — some new approaches were needed. But
he had spent the last four years in the doldrums of indifference, and
his attitude only began to change when a new Viceroy was appointed.
He described him as "His Grace the Duc de Ventadour, . . . [one]
favourably inclined to this holy undertaking . . . being himself urged
thereto by no interest except the zeal and desire that he had to see the
glory of God flourish in those barbarous countries" (V:139).

A nobleman, twenty-nine years of age, Ventadour had purchased the vice-regal title from his uncle, Montmorency, for 100,000 livres. This sum, which acquired for its holder the nucleus of an empire, was far more than the auction price of a horse (which was the equivalent amount paid previously), and it reflected a certain commitment on Ventadour's part. For Champlain, Montmorency's nephew was a welcome replacement who seemed to be personally and financially dedicated to the colony.

Like the Sieur de Monts, the duc de Ventadour had been the governor of a southern province, and, like Champlain, Ventadour had married a child bride. At the time of his appointment, Ventadour was plagued with marital problems, which in the Viceroy's case prompted a marriage separation.

Ventadour was the perfect partner for Champlain. He was a religious devotee, closely affiliated with the Jesuits. And, as had been the case with de Monts, he was also a Catholic who had influence in the halls of power. Unfortunately for the commander of New France, Ventadour's vice-regal stewardship lasted only two years; his personal religious interests within France became all-consuming, and he left the colonial business altogether.

In reference to the duc de Ventadour, there is only one significant document available: his directive to Champlain dated February 15, 1625. In this ponderous piece Champlain received professional recognition for the first time, for "His [Champlain's] intelligence, capacity, practical skill and experience in respect thereto, his good diligence and the knowledge he possesses in relation to the said country . . . " (V:142). For Champlain, this was welcome appreciation, even though the Viceroy's ensuing instruction circumscribed each expectation like a catechism. As with the first commission to de Monts for Acadia, Champlain was once again given full authority "to maintain, keep, and carefully preserve the treaties and alliances he may enter into with [the Indians], provided they fulfill the conditions thereof on their side, in default of which he may make open war upon them, to compel and bring them to such terms as he may judge necessary for the honour, obedience, and service of God" (V:145).

The Viceroy issued a four-part sermon: to complete his mission, Champlain was "commanded to this end to take up residence with all his people at the place called Québec, . . . to bring into subjection, submission and obedience all the peoples of the said country and those bordering thereon . . . to endeavour to find the easiest way to go through the said country to the kingdom of China and the East Indies." And finally, he was to deal with those "Frenchmen, or others, trading or negotiating" outside the monopoly license and to "conduct and bring the men themselves to France, and deliver them into the hands of justice, in order that they may be proceeded against according to the rigour of the royal ordinances" (V:143-47).

Yet, even with these new instructions well in hand, Champlain stalled and did not voyage in 1625. Instead, he chose to concentrate on pushing others to proceed overseas. The politics of religion was the reason for this delay. The details are not known, but there was to be a switch regarding the religious administration of the colony. Viceroy Ventadour became high priest and the vanguard he wanted marshaled to spread the word of God was the Jesuit Order. It was at Ventadour's instigation that Father Énemond Massé (1575–1646) headed into the wilderness in 1625 along with Charles Lalemant (1587–1674) and Jean de Brébeuf (1593–1649), who in years to come would be martyred in Huronia.

The journal for this new period opened with Champlain's jumping right back into the power struggle. And as was most often the case, the details were sketchy but this time there was more than a hint about what had been going on at Québec for the last year and a half. The evidence from Champlain in the journal was a note of smug satisfaction concerning the dilemma in which the de Caën cousins and other members of the "new company" now found themselves. It had been five years since Guillaume de Caën and his cousin, Émery, appeared at Tadoussac and, manipulating the King's authority, had humiliated Pontgravé and Champlain. At that time, Champlain apparently had skulked away hopeful of legal redress, and the opportunity to fight in other ways. Here, we learn the details of how the revenge was orchestrated:

> The Sieur de Caën . . . met with a good deal of opposition from the old shareholders which brought on proceedings amongst them before the Council . . . . Besides his Lordship [the new Viceroy, Ventadour] was dissatisfied with the Sieur [Guillaume] de Caën owing to the report which had reached him that he had caused the prayers of their so-called [Huguenot] Religion to be said publicly within the river St. Lawrence, and had desired the Catholics to attend them, a thing which his Lordship had forbidden him to do.

It was a sleazy sidestep to regain the initiative and there was no doubt as to who tattled to instigate this discomfort. With legions of theological scrutineers policing the French countryside, Guillaume de Caën was easily impeached and now, as insurance for the future, he was ordered to "appoint a Catholic, acceptable to my Lord the Viceroy, to command the vessels" (V:150-51). To drive the point home, Guillaume de Caën was also forever prohibited to voyage. What sweet revenge for Champlain and Pontgravé.

Following instructions, Guillaume de Caën chose Vice-Admiral Raymond de La Ralde, a Catholic, as fleet commander. A man of considerable experience, La Ralde had kept a watchful eye on the merchant fleets of other nations in 1621 during the corporate fracas between the old company and the new. La Ralde was the naval officer who had successfully established the supply outpost at Miscou Island in Chaleur Bay (fig. 40). This appointment had a special twist, for according to Gabriel Sagard, this same commander despised the Jesuits to such a degree that at one point the Order had found it necessary to censure him on the charge of trying to bring about the downfall of the Church.

The departure from Honfleur in 1626 was the highlight of Champlain's and Pontgravé's revenge for those weeks of anguish during the corporate piracy at Québec in 1621. What theatre! As the sails were being readied, the assembled seamen squirmed and snickered as the discredited Guillaume de Caën delivered a farewell speech exonerating himself from any faults concerning the colony's administration. "About six o'clock in the evening de Caën arrived, administered the oath to the said La Ralde . . . after which he read publicly before the whole crew, and others a small book containing a number of things which he was accused of having done. There were some present, as I believed, who were not particularly pleased with this reading" (V:154). The peevish performance was as much a revelation as was the telling of it, and it was obvious there would be endless trouble among the competing factions forced by the King into such an unhappy union.

With all this jostling for position, only the Jesuits presented a united and organized front by sailing time. These stalwart soldiers of God had rented one of the de Caën vessels themselves and they departed loaded with provisions and twenty willing workmen on the church payroll.

On this voyage, Champlain's wife, Hélène, remained alone in

France. Champlain left the harbor in a convoy of four pinnaces with the *Catherine* as the lead vessel. During a lengthy crossing, Champlain, almost in celebration after an escape from those carping over clerical trivia, mounted his most comprehensive navigational account of the route and the shorelines from Cape Race on the south-east coast of Newfoundland, to the settlement at Québec. Joy and confidence radiate from these journal pages.

After the longest crossing of Champlain's many crossings — two months and six days — anchor was dropped near Bonaventure Island, just off the east coast of the Gaspé peninsula, in late June. On arrival there was an incident of black humor. Just prior to his departure on a mission to refurbish the storehouse on Miscou Island, on the other side of Chaleur Bay (home of the Gougou monster), fleet commander La Ralde was forced to warn Émery de Caën, the man in charge, to "tell the so-called Reformed sailors, he did not want them to sing their psalms in the river St. Lawrence." De Caën obeyed but the sailors "began to murmur and say that they ought not to be deprived of that liberty. Finally it was agreed . . . they should assemble for prayer, since nearly two thirds of them were Huguenots. And so out of a bad debt one gets what one can" (V:194-95). The Wars of Religion were just as alive and well in the New World as in the Old.

The *Catherine* arrived at Québec on July 8, 1626, and the good news at the beginning of this season was that except for Pontgravé everyone was in good health. Ever the bear for punishment, the grand old man, having returned the previous year after a brief period of recuperation in France, had been seriously ill for months with gout during one of the worst winters ever experienced in the colony.

But the good health of the colonists did not offset the larger setback. Physically and spiritually, the settlement had deteriorated. Morale, a reflection of the indifference of home rule, was now at an all-time low. Champlain, who had been away only two years, had once again returned to chaos. Nearly ten years had passed since 1618 when he had departed for France with those first sparkling reports of self-sufficiency and the promise of agricultural independence; now there was only a listless settlement, dispirited and immobile. Only the Jesuits were filled with enthusiasm. "Would to God that, during the last twenty-three or twenty-four years, the Companies had been as united, and as motivated by the same desire, as these good Fathers!" (V:206)

During the two-year absence, the settlers had "left undone those things which they ought to have done, and done those things which they ought not to have done." The instructions for the continued construction of the new Fort St. Louis left by Champlain on his departure in 1624 had been totally ignored: "I saw a lot of work at a standstill . . . . The workmen made great mistakes in not following the plan I had made and explained to them" (V:201). After two years, only one room inside the new fortress had been completed, and into this limited space were crammed nearly all the residents not employed by the missionaries. Even the precious 1,800 newly sawn boards that were left on the site in 1624 to complete the assignment had since been wasted on lesser priorities.

With a flair that brings a flicker of life back to the saga, Champlain blew renewed energy into the depressed community. He began by demolishing the entire habitation structure in order to rebuild on a larger scale. He arranged a scheme to cut down the time wasted hauling hay upstream in small boats from the salt meadows at Cap Tourmente thirty miles (48 km) east of the settlement at Québec. The new plan called for the relocation of the cattle to those notorious meadows where the murders had taken place, and the building of appropriate accommodation for the animals and a small number of residents.

These moves were all a gamble and, in a revealing note, Champlain confessed the proposals were the subject of prior review with the shareholders. The concerns were strategic and were made because of international competition in trading matters. La Ralde was attempting to enforce a French monopoly on the fur trade from the St. Lawrence to Acadia and the naval base at Miscou Island off the Gaspé. He was swamped with security matters as the French Crown's territorial claims were being violated with increased daring by all nations who cared to try regardless of the military risk. Time was running out and new strategies were desperately needed to galvanize the colony to self-sufficiency. As it stood, the present conditions of token settlement were as much an invitation to conquest as an expansion program. Strategically, the lines of defence were spread thinner with each tiny new settlement. Moreover, the farther the French pushed inland, the longer their supply lines and the greater their need for self-sufficiency.

Finally, to cap the difficulties of the year's voyage, there was a report in late summer that the Iroquois had murdered five Dutchmen on the Hudson River. This was the worst news yet. The fragile threads of peace negotiation spun so carefully with the Iroquois three years ago were no longer connected, and the news of this attack emphasized the added risk of a confrontation with this powerful enemy federation. The threat to New France's survival was awesome to contemplate, and Champlain noted that the residents were in "mortal dread and apprehension" (V:206).

While Champlain's race for some evidence of progress continued throughout New France, supplies were getting low. A report of La Ralde's men at Miscou Island the previous year stated that many had died of scurvy the previous winter and that more hardships were expected at the post in the coming year. There were also indications of problems to come involving the barn builders on the meadows of Cap Tourmente. They had squandered their precious summer allotment of food supplies, and on August 25 when Champlain personally inspected the latest provisions from France he noted that "The quantity was small, leaving us liable to fall in distress of disappointed hopes . . . unless God should help us by the early return of the ships" (V:209). New France was still far from her goal of self-sufficiency.

Champlain laid the blame for all the ills of 1626 squarely on those in France who had failed to adequately aid their overseas settlement "owing to provision not having been made in good time" (V:213). The level of snow reached a record height of eight feet (2.4 m) that year. The starkness of the white winter curtain that shrouded the struggling colony at year end could have been an omen.

CHAPTER TWENTY-FOUR

More Murders and the Alliance Cracks: 1627-1628

"Je ne doute point d'apprendre, par la grâce de Dieu,
et un peu de temps . . ."

William Shakespeare (1564–1616), *Henry V*

IN LATE JANUARY OF 1627, THE BELOVED LOUIS
Hébert fell to his death; on this sad occasion, Champlain wrote a tribute. He recorded Hébert's accomplishments: "He was the first head of a family resident in the country who lived on the produce of his land" (V:212).

As if Hébert's death was a sign of coming unrest, it was now learned that a band of Indians from the alliance had sneaked through Iroquoia in order to secretly sit in council with the Dutch settlers located on the Hudson River. Such a development was trouble in the making; although the Iroquois were seemingly content with an unspoken armistice with the French and their allies, the same warriors had attacked the Netherlanders the previous year. Over the two-year period, twenty-nine Dutch had been killed.

An escalating conflict between the Iroquois and the Dutch could have worked in Champlain's favor for he wanted to rid the continent of all but the French. It was, however, not to be as simple as letting the Iroquois get rid of the Netherlanders. The Dutch were desperate for relief from Iroquois terrorism and were attempting to make a deal with Champlain's Indian allies. Such an alliance could only signal a return of the Indian wars on the St. Lawrence. Champlain, who had encouraged and welcomed the peace, wrote, "By renewing this war [the Indians of the alliance] were simply jumping out of the frying pan into the fire" (V:216).

Miristou (d.1628), the son of the deceased grand sagamore Anadabijou, was the new Chief of the Montagnais. He was one Indian of importance from the alliance who was against renewing hostilities, and he became Champlain's ally and confidant. From Miristou, Champlain learned stunning news: one of the major mischief makers with the Dutch was none other than that elusive personage, the perpetrator of the crime and the real "murderer," the one who, it seems, had *not* been tried in 1618! Champlain refers to this culprit as "The Reconciled." (See Notes for this chapter.)

It seems that somehow "The Reconciled" in the intervening years had undergone a metamorphosis from a complete rogue to a salvaged soul and a trusted friend. Miristou's news changed this: this one of the two murderers was now back in Champlain's bad books and thoroughly suspect. "As to the Reconciled, if he had taken these presents [from the Dutch] I did not want to see him again, nor would I consider him my friend, unless he returned them . . . . Keeping them would be an act of bad faith, like promising one thing and then doing another, and allowing oneself to be corrupted by presents" (V:217).

Champlain moved quickly. He dispatched his trusted brother-in-law, Eustache Boullé, and Chief Miristou to Trois-Rivières to powwow with members of the alliance. His hope was to initiate a reconciliation between the members of the alliance, and then to take whatever steps necessary to stave off the return of an all-out war with the Iroquois.

Seemingly well informed, the Reconciled heard of Champlain's displeasure with the intrigues and his — Champlain's — plan to prevent war. The Reconciled hurried to meet his former prosecutor and patch up matters; he claimed that as far as war was concerned, he was at this moment "as strongly opposed to it as previously he had been for it." The Reconciled's appeal failed, and Champlain dismissed him with a "very cold reception" (V:218-19).

In the next episode, however, while rushing for a restored position with the allies at the Trois-Rivières rendezvous, Champlain received another blow. He learned that in Iroquoia, at least four Iroquois had been seized by "nine or ten young hotheads" from the alliance (V:221); one of these prisoners had escaped en route from Lake Champlain: a witness to bad faith was now on the loose — ensuring chaos.

Champlain, however, still grasped at a slim chance for peace by arranging that the remaining hostages be released and returned home to Iroquoia under escort. But, as at Sorel in 1610, the captors had subjected their captives to torture. One of the prisoners had been worked over severely; he had been beaten with sticks, and his finger-nails had been torn out. "Thus by accident, all hope of the mainte-nance of the peace was destroyed" (V:222).

To compound the problems, the rejected Reconciled meddled in whatever remained of the French peace plan. Before Champlain arrived at Sorel to attempt a stay of execution for the captives, the Reconciled, aware of Champlain's anger, rushed to the scene and quickly cut the cords of the two surviving prisoners who were awaiting their turn at the beating post. The two Iroquois were to be held for Champlain's further disposition and would most certainly have been part of a French move to reconcile the alliance members. It was another chance missed. The Reconciled couldn't seem to make up his mind which side he was on; he was about to be tried and tested, however.

No longer to be outmaneuvered, Champlain contrived another plan; for this initiative he enlisted the help of Pierre Magnan (d.1627), one of the more undesirable members of the settlement. Magnan had received a murder conviction in France for clubbing someone to death. Champlain also called on the Reconciled and others who were persuaded to undertake a good-will mission to repair the damage already done. As a gesture, they were to return the captives to Iro-quoia. An unfortunate surprise awaited them.

When the ambassadors arrived at the Iroquois camp, they were confronted with the news that their hosts had already been attacked by another band of alliance Indians. The judgment of the Iroquois was swift: "While you come here to arrange peace, your companions kill and massacre our people" (V:230).

It was not until two years later that Champlain learned the details of how the Reconciled had died: "One of these Iroquois . . . drew a knife, cut some flesh off his arms, put it into the kettle, and ordered him to sing, which he did. He then gave him some of his own flesh, half raw which he ate; they asked if he wanted more, and he said that he had not had enough, so they cut pieces of his thighs and other parts of his body until he had had enough; thus the poor creature came to his end in an inhuman and barbarous manner" (V:310). To describe his end, perhaps as an absolution and out of guilt, Champlain referred to his longstanding Indian adversary, the murderer, or the Reconciled, by his real name, Cherououny, for the first time.

As for Pierre Magnan: "The Frenchman was burnt with lighted brands and the flames of the birch bark, by which they made him endure intolerable agonies before he died" (V:311).

Rationalizing the outcome at the time, whatever Champlain's motives for the Iroquoia mission might have been and apart from some concern over the effect of Magnan's murder on overall security, Champlain relished the final moment: "As far as the Reconciled was concerned, he fully deserved death for having murdered two of our men just as cruelly at Cap Tourmente; and the said Magnan . . . had killed another man by beating him with a club" (V:230).

Aside from the satisfaction of seeing the murder matter resolved after all these years, Champlain recognized that a price would have to be paid for this failed mission: "It destroyed all our hopes of peace . . . [and] on receipt of the news of the death of the ambassadors, our Indians were so exasperated and enraged that they took a young Iroquois boy, whom they had retained as a hostage and tore off his nails and burnt him in a slow fire" (V:231).

Champlain's difficulties moved from one arena to another; indeed, from one hemisphere to another. A warning sign appeared in a communiqué to Champlain from the untrustworthy Guillaume de Caën in France who informed him of an English raiding vessel headed toward the settlement from the French coast. Shortly thereafter, rumors were rife, and they were fueled by the Jesuits.

The Jesuits, ensconced in their settlement just east of the habitation on the Charles River, were anxious about a missing supply ship. They suspected a hijacking on the high seas by the English; owing to the lack of supplies, they had been forced to send all their hired workforce home, leaving them with a token complement of nine support staff in New France — "so as not to abandon their home" (V:233). To make matters worse, half the cattle in another supply ship destined for Tadoussac had died at sea.

Out of the original fifty-five residents included in the entire colonial population for the year, Champlain now had only eighteen left at the settlement to continue the reconstruction work on Fort St. Louis — and of these, half were deployed at the grain fields at Cap Tourmente. Lacking support from France, the Fort St. Louis defense project had been cut to the bone; the exiled Guillaume de Caën in France was blamed as the one who "ought to have given me ten men to work at His Majesty's fort . . . for although His Majesty and the Viceroy desired it, still [de Caën's men] were opposed to it and hinder it to the utmost of their power" (V:236).

In an attempt to rally some sense, Champlain fired off a complaint to Vice-Admiral La Ralde at Miscou. He hoped that with business and family connections to the de Caëns and a military mandate, he might help; but he couldn't — or didn't — and with no one recognizing the danger to the colony now standing alone, Champlain concluded that "the majority of the shareholders did not care . . . so long as they got forty percent interest on their money" (V:237-38). According to Champlain, de Caën even objected to measures undertaken for the direct security of company assets.

It was a deadlock; so Champlain dumped the dilemma into the lap of the new viceroy in writing — but considerable cynicism was evident in his words for the first time: "those who hold the purse strings can make and unmake [and] in the meantime, I did my best to employ a few men on the fort, while the rest worked at the settlement . . ." (V:238-39).

By the fall of 1627, while the colony was still threatened from overseas, there was another warning that the Iroquois were becoming more aggressive; and finally setting the stage for disaster, in October there were two more murders that threatened whatever remained of the alliance.

Two French settlers had been butchered at the Cap Tourmente meadows, the site of the previous murders. Dumoulin and Henri, the servants of the Hébert family, were murdered in their sleep. Their bodies had been dragged into the St. Lawrence. For Champlain, a vengeful ghost of the Reconciled might just as well have been the one accused because — in this second case of the meadowland murders — there was evidence of even more violence than before: "their skulls had been smashed by blows and axes and there were many other wounds made by swords and knives" (V:241).

Everyone in the colony was frantic with panic, at a time when supplies of all essentials, including munitions, were below the critical point. Champlain bluffed and, in an attempt to ward off a potential uprising, he confronted his unreliable allies with the evidence of the latest crime. At first the Indians blamed the Iroquois. The deceit didn't work, so they produced a ready-made scapegoat — someone already under suspicion but uniquely qualified to ask for mercy: a family man with children.

Threatened with war from all directions — from Iroquoia, overseas from the English, and now nearby from their former allies — the French were still in the mood to cut a deal. Even though the risks were greater than ever, the problem of the murder was deferred to allow the Indians to reflect on the consequences. During the lull the allies were also expected to produce hard evidence to support their allegations against the Iroquois. At this stage, these were only ploys to buy time. In France, there was more horse-trading over the control of the colony; on the frontier, it was a game of hostage trading — the living for the dead. In the opening move, three Indians were turned over to Champlain. From the start, it was a delicate business as one of the unlucky hostages was the son of the much respected Miristou, a chief who had secured his own tribal command through the French commander's persuasion. Despite this difficulty, the three bartered souls were handed over for a long incarceration.

The colony was on the verge of breakdown on all fronts. With only fifty-five settlers in Champlain's complement for the year 1627, and the remaining force of the Jesuits at nine, at year end there were only sixty-four plucky souls living in New France — in apparent defiance of the near indifference of home rule. In a later review of the period, Champlain complained that in twenty-two years, the "Companies had only managed to clear [about] one acre and a half [0.6 ha] of land" (V:257), and even five years later this clearing had only grown to twenty acres (8 ha) — "The Companies having refused to give them the means of cultivating the land." As far as Champlain was concerned, this neglect took away "all reason for them to become settlers." He verified in his journal that it was not until the month of April in the following spring of 1628 that there was even a plowshare drawn by oxen (V:326).

By comparison, in 1627, Virginia could boast more than 2,000 settlers. Even the threatened Dutch settlement on the Hudson River was thriving at 200.

CHAPTER TWENTY-FIVE

Treason and the First English Attack: 1628

"No other American colonial founder was so versatile as Champlain; none had a more attractive character."

Samuel Eliot Morison (1887–1976), U. S. historian,
Samuel de Champlain: Father of New France

B Y JANUARY OF 1628, AN ARRAY OF PROBLEMS threatened the habitation at Québec. Among the critical difficulties were relations with the Indians and the fact that supplies were exhausted.

But there was an even greater danger: war had broken out between England and France. Champlain certainly wondered about this in 1627; he suspected that one of the French pinnaces had been taken by the English at the end of the season when it was returning to Honfleur. His comment, however, that earlier in the same season Guillaume de Caën had written to him at the colony providing information that was only described as "not much" leaves the entire question of his knowledge of the European conflict up in the air.

The conflict abroad whose effects were eventually to spill over on to the shores of New France was sparked by a particularly complicated sequence of events. Although King Charles I (1600–1649) of England was married to the sister of King Louis XIII of France — a marriage designed to keep peace between the two nations — the Earl of Buckingham had led an English attack by sea to help the Huguenots on the Île de Ré, off the port of La Rochelle. This ill-conceived venture failed; but, as a result of this — and for other reasons as well — warfare between the two countries in the form of piracy on the high seas was resumed again.

The rebellion of the Huguenots on the Île de Ré and in La Rochelle, the fact that it had been brutally put down by the Crown, and the resulting attempt by the English to help the Huguenots in 1627 was seemingly all unknown to Champlain in New France until June of 1629. For months, Champlain had been uncertain and worried — largely because supplies had not been delivered and he suspected the worst. By the first of the year, he had concluded that to maintain any semblance of law and order, his first priority had to be finding a solution to the second set of murders. The continued incarceration of the hostages taken the previous year — that is, those given over by the Indians to "compensate" the French for those murdered — had not resulted in the Indians turning over the real killers; indeed, it only meant that there were three more mouths to feed.

The opportunity to bargain with the Indians on this matter came late in the month when thirty starving Montagnais appeared at the settlement begging for food. The French usually shared food in such cases; but, acting out of character, they held back what meager provisions they had to share and seized the opportunity to bargain. Stubbornly pressing for an advantage, Champlain insisted the killers be identified.

But the Montagnais were also bargainers par excellence, and they presented their own solution. It was a solution based on their cultural belief of compensation for the aggrieved rather than capital punishment. They did not offer to identify the guilty, but rather they tempted the French by offering them a gift of three Indian girls: Faith, Hope, and Charity, aged eleven, twelve, and fifteen respectively.

The Montagnais knew their target well. They were dealing with a company of lonely bachelors; and it was noted in the journals that for some time the surgeon had been seeking a woman, "desiring to have a young girl in order to have her educated and afterwards to marry her." Thus far, he had been unable to "persuade any of the savages to let him have one, no matter what he offered, although his whole object was the glory of God" (V:250). Champlain recorded this without comment, though given the circumstances the modern reader may well question the surgeon's motives.

François Pontgravé, now in his seventies and still going strong, for "cause and just impediment" fired off a written objection to the whole business. He pointed out that should these young girls be taken on, there would only be three more vigorous appetites chomping at the dwindling rations as well as the three hostages already in tow. Acceptance of this "gift" was a bad move for the French, and one that the Indians had calculated would soften them up. It was a successful ploy.

According to Champlain, he himself stepped in to claim the prize in this trading game; he adopted Faith, Hope, and Charity. Nonetheless, he did so only on the condition that his acceptance did not in any way obviate the French protest of the murders, and the hostages previously taken were to remain in custody. As Champlain saw it, he gained three souls for God, and of course some good will from the Indians as well as more time to resolve the murders. Faith, Hope, and Charity won a secure home and a cultural opportunity, and the French saved face following their first stratagem of withholding food. But nothing was really solved, and, given this stalemate, there was soon another attempt to free the three original hostages.

Chief Erouachy of Tadoussac, the noted ambassador of the Montagnais, appeared just as he had at the ceremonial *Tabagie* in 1623. Then he had come to gain the restoration of rights for one of the murderers, probably the accomplice who was at the trial in 1618. This time he was to make an overture on behalf of the hostages. He began his presentation with dire warnings that unpleasant times were in store for the settlement if this matter wasn't soon resolved with the release of the hostages. Then the chief repeated the flimsy allegations against the Iroquois. Erouachy's purpose was clear — to get back to the business of war in a big way.

Champlain was unmoved, and Erouachy retired only to return within a few weeks making accusations against the Algonquins. Champlain rejected these arguments as "feeble and unsound." He determined not to "temporize any longer"; in one swift move, he released the three hostages in exchange for Erouachy's son. This was a bargain that reduced both risk and cost. Just as important for peaceful relations, it also took Champlain off the hook with his friend, Chief Miristou, whose son had been one of the hostages. As an added bonus, Champlain gained some leverage over this meddlesome Chief. Nonetheless, the matter of the murders was not at an end.

Erouachy, now the one with a son at risk, left. But he returned six weeks later to inform the French that no vessels had come from France. This was a ploy designed to encourage deep feelings of insecurity; but Champlain was already alarmed as all the "provisions were exhausted, excepting for four or five barrels of quite poor biscuit . . . some peas and beans . . . . Such are the straits to which we are brought every year . . . . I have already fully pointed this out in many places . . . . All is well if only the fur trade is secure: the profits go to the shareholders, and to us are left the hardships" (V:266-68).

By late June, other Indians came to the settlement seeking relief from hunger. In desperation, the French decided to make a run for La Ralde's naval storehouse and staging center at Miscou. Here it was hoped the settlers might "secure supplies from ships that might be along the coast and obtain passage for some of those we must send home." Suddenly, it was realized that there wasn't a seaworthy vessel at Québec to transport the ten people who proposed to return to France. In a scathing denunciation, Champlain blamed Vice-Admiral La Ralde not only for this, but for the fact that the settlement was "without a single sailor, or any man with knowledge enough to fit out or navigate a vessel . . . . We are in fact destitute . . . as if we had been deliberately abandoned" (V:267-68).

This was another of Champlain's puzzling comments, similar to the one made in Acadia. In that incident, Pontgravé had been ill below deck and the carpenter Champdoré had been at the helm. For some unexplained reason, Champlain, the master of the seas, soon at that point to write a comprehensive treatise on seamanship, had claimed ignorance of the basic skills needed to sail a vessel. In this instance, Guillaume Couillard de Lespinay (c.1591–1663), the son-in-law of the late Louis Hébert, was chosen for the task of commanding the vessel to sail to the storehouse. Couillard, although highly valued as an experienced sailor, refused, fearing to leave his family should there be an attack on the settlement in his absence.

In the meantime, the plan was interrupted by the arrival at Québec of two settlers who had come up from the granary at Cap Tourmente. They brought exhilarating news. The farmhands stated that they had met with a Montagnais runner from Tadoussac who carried a report that six French vessels under the command of a certain Captain Michel had arrived at the trading post.

This story did not make sense to Champlain because such a fleet would invariably be commanded by a more senior commander than Michel, whom Champlain knew well as a river pilot. No one was promoted that fast in the French Navy, or in any other navy.

Having touched base at Cap Tourmente, the Indian runner, continuing his marathon, arrived at Québec. Here he was subjected to stern cross-examination. Suspicious that something was amiss, Champlain smartly dismissed the messenger and, in desperate need of reliable information, he sent a language-proficient settler, a Greek — who was the first colonist of his nationality recorded — with two companions to investigate. Disguised as Indians, they headed for Tadoussac. They returned within an hour with devastating news: the English had captured Tadoussac and were already at Cap Tourmente; possibly they were only moments away from the settlement with its partially constructed Fort St. Louis. As witness to their story, the Greek and his companions produced refugees who had escaped English captivity. These included Monsieur Foucher, the manager of the Cap Tourmente farm.

Foucher poured out his heart, describing the skirmish to his anxious comrades at Québec. According to him, the conflict had begun on July 9 when, just before daybreak, some sixteen English soldiers had arrived at the Cap Tourmente meadows by pinnace. They had disembarked and advanced on the farm along the edge of the surrounding wood. When they were discovered and challenged, the attackers were momentarily stalled before tricking the sleepy custodians. With the English vanguard were Frenchmen known to Foucher from a visit the previous year. The renegades claimed to be ambassadors from Cardinal Richelieu (the King's first minister) and the Sieur de Roquemont (commander of the French fleet). With their masquerade, the traitors bought enough time for an English platoon to surround the farm and capture it.

Gabriel Sagard reported that in taking Foucher so much by surprise their enemy had "singed his moustache." Champlain added that "he told us that he had escaped with three of his men, a woman, and a little girl, whom [the English] had taken on board in a boat . . . after having killed what cattle they wanted and burnt the rest of their stables, where they had them shut up. They also burnt two small houses into which Foucher and his men had retired, and destroyed everything they could, even to the cap worn by the little girl" (V:275).

Threatened on his own doorstep, Champlain struck like lightning: "I set all hands to work to make entrenchments around the settlement, and barricades on the ramparts of the fort which were not completed" (V:277). With Tadoussac taken, the company assets razed at Cap Tourmente, and Québec under siege, Champlain had a clear response to his request a year earlier to the Viceroy calling for a clarification of priorities. He had received no answer. Perhaps now that the colony had actually been invaded, someone in France would listen to his voice in the wilderness; but then, too, perhaps it was already too late.

The crisis intensified. On the next day, a vessel arrived in the vicinity, appearing to make a sortie to the Jesuit encampment up the nearby St. Charles River, minutes east of Québec. Swiftly, Champlain hustled riflemen at the ready to the woods in defense. It was a false alarm; there was no immediate danger. The intruder was a Basque trader returning the captives taken by the English at Cap Tourmente — including Madame Pivert and a little girl. Inveigled somehow into the service of the English, the Basques were in the thick of it to return the prisoners and deliver a written message to Champlain from the commander of the English forces, David Kirke (c.1597–1654). As accorded with tradition, Champlain politely entertained the six Basque emissaries and agreed to a public reading of the enemy demands.

The invaders, the Kirkes of England, would be on center stage in the Champlain drama for the next four years. David Kirke, the eldest of five sons, was the leader of the English expeditionary force, which comprised a family contingent of brothers: Louis, Thomas, John, and another in this enterprise named James. The father of the five was Jarvis Kirke of Derbyshire, a merchant who operated in both London and Dieppe; it is believed that his wife, Elizabeth Dowding, was the daughter of another English merchant who was said to have settled in France. Whatever the case, all five sons were citizens of France by birthright. Fully bilingual, these free-roaming seamen could legally play on either side at will; having chosen the side of England, they were hated in France for their treason and were burned in effigy in Paris.

The English commander's written message to Samuel de Champlain, lieutenant of the Viceroy and commander of New France in Québec, was a note of contempt. General David Kirke, also known as the Vice-Admiral, claimed authority from his King, Charles I of England; and then, to intimidate Champlain further, he boasted of his conquests to date, including La Ralde's naval base at Miscou, a flotilla of French vessels, the post at Tadoussac, as well as a provision ship headed for that same port, and finally the Cap Tourmente farm, which had been torched. Now, having accomplished a complete blockade, Kirke taunted Champlain: "For I know when you are distressed for want of food, I shall more easily obtain what I desire — which is to take your settlement." The Englishman even claimed to have had better knowledge than Champlain about the Company's affairs in France, and he urged Champlain to consult the Basques for the details regarding the direction "affairs are taking in France touching the New Company created for this country." Then, cutting off the directive, Commander Kirke put the case bluntly: "Send me word what you wish to do . . . send me a man" — softened at the end, of course, with the usual courtesies of the times: "I remain, Sir, your affectionate servant" (V:280-82).

Sensing a mistake in judgment on Kirke's part and with nothing but gall in his scabbard, Champlain replied with a bluff about the conditions at the settlement, acknowledging the hardship on hand and the risks, but insisting that "nevertheless, the place can make good its defence on slender supplies when good order is maintained in it." And as for those courtesies promised for a quick surrender, Champlain responded that "I know that you will think more highly of our courage if we firmly await the arrival of yourself and your forces, than if, in a cowardly manner we abandoned something that is so dear to us without first making proof of your cannon, your approaches, entrenchments and battery against a place . . . which I am confident . . . you will not judge to be so easy . . . nor its defenders to be destitute of courage . . . seeing they are men who have tried the hazards of fortune in many different places." Champlain the professional! Superb! And it worked. The Lieutenant of the colony touted commitment and experience with just enough sprinkling of the truth to be convincing. He too closed with a nicety: "Your affectionate servant, Champlain" (V:283-84).

The ruse put off the English commander for the season and Champlain won round one at Québec. Whipped with words, Vice-Admiral Kirke retreated, but not before burning all the vessels at Tadoussac save the largest, which he took as a prize. As the English brothers retreated from the Gaspé in a blaze of revenge, they captured four more of Admiral de Roquemont's vessels. Closing the matter, Champlain, pleased with his own situation, reminded the reader in his journal that it "shows on such occasions it is a good thing to put on a bold countenance" (V:286).

Throughout the upheaval, Champlain had been without adequate communication to enable him to interpret recent events in France. Reflecting the colony's state of isolation, the journal bounced wildly from optimism to despair. In one instance, after the Kirkes' retreat, there was mistaken news of a French naval retaliation at the Gaspé, news brought to Québec by Captain Thierry Desdames (fl.1622–46), the officer in charge of the storehouse at Miscou. Uninformed of Kirke's success, Desdames gleefully told of the arrival of Admiral de

Roquemont with a fleet of relief vessels from France. Hope at Québec surged with the good news that there were workmen, settlers, and "supplies of all kinds" on the way; but the letdown came just as quickly when it was learned that Desdames didn't meet de Roquemont and hence didn't have a written message. And further, Desdames chose not to verify the sound of cannon he had said he had heard as he departed for Québec. Had he been more careful, he would have learned that the entire fleet was captured by Kirke, and that de Roquemont was shot in the foot. Empires are lost over such bungling.

Sometime during the summer, and recorded as an event *after* the battle with the English, Champlain learned of instructions en route from King Louis. This fourth and last letter from the Crown, dated April 27, 1628, before the hostilities began, documents the apparent apathy; but, to appease, the opening was more flattering than usual: "To our dear and well-beloved Sieur de Champlain" (V:288) Notewor thy! In one move and without formality, Champlain had risen to membership in the nobility to be addressed with the title "Sieur." But in the next breath, the tone radically changed.

The King, acting as an auditor-general, delegating duties in wartime, instead of greasing the way with an increase in pay as in 1621, in a terse directive, essentially reduced Champlain to the role of bookkeeper and there was also a no-nonsense command: "To do this we give you power, authority, commission and a special mandate; to carry it out, notwithstanding all oppositions or appeals whatever . . . for which we refuse to allow delay . . . FOR SUCH IS OUR PLEASURE." Through this one royal and absolute directive, Champlain was back on line as the unrecognized quartermaster of Québec. To ensure complete compliance, he was also ordered to make an inventory of de Caën's assets including "all the munitions of war, goods, victuals, furniture, utensils, . . . with all the cattle" (V:289-91), and if there were any objections from the de Caën interests, Champlain was to press further with a title search on all Company property. It was hardly a move calculated to help Champlain repair and build longterm relations with the de Caëns, and if there was any sweet revenge to be enjoyed at their expense for past humiliations, the cost was high.

The most important message to be gleaned from this latest royal cannonade was the fact that Champlain now had evidence that he no longer necessarily reported to the Viceroy; for the present he would report directly to the King. With the de Caëns apparently out of favor and the monarch acting as an interim-receiver, it was obvious that major events were in motion in France. At last Champlain had a royal written answer to his written request to the Viceroy to establish priorities.

Although there was no explanation in the journals for this latest organizational contortion in France, other sources confirm that the duc de Ventadour's resignation had been secured by the first minister, Richelieu, who in turn had merged the office of Viceroy of New France with one that he himself held, Grand Master of Navigation. Owing to another rebellion in La Rochelle, France was on the verge of devastating civil strife, and the nation's security depended upon the strongest of navies. Thus, during these times while Champlain's stature may have risen in the immediate past, in fact his power had been curtailed. The reasons for this were not as thought by many historians, deliberate neglect of the colony, but rather that during this past summer, the monarch and first minister of the land had been totally preoccupied with a series of events that threatened the very survival of the throne of France. (See Notes for Chapter Twenty-Five.)

For the remainder of the year, however, Champlain was completely out of touch with France, and the journal offered only a post-mortem on the failures of the Sieur de Roquemont, who was unmercifully castigated in absentia as incompetent: "courage must be accompanied by prudence, which is what wins esteem as implying the employment of ruses, stratagems, and inventions" (V:296). And in his final outburst of complaints about the past year, Champlain confirms that Captain Jacques Michel, the former river pilot of the St. Lawrence, was indeed a traitor; for this Champlain raged against him for pages and pages.

With the season lost for any constructive purpose, the winter that followed was one of the roughest the colony had ever faced. There were only meager supplies for distribution, and all residents were forced to hunker down for a long stretch of cold and misery. To stiffen the backs of those that might falter, Champlain served a sermon instead of food: "I was always preaching to all our people: that they should try to have some patience while awaiting our relief . . . " (V:302).

On a positive note toward the end of those miserable months, want, instead of absolute authority from France, was the mother of invention: "The necessity we were in caused us to devise what in the previous twenty years had been considered impossible" (V:297). The settlers were forced unaided, to drag wood for fuel some 2,000 yards (c.1,800 m), in order to begin construction of a flour mill. Previously, the colony had awaited the pleasure of craftsmen in France to fashion the necessary mill stones, which had been dumped at Tadoussac as they were too heavy to move upstream by ship; now the stonemasons on site quarried the bedrock of the surrounding environment. For the French at Québec, this was a first step toward self-sufficiency.

There was one pleasant note of hope to end the year 1628. During all this trial and tribulation, a newcomer and friend of Champlain appeared on the scene, another Chief from Tadoussac, Chomina (fl.1618–29). This Chief had more names than fingers. Known to some as "The Grape," his neat appearance and superb manners had prompted the French to call him "Le Cadet." He was a welcome addition because help was needed — and badly. The growing fear in the colony was soon to be justified — a second assault from the English was forthcoming in the spring.

CHAPTER TWENTY-SIX

Québec Falls to the English Raiders: 1629

"I am going to seek a great perhaps."

François Rabelais (1404–1553), French satirist

A S WINTER MELTED INTO SPRING AND, WITH SUP-
plies nearly exhausted, Champlain was forced to set June 30 as
the deadline for the arrival of the relief ships from France. If no vessels
from France were sighted by that date, then he knew he had to resort
to drastic measures. At first, he considered only two options: surrender to the English if necessary, or close down the settlement and
escape to the Gaspé.

In April, after an absence of just over a year, Erouachy, the Chief
from Tadoussac, reappeared. He had not warned Champlain of the
impending English attack the previous year, nor had he reported on
the piracy committed by the Kirkes at Tadoussac. Moreover, it seemed
that he was expected to visit the previous year in order to bring
evidence as to "who was the murderer of those poor men" (V:305).
Unwise in the ways of diplomacy, Erouachy arrived at the settlement
and bluntly demanded the release of his son, who had now been held
for some fourteen months and who, it seemed, was ill. Champlain was
displeased, mistrustful, and unsatisfied over the murder business; so
he refused the chief's request.

Annoyed, the Tadoussac chief again proposed an attack against the
Iroquois. Champlain, however, was more concerned with survival
than with attacking the Iroquois in order to push out the English and
the Dutch. But as a last resort, he was willing to toy with the idea of
attacking them to grab food supplies. He made it very clear to

Erouachy that such an undertaking would only be initiated with the full support of the old alliance: "I showed him the means and inventions that we had for promptly carrying the fortresses of the enemy, which he was greatly pleased to see" (V:316). With the Indian alliance crumbling before him, Champlain was attempting to move from damage control to damage repair. But should there be a third confrontation with the Iroquois, then there was to be no repetition of the débâcle at Syracuse.

Pragmatism was to rule the day as the plans and expanded options were carefully considered. On May 16, Champlain made his first move. He decided to carry out a series of reconnaissance missions throughout all New France, and elsewhere, in search of a possible refuge. And, even as he meditated on the wisdom of carrying out the destruction of an Iroquois settlement, he sent an emissary to Iroquoia to explore the prospects for peace. In the meantime, he also sent a party of three, including two settlers, downstream to Pontgravé at Tadoussac to be on hand to warn of any threat from the English; "Thus we omitted nothing that we could think of that might help us out in our difficulties" (V:320).

Though many such reconnaissance missions were launched, they were not mentioned in the journal until later. By mid-May, in desperation Champlain was forced to change the self-imposed retreat deadline of June 30 to July 10. He noted in passing that, "out of nearly 100 persons, few could probably survive, unless God had pity on us" (V:321-22). A crash program was already under way to reduce the settlement to fifteen persons by relocating most to the Gaspé or to Huronia.

Captain Desdames, the same over-anxious fellow whose incomplete report of the naval battle the previous year had confused everyone, had been given a chance to redeem himself by leading the exodus to the Gaspé. On May 17, a vessel with a crew of six sailors sailed from Québec under his command. This was a mercy mission, and Desdames was armed with a written plea from Champlain to the captain of the first friendly vessel he could find. In it, Champlain begged for supplies, assistance, and a passage homeward for all, including those who still remained at Tadoussac and Québec.

As in the previous year, no one was willing to promise that, once safely away, they would return to assist their comrades. Tempers were short, and Champlain was furious at those who would "put so pernicious a purpose into effect" (V:323). Getting tough, he threatened anyone who might be involved in a plot to mutiny with the gallows. His threat was successful and Desdames made good his getaway.

It was a race against time. Those left at the settlement had to search the woods for tree gum, a natural glue that, when mixed with seal oil, created a superb pitch for caulking the one remaining leaky vessel. If it could be repaired, then thirty more settlers could make their escape. But even if the vessel were to be repaired, and even if Desdames's pinnace returned for a second load of passengers, there were still not enough vessels to transport everyone to the Gaspé.

On May 20, in the midst of these frantic preparations, twenty "strong and robust" Indians from Tadoussac, all fired up, reported in at Québec on their way to war against the Iroquois. An attack on the Iroquois would end any chance Champlain's lone peacemaker might have had, and the Indians boasted of the great disruption to come. From them, more was learned of the battle the previous year between the English and the French. Apart from the successful siege at Tadoussac where the prize vessel was taken, the English had also followed a scorched-earth policy at the Gaspé, killing a number of Frenchmen. Admiral de Roquemont not only was shot in the foot, but, along with Vice-Admiral La Ralde, had been taken prisoner. And the Jesuits had been taken into custody after the Kirkes had burned their supply of corn. All the remaining French had been taken to England as proof of military success. Whatever satisfaction Champlain had gained with his successful bluff at Québec had now turned somewhat sour.

On May 30, yet another group of emissaries in search of sanctuary arrived back in Québec bringing with them more confusion. They brought information concerning new hostilities between the Algonquins and the Iroquois; by June 6, there was additional evidence that confirmed the spread of this year's conflict to Trois-Rivières, only a few miles from Québec itself (fig. 40). In New France, the crush of events signaled the most serious threat since the beginning of the colony.

On June 11, the exploratory party sent on May 17 to Tadoussac returned empty-handed. With no relief in sight, Champlain mustered a work party to go to the islands off Cap Tourmente to hunt seals for the oil to mix with the tree gum being harvested. Champlain had hesitated over this assignment because he was well aware that sealing was the toughest work for his famished and fatigued colonists.

In the midst of the race, the Desdames mission to the Gaspé returned with the first good report of the summer. He reported that thus far there was only a hint of trouble ahead for the season. Some eight English vessels had been sighted sailing the Acadian coast, but they had not appeared to be hostile. Even better news, however, was an invitation from the Gaspé from "Juan Chou, an Indian Chief and his Canadians . . . [who did] their best to welcome the French, promising that if the Sieur [du Pont-Gravé] wanted to go to their country, in case our vessels did not arrive, he should want for nothing." It was a grateful Champlain who noted: "It was not a small thing to find so much courtesy and kindness with an assured asylum amongst them" (VI:26-7).

This particular overture was also a reminder to Champlain of the need to extricate his seventy-four-year-old, ailing companion from the danger zone.

The lovable curmudgeon Pontgravé was still peppery in spite of his health, and torn between staying on to the end and going home to a well-earned retirement. True to form, he balked at the way he was being handled and, just before departure, he insisted on a public reading of the directive to him from Guillaume de Caën. For Champlain, this performance was all too familiar, for old Pontgravé was having a tantrum similar to the one that Guillaume de Caën had indulged in at Honfleur nearly a decade earlier. This time, however, Pontgravé was concerned about money, not religion. He was owed monies from the de Caën interests and, long experienced in such matters, he knew the need for properly conditioned witnesses. Then, in a sudden switch of position, the old gentleman decided to hang on for the next round in the contest for New France.

With the Pontgravé matter clarified, the only loose ends were the matter of the murders and the single Indian hostage still in custody. Since Erouachy's visit two months earlier, there had been no progress on the matter. In the face of so much trouble, it was decided to bargain further with those who sought the release of the hostage. With food supplies exhausted and the threat of a second attack by the English looming, the long-held charge was a growing liability, not likely to be of any use. The poor soul was near the end, crippled in the leg and suffering from severe stomach problems.

To negotiate a solution, Champlain sent for the trusted Chief and his good friend, Chomina. In a quick shift of position, Champlain announced that he was prepared to "set the prisoner at liberty" under certain conditions. There were six in all: the prisoner was to "leave his little son" with Father Le Caron; corn was to be supplied to the settlement; eels were to be supplied; Chomina was to be elevated to the rank of a Captain amongst his own people; and, while the reparations were undertaken, Erouachy was to continue to hunt for the person now being touted as responsible for the murders. It was a long list for the release of one sickly hostage; but it was accepted, and "Captain" Chomina even offered to assist should there be a war with the English.

As in the past, however, Champlain fretted over the final outcome of the murders: "We were compelled to let him go . . . by the scarcity of our supplies"; but at the end, as if to reinforce his decision for compassion, Champlain recorded a promise from the prisoner in his journal: "when I am cured, I want to prove . . . that I am not a wicked man." Perhaps the fellow had learned somehow a lesson or two in the past from that master quick-change artist — the Reconciled. Regardless, Champlain had his own assessment: "The truth is that, to these people, who are accustomed to great freedom of movement, the imprisonment for fourteen months is a very distressing mode of punishment, and they would almost as soon be put to death at once" (VI:24-5).

By this late date, even with the second set of murders tidied up and the promise of tangible support from Chomina, the prospects for survival were slim. Although scouts had been sent to Iroquoia, Huronia, the Gaspé, and Acadia — as well as to nearby Tadoussac and Trois-Rivières — apart from the lone runner to Iroquoia (whose fate one can only guess in view of the renegade alliance Indians on their way to attack), all the scouts had reported in, except the contingent sent westward to Huronia. This one mission was the last hope.

While awaiting this last report, Champlain commenced the closing rituals that signaled the end of the colony. There were final dispatches drafted for brother-in-law Eustache Boullé to courier homeward to the King, the Cardinal, and the Council. On June 26, primped up to beg for the relief of the settlement, Boullé's party, including another group of émigrés, departed in the last pinnace, now repaired and seaworthy. But of the thirty who left, a sturdy twenty of them wished to try their luck at the settlement on the Gaspé. Those unlucky few who remained had to forage in the forest, surviving on a miserable diet of wild roots. The hero of the occasion was Chomina, who was so moved by the pitiful sight that he joined in their search.

Just when all seemed lost, news arrived at the settlement from Acadia on July 15. Hospitality could be expected from Indians in the region of the Kennebec River (fig. 12). At this moment of joy, Champlain undoubtedly recalled his explorations of this same region twenty-five years earlier as he wrote of the "hope I entertained of the benefit we might derive from it in our time of need," or the desirability he had first expressed that there be a detailed exploration of this region: "of the river which abounds in fish," (I:321) but is so "very dangerous for vessels" (I:326). Just as euphoria over the good news took hold, there came equally disheartening news. On July 17, the flotilla of twelve canoes and the twenty "emissaries," including the Récollets who were sent to explore the option of sanctuary in Huronia, returned. They had been rejected and had only managed since mid-May to scrounge a paltry supply of foodstuffs from those good "Farmers of the North." The Hurons were reported to be angry at the mass exodus of their French tutors who had come on a mission from their God to bring salvation. It now seemed as if the God of the French was less than almighty, or at the very least, less than pleased.

For the next forty-eight hours the settlers meditated on this bitter harvest. At this point, every effort short of an all-out attack against the Iroquois had been explored and failed; now, even a skirmish to grab a cornfield in Iroquoia was unthinkable because "powder for hunting was so precious that I preferred to suffer rather that to use the little that we had, which was only between thirty and forty pounds, and that of a very poor quality" (VI:41). In fact, even the fishing had become an unrewarding chore for the remaining settlers, "owing to the lack of nets, lines, and hooks," and the required effort that was "at a cost of great trouble and patience" (V:40), and "very fatiguing." With an English attack only moments away, the French were exhausted, but not for long (VI:40-1).

On July 19, La Nasse, a Montagnais Indian attached to the settlement, brought news that the English had arrived. Champlain was greatly astonished that even a small relief vessel from France could not, by this late date, have been dispatched on a mission of mercy. "When the news came I was at the fort, with some of my companions having gone to fish, and others to look for roots; my servant and the two little native girls [Hope and Charity] had gone with them. About ten o'clock in the forenoon some of them came to the fort and to the settlement; and my servant arriving with four small bags of roots told me that he had seen the English vessels a league distant from our settlement" (VI:51-2).

It was over before it even began. This time there was no fighting, no barn-burning — no action at all, for resistance would have been pointless, and the settlers knew it. In the negotiating arena, however, Champlain, the great colonial advocate, was resolved to turn the confrontation into a mighty battle of words. When a single English soldier arrived on the shore at Québec, he was carrying a flag of truce. The communication he also carried was dated July 19, 1629, and came from Louis and Thomas Kirke, the two brothers of Vice-Admiral David, who awaited a reply at Tadoussac. This time they could not be bluffed: they only made a simple demand for unconditional surrender. Even so, for Champlain, a master of such legalities, there was room to maneuver: in drafting the conditions of capitulation, he requested that the Kirkes prove their legal authority from the English King, and also prove legally that there was a state of war between England and France. During this quest to assure notarial justification on record, Champlain even went so far as to insist that captains Louis and Thomas Kirke must prove they were duly authorized by their own brother, the Vice-Admiral. It is a wonder Champlain did not demand the right to study the enemy logbooks!

Stripped to its essentials, the transfer of power called for the customary demands, including the right of the defeated to retain their personal weapons and a safe passage home for all, extending to any other wayward resident souls who might be discovered at a later date. The surrender was all very civilized and reasonable; but there was one major stumbling block. Champlain insisted that he be allowed to keep his two adopted children, Hope and Charity, and take them to France with him. (Gabriel Sagard reported that at this time the third child, Faith, had already returned to her people.)

The response from Vice-Admiral David Kirke of the English fleet at Tadoussac was swift. He agreed to all conditions except that pertaining to the personal matter: "[Regarding] the native girls, I cannot grant you the request for reasons with which I will acquaint you if I have the honour to see you" (VI:60). Champlain sensed trouble; but, persuaded that Louis Kirke would argue positively on his behalf before his brother at Tadoussac, he gave in without further fuss.

As arranged, on July 20 the English vessels arrived at Québec to take possession of the settlement; there were three vessels and 150 troops to enact the first conquest of New France. For the French, greatly outnumbered and isolated from their mother country, there was no choice; but Champlain, the old quartermaster, was not yet ready to accept defeat. Far from it. For legal purposes he requested there be a written inventory of all the spoils confiscated by the English as this was a perfect opportunity to have an outside source corroborate the sorry state of the colony. Louis Kirke agreed, and the list was completed on July 21. According to the journal, David Kirke later commented on "how very little [there was] in the way of arms and munitions" (VI:128). The one "old military tent" found and listed on this scavenger hunt was an appropriate indication of just how far conditions in the colony had fallen.

With the conquest complete on July 22, 1629, the English flag was "hoisted on one of the bastions," and Louis Kirke "had a salute fired from the ships as well as from the five brass guns at the fort . . . the whole in sign of rejoicing" (VI:67).

For Champlain, this was the lowest point in his career. For almost three decades he had warned of such a catastrophe; but just as excruciating to him was the betrayal from within. Added to the sedition of "that downright traitor and rebel, Jacques [Michel] the river pilot" who "sold out to the English" (VI:81), Champlain's list included four others: his two interpreters, Étienne Brûlé and Nicolas Marsolet (1587–1677); Pierre Raye, the wagon-maker, "one of the most perfidious traitors and scoundrels in the lot" (VI:63); and finally, Le Baillif (a word taken from the Old French, meaning "one who is in charge"), a fellow accused of stealing gold and a silver chalice belonging to the church. Champlain's desolation was complete: "From the time the English took possession of Québec, the days seemed to me like months" (VI:69).

Through all this heartache, Champlain was able to derive some comfort from the fact that the English were accommodating to those willing to stick it out as residents in the conquered territory. Everyone, it seemed, "expected nothing less than [that] they would have to go back to France . . . . The English, however, did nothing of the sort; on the contrary, they offered them all of their assistance, and said that if they wanted to remain in their homes they were as free to do so as they had been under the French." Pleased, Champlain reasoned that Louis Kirke "always had a liking for the French nation . . . finding intercourse and conversation between them more agreeable than with the English, to whom his nature seemed to be adverse" (VI:70-1).

The orderly exodus aboard the English vessels began on July 24 from Québec. While the war for possession of the settlement was over, the battle for the seas and trade had never been fought. At La Malbaie, east of Québec, this conflict began between an armed trading vessel commanded by Émery de Caën and the English warship captained by Thomas Kirke. As a captive aboard Kirke's vessel, Champlain rendered a running account of the first recorded naval engagement on the St. Lawrence River.

As the English vessel, loaded with some thirty captives, sailed downstream on the great river of Canada, Émery de Caën, on the shoreline at La Malbaie, was caught red-handed trying to tidy up commercial matters before his flight for France. Ranking profit ahead of country and common sense, and in anticipation of the English attack, de Caën had been working on a scheme to filch the entire inventory of beaver skins from Québec.

Catching sight of the English, de Caën tried to catch a favorable wind for escape down to the open sea; but, anxious to bag him, Thomas Kirke quickly closed in for battle. As the gap between the opposing vessels narrowed, cannon suddenly roared fire from both ships. Within minutes there were about thirty shots exchanged, "one of which fired from the vessel of the said Émery, carried off the head of one of the able seaman of the said Thomas Kirke" (VI:75).

Still scrambling to escape, de Caën made "several tacks in order to gain the wind"; but he was too slow, and the French and English vessels were doomed on a collision course. In the comic chaos that followed, the bowsprit of Kirke's vessel somehow crashed into the stern of de Caën's, and the fluke of the latter's anchor astern acted as a padlock to hold the adversaries in a deadly embrace. In all this confusion, the prisoner Champlain and his companion were locked below for the duration of the engagement, according to custom. Just to be sure that there was no interference from them, the hatches were nailed down overhead. From this restricted vantage point, war correspondent Champlain could only note the hullabaloo as the battle raged on the decks above.

Attempts by each side to board the other were frustrated by the clumsy handcuffed position of the vessels which assured that each could easily fend off such an attack by the other. Still they bashed away in the battle; "each party did what it could to vanquish and overpower the other . . . flinging stones and cannon balls and anything they could lay their hands on from ship to ship" (VI:76).

As the furor climaxed, Thomas Kirke gained the upper hand. For safety, de Caën's men on the French vessel "rushed down into the lower part of the vessel." The finale was pure slapstick, with the captain of the French vessel last reported encouraging his men to come up again for more battle by "striking them with the flat of his sword." At this signal the swashbuckling was at an end, especially when "Émery de Caën, in a craven spirit cried quite loudly, 'Quarter! Quarter!' " (VI:77).

The fight ended with the loss of three English sailors and a large chunk of French pride. With the battle over, "men came at once with pliers to open the hatches" (VI:78), following which Champlain was whisked away and ordered to consult with de Caën to ensure there would be no treachery. The dispossessed commander of New France balked at this demand. In time, the two captured "associates" were able to meet and exchange news unconditionally.

As a prisoner, and on the defensive for a change, Émery de Caën pleaded that prior to capture he was only headed on to Québec to bring news of relief to the settlement. He protested further that he had a letter from his cousin Guillaume that guaranteed that there were sufficient provisions on the way for three months — enough, at least, until the arrival of another promised relief vessel under the command of Admiral de Razilly (1587–1635). Of more interest to Champlain, though, de Caën also whispered that the war between France and England was over. This hearsay, even if true, would be of no value vis-à-vis his present situation with the Kirkes, and, from past experience, Champlain had no reason to rely on information from these commercial opportunists.

Taken to Tadoussac as a prisoner at large, Champlain found that he had time on his hands to catch up on personal matters. Unhappily, the defeated commander learned that his brother-in-law, Eustache Boullé, who had been dispatched earlier with messages to take to the high and mighty in France, was also to be found a captive in David Kirke's camp at the trading post. However, there was some hope; there was added confirmation that the war between England and France was over. This was not enough to move the Kirkes.

Frustrated at every turn, Champlain broached the issue of Hope and Charity only to discover that the prior "understanding" reached with Louis Kirke at the time of the surrender had now been skewered by brother David. The situation was an infuriating and emotionally charged one; but even on legal grounds, Champlain was defeated, having accepted the terms of surrender with this matter left unresolved. It turned out that there was a web of intrigue, and both Étienne Brûlé and Nicolas Marsolet were accused by Champlain of "indulging . . . in unrestrained debauchery and libertinism." He raged at both; but the treason of Étienne Brûlé was an especially cruel blow:

"whatever happens you will always have a worm gnawing at your conscience . . . . Following this I said a good deal more on the subject" (VI:99-100). Champlain was angry — as angry as he ever revealed on record. There was nothing more ever learned about this culprit in the saga, however, and from this point onward, the tale of Étienne Brûlé was forever relegated to one of the great mysteries of early American discovery history.

As for Nicolas Marsolet who had written to General Kirke claiming that there had always been an agreement amongst the Indian chiefs that Champlain would not be allowed to keep the girls, Champlain was enraged. He claimed that witnesses to these gatherings could verify that this was nonsense; livid, he outlined his view of the more likely problem: "the rascal had invented this piece of malice in order to keep back these girls whom, it was believed, he wished to debauch, as did other Frenchmen like himself "(VI:105).

Champlain's circuitous record of gossip included testimony that Hope and Charity had whispered to him that Marsolet had been sidling up to Hope and that he had already "asked her to go away with him, and had offered her a number of things to induce her to do so . . . . But she always refused and had even complained." According to Champlain, Hope and Charity defended their decision publicly to retain the family unit with a protest that "We have an affection for him [Champlain]; if we had not, we shouldn't wish to follow him to France" (VI:106). After all these entreaties, the case for the sibling damsels in distress was scrutinized by the English for any signs of weakness, and in the process, Commander Kirke lost his temper.

Getting nowhere with Louis Kirke and David Kirke, Champlain next turned to Thomas Kirke; thwarted there also, in desperation he even made an overture to the traitor Jacques Michel. Nothing worked; despairing, Champlain offered the English commander a bribe of nearly two years' salary in beaver pelts. It was pointless as the Kirkes had already grabbed the full inventory of pelts, and they commanded the oceans for the foreseeable future.

Humiliated at every turn, and swallowing whatever pride he had left, Champlain pleaded with Marsolet; after this overture, he reported being cast aside by a stunning act of duplicity: "Sir, you can believe what you like in this matter . . . when I serve a master, I must be faithful to him" (VI:116). Et tu, Brute! With this effrontery and other twists of the tale, it was not clear whether Marsolet was acting as the Admiral's pimp or if Admiral Kirke was performing the same service for Nicolas Marsolet. In all this, nothing was certain; months later, fair-weather friend Jacques Michel, in another spin, turned on his English commander, claiming that the English Admiral was the real instigator who had directed the kidnapping of the girls in the first place.

Now exasperated, and as a last resort, Champlain orchestrated a theatrical ploy to turn the tables, and this time the two girls, Hope and Charity, were part of the production. The precise location is not known; but as the curtain rose in the company of the English ensemble, the "poor girls, seeing there was no remedy left for them, began to grieve and to weep bitterly, so much so that one fell into a fever, and went for a long time without eating, calling Marsolet a dog, and a traitor, and saying, 'Since he saw that we would not yield to his desires, he has caused such distress that I can conceive of nothing like it short of death' " (VI:117). Act one, however, won no applause from this hostile English audience.

In the second act, the girls expanded the stratagem with a dramatic entrance to a dinner party hosted by the English commander for all the captains, including Marsolet. During the festivities, Hope, the older girl, suddenly interrupted the banquet and, to gain attention, she opened her presentation by "sighing." Egged on by the English, she confronted Marsolet in a face-to-face encounter and with a well-concocted salvo she blasted her tormentor: "You maliciously persevere in your falsehoods . . . [because] I would not yield to your foul desires." She was unrelenting: "My sorrow is so great that I shall have no rest until I unburden my anger . . . . Remember that, though I am only a girl, I will procure your death if I can . . . . If you come near me again, I will plunge my knife into your heart" (VI:117-20).

Unmoved, Marsolet scoffed, "You have studied that lesson pretty well." Charity was taunted by Marsolet in her turn: "Won't you say something to me?" She was ready for this and let him have it: "if I had your heart in my grasp, I would eat it more readily and with better courage than the meats on this table." During all this indigestion-making oration, Commander Kirke did nothing to relieve the situation. Champlain noted that as when Pharaoh was confronted by Moses for the release of the children of Israel, "nothing could move or soften the heart of General Kirke" (VI:120-21). This was a bitter blow for Champlain, and the children were never again mentioned.

In the final weeks of autumn, before the departure for England, another matter gnawed at whatever good-will might have been preserved between these adversaries. As a result of the conquest, religious rivalry moved to the forefront. For the first time, the English Protestants had the upper hand, and Catholics were forbidden to worship publicly.

At the end of this era, the only relief for the deadlocked enemies was a massive slaughter of wildlife. In a senseless rampage, Champlain and General Kirke on the hunt together managed to kill "more than twenty thousand" birds (VI:142). Even without war, these European intruders managed to vent their violence on the environment. With more than a season at an end for this year, it was time for both sides to quit this commerce and empire business and return to more peaceful pursuits in England and France.

CHAPTER TWENTY-SEVEN

Champlain in England and France: the Paper War: 1629-1632

"Champlain alone, among the men of his days, had sufficient patriotism and confidence in the future of the colony to maintain and hold aloft under great difficulties the lily banner of France."

Narcisse-Eutrope Dionne (1848–1917),
Samuel Champlain, 1905

IN SEPTEMBER OF 1629, THE PRISONER CHAMPLAIN WAS taken to Britain aboard the Vice-Admiral's vessel. It was a difficult trip, and en route eleven English sailors died of dysentery. On arrival at Plymouth, the Kirke brothers received news that was another blow: the war between England and France had been over for almost half a year. The seizure of Québec months after the signing of the peace treaty was therefore illegal and may even have been known by the Kirkes to have been so. At this loss, the English commander was "greatly angered." So was Champlain.

After sailing on to Dover, most of the French were released to seek their own passage homeward and everyone now sought a fresh purpose. Not so Champlain. The uprooted commander had other plans. Below the great white cliffs of Dover, after his compatriots had returned to France, he carefully penned a list of charges against the Kirkes. Instead of first returning to France and deferring to the central authority in Paris for further instruction, Champlain for the first time boldly took charge of a major political issue. He sent the French grievance directly to Monsieur Châteauneuf, the French ambassador in London, for immediate action. Invigorated by the challenge, the great warrior, now fifty-nine, was back in the battle fighting for the colonial foundation. His demands were simple enough — all property was to be restored, and at once.

Preparing for the forthcoming battle, in his last moody moments with the enemy, Champlain was escorted aboard Kirke's vessel to London and, within a week, the ten-cannon, one-hundred-ton English flyboat with its cargo of one angry Frenchman entered the Thames for anchorage at Gravesend. Champlain was ferried farther upriver on a smaller craft to arrive at the enemy citadel on October 29, 1629. Alone, on his quest for redress, the anxious colonial advocate wasted no time. The next day he was off to see Châteauneuf "to whom I related all the reasons for our voyage" (VI:146). Champlain provided a copy of the document of surrender when he made his verbal appeal and his latest cartographic endeavor, the largest survey he had ever made (fig. 40). Convinced, Châteauneuf quickly took up Champlain's standard and, after an audience with King Charles I of England, he reported news of progress. But after three weeks' effort, the French emissary was in a state of frustration, and was reduced to sending missives to the King's Council in Brittany as well as to Cardinal Richelieu in Paris.

It was no use, after five weeks of disappointment, "awaiting news from France all the time, and marking how little diligence they showed in sending anyone over, or in advising me of what they wanted done" (VI:149). Champlain, bereft of a relevant strategy by France, and accomplishing nothing in England, left London disgusted and empty-handed on November 30, 1629. In anger over this interlude, Champlain did not write even one syllable about the English capital in his journal.

Champlain had been ill-prepared for the diplomatic mission he had attempted in London. Although he was undoubtedly aware that King Charles was married to King Louis's sister, the Catholic Henrietta Maria, and he may even have known that the English monarch had sworn to protect Catholicism in the land, Champlain gave every indication that he had no knowledge beyond that. He did not seem to know that King Charles was also deeply embroiled in financial and political difficulties. To Champlain, time had been wasted and the timing could not have been worse.

On arriving in France, Champlain's only option was to go alone to the center of the cobweb, the court of King Louis. En route, he spent two days in Dieppe and two in Rouen, two great ports of commerce and information. For two years, Champlain had been forced to survive on a mixture of silence and propaganda, and now this hornet, woefully out of touch, was stinging mad.

For a start, he had yet to learn from the authorities the details concerning the restructuring of the corporation formed in 1627, which was called the Hundred Associates. In addition, he needed to understand the direction of the current political winds. This knowledge was particularly important where the de Caëns were concerned. Recently, it seemed, these survivors and plotters for power had again gained some commercial advantage. Émery de Caën was one who, during the first year of the English occupation, had been granted a license for fur trading on the St. Lawrence. But there was much about this that was uncertain; for while elder partner Guillaume de Caën had been ordered to spearhead the relief effort for Québec, the old proviso remained that the latter was not to go there himself. The penance for the psalm-singing business on the St. Lawrence was eternal. Even though seemingly almighty at times, the de Caëns were forever on a short royal leash.

Champlain completed his quest for useful information and then journeyed on to Paris, where he took up residence with his wife, Hélène. At this point, an unemployed but financially well-off Champlain embarked on the most dangerous trail of his career. During the coming months there were moments when his conduct bordered on treason: "But what is the explanation of their [the English] having taken possession of our places so easily? It is because the King has not, up to the present, attached importance to these matters" (VI:149). It was not unlikely that this outburst when published would be the shot that finally ended any prospect of personal recognition.

By January of 1630, when Champlain picked up the prodding iron he had left in London and used it to poke at the center in Paris, there was no evidence that he was aware his beloved New France had become a plaything in a royal dowry dispute between Charles of England and Louis of France. Indeed, there is no evidence that he was ever aware of this fact. Champlain saw the colonial defeat in simplistic terms. He thought that it could be remedied if a diplomatic team pressed for English recognition of the legal rights of France. At first there was some indication of success, for in the spring a royal edict staking the French claim was issued by the King. The royal action appeared to be a breakthrough even if somehow, in the drafting of the document, a description of Acadia had been left out. But nothing came of this maneuvering as France was truly enveloped in a malaise of other priorities, none of which included thoughts about the overseas colony.

Persisting with his own assessment, Champlain believed the loss of direction was owing to "the distraction of His Majesty's attention in

Italy," and that for this reason "no reply was given, awaiting the end of these wars" (VI:171).

He was wrong. The piccolo Italian affair was not the problem. The English and French kings were at loggerheads over a debt. King Charles of England was owed 400,000 crowns by King Louis of France; it was the balance of the dowry settlement due for his marriage to King Louis's sister, Henrietta Maria. Parliament had refused to provide him with funds and the British monarch needed the money.

And there were additional grievances wearing away at the royal relationship between the two Kings. There was no love lost between Charles and Henrietta. Shortly after their marriage in 1625, there was one incident reported where Charles dragged Henrietta into a room and, in a struggle to attract attention, Henrietta had smashed her hand through a window. In anger King Charles kicked Henrietta's entire retinue of French servants out of England, leaving her isolated in a strange country. The relationship between England and France was not much happier than this royal marriage of convenience.

There were, however, fleeting moments of promise for the colonial advocate. In one move, after an overture from the Company directors, King Louis promised naval assistance to effect the restoration, and all seemed well enough when on April 14, 1630, a royal directive was issued to send a fleet of six vessels to retake the conquered lands. Champlain was restored to his position as Lieutenant; but, in an unexplained turnabout, Richelieu and the King reversed the decision to proceed with the restoration. In the ancien régime such intrigue was routine.

Seemingly blocked at every turn, Champlain reverted to his practised role of promoter, and he conducted his final crusade like a marketing director using all his verbal, written, and graphic skills. Included in this tour de force were all manner of briefs, journals, and letters to the nobility, and for one last grand effort, a magnificent map (fig. 40) — no doubt a more polished version of the same he had handed over to the French ambassador in London a year earlier.

Champlain fervently gathered whatever useful information he could, such as current data concerning the captured settlement. One particularly interesting piece of news came to his attention. He learned that in the fall of 1630, the Kirke brothers had returned to London with a booty of furs worth 300,000 livres, the largest booty ever reported to date. Moreover, news came from overseas that in spite of a good beginning at the business of managing the settlement, the

English had proved that, up to this point at least, they were no more interested in western colonization along the St. Lawrence River than Champlain's superiors had been — and for the same reason: seasonal investment for quick profit was more attractive. The habitation was in disrepair, with the only noticeable sign of change being makeshift alterations. Champlain also learned that the fort had been struck by lightning, which had killed two dogs and blown up its chimney. There was much pain for the profit gained: "fourteen died of want and misery during the winter, and others had been quite ill. No building or clearing of ground had been done since our departure . . ." (VI:183).

While waiting out the resolution of this title dispute between nations, Champlain prepared the last and largest of his journals, *Les Voyages*, which was published in 1632. In this work, which covered events from July of 1618, there was a repeat of the events already recorded in the two previously published works, covering the years from 1604 to 1618. Although the reworking was largely repetitious, there were many subtle changes and curious omissions, such as the great trek of the Récollets into Huronia. In the revised version, the Jesuit contribution was emphasized, and for this, there was no explanation. Although the Jesuits have been accused of tampering with Champlain's manuscript, there is no evidence to support this theory. As it stands, Champlain alone must be held accountable.

The main thrust of this publication is the documentation of the saga from 1620 to 1632, and this is the major source of information about New France during this period. The "1632," as it is affectionately known, includes a bonus: in addition to the spectacular summary map to which we have been referring, there is a valuable supplement included — the *Treatise on SEAMANSHIP and the Duty of a Good Seaman*.

The *Treatise* is easily Champlain's most important literary achievement. The account is full of confidence, life, and buoyancy of language not found elsewhere in his writings. Yet, Champlain's contribution as a geographer, naturalist, and cartographer is completely ignored in the annals of French scientific achievement for the period. Recognition is long overdue, and the *Treatise* is a good place to start.

In this little guide, Champlain outlines the essentials of sound management at sea. To be a "good seaman" — from the lowest rank to a fleet admiral — there is much to learn: the appropriate attitude and table and other manners are covered; "[the seaman] should not be

40 Champlain's Summary Survey Map of 1632 (date of publication)
Carte de la nouvelle france, augmentée depuis la dernière . . .

Champlain's map of 1632 is the last he made and it is an overdue and welcome surprise for at that time he had published no summary surveys since those of 1612 and 1613 (figs. 29, 31, and 32). Apart from the unpublished single sheet proof map of 1616 (fig. 37), he had added nothing to the cartographic record for more than two decades.

Unlike any of the others, however, this final chart is a political statement. It not only shows the impressive extent of the French empire in America, but locates all the known settlements from the period 1603 to 1629 to which the French had ever had title or any interest. It was probable also that this was the same chart, or some later version of the one, that was presented to the French Ambassador, Monsieur Châteauneuf in London, as a "map of the country to show to the English the explorations we had made and the possession we had taken in that country of New France before the dainty about his eating, nor about his drink"; and he needs a "strong voice" to give orders (VI:258-59). One must be "affable in conversation," but "not too ready to talk with his fellows," and "courteous to defeated enemies" (VI:260-61). Full of common sense and insight, the book includes, for example, strict health rules where one must "take great pains when there are sailors and soldiers [aboard] to make them keep as clean as possible . . . [and] often have the space between decks cleansed of the filth that accumulates there; for it frequently causes a stench and gives rise to deadly disease, as if it were an infectious plague" (VI:266). The student of ocean matters is admonished that it is important to include "good surgeons who are not ignoramuses, like most of those who go to sea" (VI:267). And finally, to ensure a state of well-being, there is a sermon that one must "take good care to have wholesome food and drink" (VI:264).

Finally, personal information about the author is included. From the *Treatise* it is learned that Champlain had spent thirty-eight years on voyages at sea, and he indirectly confirms that he is a competent artist, as well as a cartographer. As a proficient seaman, one "must know how to draw . . . an accurate chart, on which it is sometimes necessary to depict many particulars in the countries or regions, such as representing mountains . . . the birds, animals, fishes, trees, plants, roots, medicinal herbs, fruits, dress of the peoples of all the foreign countries, and everything worthy of remark that may be seen or met with" (VI:284). Champlain had not wasted his time in exile. The *Treatise* was the first of such professional manuals in France and was published centuries ahead of any other such contribution.

English had entered it, they having only followed in our tracks."

To emphasize French title claims, Champlain takes pains to place flags on French settlements and to emphasize French discovery and naming. This time he emphasized a vast bustling empire of Indian settlements over his earlier, more whimsical illustrations. The chart includes lakes discovered and others known only through second-hand information. For the first time, too, La Ralde's Miscou Island naval base and the Gaspé Peninsula were shown in detail. As a statement of proprietary interest, all the ports on the New England coast are labelled with the names originally assigned them by the French, regardless of the English occupation which in some areas had entered a third decade.

To fully appreciate the minute detail of the chart, the extensive legend that accompanies the original can be found in Vol. VI of the Champlain works, p. 224, entitled "Table for Identification of Noteworthy Places on this Map."

CHAPTER TWENTY-EIGHT

The Rescue of New France and the Death of Champlain: 1632-1635

"Samuel de Champlain — artist, writer, explorer and mapmaker who accurately charted the northeast coast from Newfoundland to Cape Cod — did more than anyone else to further France's territorial ambitions."

The National Geographic, February 1985

CHAMPLAIN ASSUMED THAT SHORTLY AFTER THE signing of the Treaty of Saint-Germain-en-Laye on March 29, 1632, and with the Sieur de Razilly, the Governor of Acadia, now nominated as his successor, New France would be restored to her rightful owners. Free at last in retirement to put the finishing touches on his final work for publication, *Les Voyages* (1632), he had nothing to add but a prayer: "There is no doubt that, with God's help, great progress can be made in the future, since everything will be controlled by persons of the competence of the Sieur Commander de Razilly. God there will be served and worshipped, Whom I pray to make to prosper the good and laudable intentions of that officer, as also those of the New Company, which, I may add is not discouraged by past losses, having the support of his Majesty and of my said Lord Cardinal" (VI:220).

But Champlain's work was not yet completed. He was needed still; for the moment, those in authority in Paris were determined to move along with the next generation of players, just as they had in the previous year 1630 when Émery de Caën was given the opportunity to challenge English control of trade on the St. Lawrence. Even though de Caën had failed, many moves were yet to be made before Champlain would be called back into service. For the time being, the retired lieutenant had outworn his welcome in the halls of power.

Unlike Champlain, the Kirkes of England were not so easily dislodged. First, they ignored the Treaty of Susa in 1629, captured and kept the colony, and were not persuaded otherwise by the new treaty of March 29, 1632. For, in the interim between the year 1628 when they had made their first attack on Tadoussac and the current year of their occupation, they were granted a patent from King Charles to join forces with Sir William Alexander and others for the purpose of creating a new enterprise — to be called "The Company of Adventurers to Canada." This strategy with royal endorsement envisaged the creation of an Anglo-Scottish colony centered at Tadoussac with all associates having the right to trade freely on the St. Lawrence and share the use of all harbors. The Kirkes intended to stay, and the vacillation of the French in the past was the precedent for their holding on.

For the French, the de Caëns too were made of stubborn stuff, and although Émery de Caën was the forward arm of the family operation on the frontier, Guillaume de Caën was busily at work behind the scenes in France. Through a series of moves, he managed to secure a new vessel for his nephew, operating funds for general use, and an exclusive license as compensation for the de Caën losses that resulted from the French military failures on the St. Lawrence.

To implement the terms of the new treaty, it was the de Caëns that were expected to restore the colony for the entire 1632 trading season. Informed more than three weeks in advance of the agreement, on March 4, Émery de Caën was designated to take up the position of interim commander at the settlement prior to Razilly's permanent appointment. However, it took him over three months to show up at Québec. When he arrived on July 6 in mid-season, the Kirkes seized the opportunity to test him and balked at the transfer. Twice before the Kirkes had dealt with de Caën: once they had humiliated him at La Malbaie in 1629 and the second time rebuffed him at Québec in 1630. This time, the Kirkes neatly managed to squeeze in another week of trading before yielding the colony on July 13, 1632.

The event that brought Champlain out of retirement was Richelieu's appointment of Captain Isaac de Razilly as the new commander of the colony on April 20, 1632. The nomination backfired when Razilly, a widely respected naval officer, openly challenged the First

Minister in one of the rare tributes ever paid to Champlain: "because he [Champlain] is more competent in colonial affairs." One suspects that only as a last resort was Champlain brought back into service; but in the interim, Émery de Caën sat in residence at Québec as the acting commandant for the next ten months. It was not a happy situation. The interim commander was not motivated to initiate the badly needed restoration of the settlement; as before, Émery de Caën was driven by commercial concerns such as the opportunity to harvest the fall and spring trade, prior to relinquishing his command to the more permanent administration.

Rigged out for the rescue mission, sixty-three-year-old Samuel de Champlain sailed on his final voyage to Québec on March 23, 1633. He arrived without fanfare on May 23, 1633, to accept the keys of the fortress from a custodian who had received them the day before from de Caën. The latter had left without greeting the victorious leader. The longstanding grudge between Champlain and the de Caëns dated back more than a decade, and was as preserved and tightly packed as gutted and salted sardines for a long voyage.

Just like his previous return to the colony after a six years' absence, Champlain found everything in a shambles. On this occasion, he had been away for twice as long and the property had been in the hands of the enemy for more than three years. Moreover, for ten more months Émery de Caën had done nothing to repair the damage. Burned, pillaged, and struck by lightning, the ruined fortress would have to be rebuilt, and, as before, it was vital to restore morale. As a signal of the new era, the chapel Notre Dame de la Récouvrance was constructed.

By spring, Champlain learned that nothing remained of the former Indian alliances, and the ever-present threat of attack from the Iroquois was his main consideration for all planning. There was much to be done to recover the three decades of colonial spadework already invested. Starting with security matters, a cannon was placed at what is now Sorel at the mouth of the river of the Iroquois (Richelieu) to prevent Iroquois warriors from coming upstream from Lake Champlain. With trouble brewing elsewhere, the colonizers commenced building a new fortress at Trois-Rivières. It was a powder keg in which even seemingly harmless events could prove to be explosive.

In one incident, while practising the tossing and handling of drumsticks on parade, a French drummer boy accidentally hit an Indian in the face and drew blood. Overreacting in the belief of defending good relations with the Indians, Champlain had the show-off flogged; this prompted the Indians to rush to the aid of the drummer. As ever in the case of crime and punishment, the Indians and the French were out of sync. The cultural gap remained a gulf of misunderstanding.

In another observation of these latter years, Father Le Jeune, the Québec Superior, wrote to Paris:

> I saw a savage dragging his mother behind him over the snow. The coaches and wagons of this country are sledges made of bark or wood, the horses are the men who draw them. Now this poor old woman was tied upon one of these sleighs; and her son, being unable conveniently to take her down by the common path of a mountain which borders the river along which he was going, let her roll down the steepest place to the bottom, and then went by another route to find her. As I could not bear this act of impiety, I said so to some of the Indians who were near me. They answered: "What would you have him do with her? She is going to die anyway."

As part of this final phase of the epic, there was a fifth murder to deal with; but this time everyone was spared a rehash of the arguments over capital punishment when, obligingly, the suspect slipped away before the trial. For one last time, as if on cue, the Indians suggested compensation by offering children as gifts; but this time the negative response was sharp and final. From the only source now available concerning this event, *Le Mercure françois*, Champlain was reported to have remarked: "These innocent children cannot carry the guilt of the murderer. I desire no further hostage than the guilty one to be in my hands — a perfidious traitor, with no more courage or friendship than a tiger."

Fortuitously, in the midst of all the restoration happenings, there was a break in the pattern. In midsummer, two months after Champlain's receipt of the keys of the fortress, hundreds of Hurons led by many great and lesser sagamores arrived at Québec full of pomp and the promise of better times ahead. For Champlain their gathering was a déjà vu of the great conference of 1603 — only this time it was the Hurons and not the Algonquins spearheading the concept of a grand alliance. Much had changed. The original trust was gone, and even with this great show of strength, the Hurons, it seemed, were skittish and still smarting over being abandoned to the English in 1629. And the French, despite many promises, enticed by their lust for trade with only a marginal benefit in colonial development at the expense of too many battles, were equally guarded. The conference failed even though it was the same old bargain on the table — the right to settle and proselytize in exchange for military aid. This time, Champlain's insistence that the Jesuits be allowed to settle once more in Huronia was not accepted as it had been in 1615. For the moment, he had outworn his welcome and the wounds of the past cut deep. It was a time for quiet diplomacy, fresh ideas, and patience, but for Champlain, now set in his ways, time was running out.

After three decades of colonial effort, neither the Indians nor the French were in control in religious matters; even after all these years, the Indian sorcerers and witch doctors held their hypnotic sway over their masses with no less authority in spite of a determined priesthood of Christian shamans loosed in a wilderness of souls. A report in the *Jesuit Relations* from Father Le Jeune to Paris in 1634 described the missionary work as "very encouraging" yet was hardly convincing on the basis of the facts cited. Of the seven baptisms on record for that year, six were for the dying and four out of seven were for minors or infant children. For the Indian, the curious Christian baptism ritual with water was only a last resort in the hopes of a cure for a litany of ailments.

Then, too, as for rumors about the white man adopting Indian ways and succumbing to all manner of degradation, for the early decades of the seventeenth century there was little evidence from which to draw any conclusions. The alleged cavortings of Étienne Brûlé and Nicolas Marsolet undoubtedly have some basis in fact; but these examples were no indication of a trend, and it must be admitted that much of our information on the subject is not without bias. Thus, in 1636, the year after Champlain's death, Father Le Jeune could with a clear conscience report to Paris that "debauchery, dissoluteness and intrigues are not yet current here."

Toward the end of Champlain's last command, the problem of securing a meaningful commitment from France remained the priority. In one final flurry of penmanship in a curious twenty-five-page pamphlet, undated, unsigned, and yet printed and seemingly intended for eventual publication, he wrote a last-ditch appeal to King Louis. It was perhaps even drafted during the "paper war," and written before Champlain's last departure for Québec; but in this piece there was little to inflame those who had already been assaulted by the previous presentations. Only one observation was new — a reminder of the age.

Now at the end of his voyages, the author claimed to have found another strange bird, even more unusual than the big yellow specimen reported on the hunt in 1615 in Ontario (fig. 35). Acknowledged as rare by comparison, this added alien to natural science was described as very large, about the size of a chicken, with gray feathers and a white undercoat, and this time it was a bird of prey — not a parrot — and it was reported to have one foot formed as a talon for catching fish and the other webbed like a duck. One can well imagine the guffaws from Richelieu and King Louis dining at Fontainebleau, or from a vengeful Marc Lescarbot rising from retirement to the bait. Yet this oddity was well within the scientific reasoning of the ancien régime. For example, one popular remedy for dysentery, which remained in vogue for two centuries — first published in 1564 in a guidebook — instructed that "one should take the dung of a dog which has gnawed nothing but bones for three days, dry and powder it and give the powder to the patient twice a day, together with the milk in which you have quenched several river pebbles heated up in a fire." Even for the more simple discomforts of life in the ancien régime, the remedies were breathtaking and bizarre: "For smelly feet, put iron dross in your shoes . . . for a tooth-ache wear a man's tooth wrapped in taffeta or a pierced bean containing a louse around one's neck." It was an age in which medical texts promoted "frequent bleeding and induced vomiting."

There were, however, no such mystical meanderings in the two letters written by Champlain at Québec to Richelieu, dated August 15, 1633, and the follow-up letter a year later on August 18, 1634. These were to be the last words on record from him, and both epistles were short and pointed. The first contained a request for 120 armed men. With these forces and a reconstructed alliance, bringing together some two or three thousand Indian comrades, Champlain believed the Iroquois could at last be brought to heel.

A year later, however, having had no reply to his first letter, he repeated his request, and this second time a little flattery was added, with a notation for posterity that the repairs of the damage done by the English during the occupation were completed. Again, there is no evidence of a reply, and with this firm silence all avenues of redress were closed. At the end of his influence, Champlain had been reduced to one reporting letter a year, and, with these unanswered, he was abandoned; on his part, there was no point in further initiative. It was best he not know the final humiliation.

In France, while Champlain was still in charge at Québec, Charles Huault de Montmagny (c.1583–c.1653) was nominated as the Governor of New France, a title never granted to the very champion who founded the colony and clearly had earned the encomium. For the officer of his country who logged nearly forty years in the service of his nation, there was nothing. But perhaps he was no longer concerned, for he was probably aware that by this time he had managed the impossible; for half a lifetime, and almost single-handedly, he had checkmated one of the world's most powerful nations into a staggering investment: the building and support of a seedling colony with great promise. It was a testament to perseverance.

In the year before his death, there was one last vignette of Champlain in full command. Writing to Paris from Québec "on the good conduct of the French," the Superior of the Jesuit mission, Father Le Jeune had the perfect tribute to close the Champlain legacy:

> We have passed this year in great peace and on very good terms with our French. The wise conduct and prudence of Monsieur de Champlain, Governor of Kebec of the river Saint Lawrence, who honours us with his good will, holding everyone in the path of duty, has caused our words and preaching to be well received . . . . The fort has seemed like a well-ordered Academy. Monsieur de Champlain has some one read at his table, in the morning from some good historian, and in the evening from the lives of the Saints.

During October of 1635, Champlain collapsed at age sixty-five. He was the victim of a stroke; he was never again mobile. Aware that the end was at hand, on November 17, with Father Lalemant as a witness, Champlain signed his last will and testament. It provided funds for the Jesuit mission at Québec and monies to buy furniture for the newly built Notre Dame de la Récouvrance. Two hospitals were also named as beneficiaries, and there were additional monies set aside for the poor. All his personal effects were passed on as mementoes; Hélène was to have his religious amulet, the Agnus Dei, a gray fox skin and a gold diamond ring — the latter thought by some to be made of the clear quartz crystals from the hills around the Québec citadel, and mistaken earlier by Cartier for the more precious diamonds. There were ten other recipients, including Champlain's valet, Poisson, who was to have his clothing. Father Lalemant, the witness to the will, was to receive a painting of the crucifixion along with the special tools of the navigation trade, a compass and an astrolabe. This was a caring disposition that touched many, but this was also a distribution that would be, in a small measure, successfully contested later and adjusted to accommodate the claim of a distant cousin peeved with the testament.

On Christmas Day in the year 1635, after receiving the last rites of the church, in a community of no more than two hundred, Samuel de Champlain died at Québec, the citadel of Canada's foundation as a nation and the foundation home of the French fact in America.

No biographer can surpass Father Le Jeune's description of the end:

> On the twenty-fifth day of December, the day of the birth of our Saviour upon earth, Monsieur de Champlain, our Governor, was reborn in heaven; at least, we can say that his death was full of blessings . . . . What tears he shed! How ardent became his zeal for the service of God! How great was his love for the families here! . . . He was not taken unawares in the account which he had to render unto God, for he had long ago prepared a general Confession of his whole life, which he made with great contrition to Father Lalemant, whom he honoured with his friendship. The Father comforted him throughout his sickness, which lasted two months and a half, and did not leave him until his death. He had a very honourable burial, the funeral procession being formed of the People, the Soldiers, the Captains, and the Churchmen. Father Lalemant officiated at this burial, and I was charged with the funeral Oration, for which I did not lack material. Those whom he left behind have reason to be well satisfied with him.

Today, Champlain's life stands as an unbroken act of faith. In this iconoclastic age the light from this beacon is a welcome ray of hope.

"Happy he who like Ulysses has made a great voyage."

Joachim Du Bellay (1522–1560), *Les Regrets*

Exeunt

Anadabijou, Chief of the Montagnais
After the Tadoussac conference in 1603, there are only two further references to the Grand Sagamore. The first, in 1611, refers to one son who received a consolation present from a party of Algonquins who had recently learned of Anadabijou's death. The second reference quotes his son Chief Miristou who apparently remarked years later that his father had "maintained peace among the other nations and the French."

Aubry, Nicolas
The priest from Paris who was temporarily lost in the wilderness of Nova Scotia returned to France shortly thereafter, and was apparently still alive in 1611.

Boullé, Eustache
After the English conquest and his repatriation to France in 1629, Champlain's brother-in-law took up residence in Italy for ten years where he converted to Catholicism from the Huguenot persuasion, took holy orders, and became a priest. Hélène Champlain took a personal interest in his career and ensured that he had a generous pension. The year and details of his death are not known.

Brûlé, Étienne
Having lived among the Hurons for two decades, Étienne Brûlé was murdered and then reportedly eaten by the Indians in 1633. There are more controversies and speculations than facts concerning the life of Étienne Brûlé. First there were doubts as to whether or not he was the first interpreter sent into the wilderness by Champlain, and numerous questions surround almost every recorded episode of his life thereafter, including his role with the English raiders.

Caën, Guillaume de
This elder cousin and leader of the de Caën interests continued as a commercial activist long after Champlain's death. In 1640, in compensation for losses at Québec during the English conquest, he was given five uninhabited Caribbean islands and he was granted the title of

"Baron of the Bahamas." By way of explanation, it has been suggested by some historians that to engineer this deal Guillaume the Huguenot, "outlawed" and censured for so long over the psalm-singing business, finally became a Catholic. In 1643 he successfully sued the Company of One Hundred Associates for a huge sum to reimburse him for the 9,000 beaver skins lost during the English occupation of Québec. But long before this de Caën was in some way involved in other litigation or compensation. In 1627, Hélène Champlain was forced in her turn to sue de Caën for the funds owed to her husband. There is no record of de Caën's birth or death.

Champlain, Hélène

After many years of dealing with Champlain's business affairs, his widow took holy orders in 1645 and became an Ursuline nun, Sister Hélène de Saint-Augustin. High-spirited and fiercely independent, she finally left the Faubourg convent and was authorized to found a nunnery in the town of Meaux near Paris. She died on December 20, 1654.

Chomina, Chief of the Montagnais Indians of Tadoussac

After the English conquest in 1629, nothing further is known about this friend of the settlers.

Darontal, Chief of the Hurons

After his visit to Québec in 1616, Darontal may have settled in the vicinity of Montréal. Champlain had promised to support his move there as proof of Darontal's idea that the Indians and French could live in harmony. Gabriel Sagard reports that as late as 1624, Darontal was still the great Chief of the Hurons.

Erouachy, Montagnais Chief of the Tadoussac District

There is no further record about this gallivanting native leader after the conquest of Québec by the English in 1629.

Henry III, King of France

In 1589 when Champlain was twenty-two years old, Henry III, the king who had done much to foster the Wars of Religion, was stabbed to death at the age of 38 by the fanatical friar Jacques Clément.

Henry IV, King of France

Like his predecessor, Henry III, Champlain's lone royal supporter was also murdered. In 1610, the religious fanatic François Ravaillac seized an opportunity during traffic congestion in Paris to invade the royal coach near the Palace of the Louvre and stabbed the King twice with a long knife. Beloved by his people, the King who reputedly had had fifty-six mistresses and still time enough to be concerned that there be a "chicken in every pot" in the land was eventually honored by the people of France with the apellation Henry the Great.

Iroquet, Chief of the Algonquins

In his journal record for 1623–1624, Gabriel Sagard offered a final familiar note on this giant. He told of a report that Iroquet and twenty of his men bagged 500 beaver in the Neutral country, but could not be persuaded to divulge the route and location. This was the same Indian policy of protectionism evident throughout the saga.

Kirke, Sir David

Following his conquest of Québec in 1629, David Kirke was knighted by King Charles I of England in 1633 for services rendered to his country during the Québec affair. In 1639, Sir David was appointed the first Governor of Newfoundland. After fifteen more years of a checkered career of local politics, fights with foreign fishermen, charges of tax evasion, and a vicious lawsuit, Sir David died in a debtors' prison in 1654.

Le Caron, Father Joseph

After returning to France in 1625, the enthusiastic Father led a spirited attack against the Montmorency Company whose business interests conflicted with church progress. After returning again to Québec and later after the conquest in 1629, Le Caron and his Récollet companions returned to France. Coincidentally, Le Caron, superior of the convent, died at age forty-six on exactly the same day that New France was finally legally wrested from the English in 1632.

Lescarbot, Marc

After his farewell to Acadia in 1607, Lescarbot returned to France where he led a stormy life as a man of law and letters. In 1609, his plans for marriage eroded into a legal action for the return of the engagement ring. In 1619, at nearly fifty years of age, Lescarbot married a widow whose only claim to fame seems to have been a lifetime of lawsuits in order to gain and secure title and possession to her properties. In 1642, this talented curmudgeon finally managed through death "to flee a corrupt world."

Louis XIII, King of France
A suspected homosexual and in his youth described as foul-mouthed
and quick-tempered; a man who, according to Richelieu, was guilty of
"slovenliness and disorder" in later life and a monarch with whom it
was necessary to speak with "words of silk," King Louis also earned an
assessment from the Cardinal that has survived the ages for frequent
quotation: "He wanted to be ruled, yet chafed when he was." After a
stormy unhappy life and years of ill health, Louis died in 1643 of
tuberculosis.

Marsolet, Nicolas
Although most of the settlers either chose to be, or ended up being,
repatriated to France after the English conquest of 1629, Marsolet
stayed on at Québec as an interpreter for the English, but ever swift to
join the winning side, again switched allegiance back to France when
the French returned in 1632. During his lifetime in the colony, he
operated a trading vessel and owned a shop at Québec where he was
accused of ripping off the customers with high prices for wine. The
"Little King of Tadoussac" fathered ten children and I was fortunate
enough to confer on genealogical research with one of his descen-
dants. Nicolas Marsolet, a colorful founding father of the Québec
community, died in his late seventies at Québec City on May 15, 1677.

Marie de Médicis, Queen of France
She was described by a contemporary as "one of the great beauties of
the century," with a bosom "beautiful and well shaped" and a mouth
that "supplemented the devastation caused by her eyes," although
Cardinal Richelieu was one who escaped the spell of her many
charms. As first Minister of the Crown serving King Louis, he ensured
that the former Regent was abandoned and then banished. Deserted,
the Queen fled to Brussels in the Spanish Netherlands in 1631, where
she died destitute in 1642.

Monts, The Sieur Pierre de
After the colony's formative years and primarily the voyages, little is
known of this great financial and moral backer of colonial develop-

ment. He seems to fade from the picture from 1617 onward. He died in 1628 and Lescarbot's tribute in his "Adieu à la France" (1606) provides a suitable epitaph for his tombstone.

"De Monts, it is you whose high courage has traced the way for such a great undertaking, and for this reason, in spite of the attack of time, the leaf of your fame will grow green in an eternal spring."

Pontgravé, Captain François

Nor is anything known of the final days of Champlain's most loyal comrade. One can imagine that it was very difficult for him to learn of the conquest in 1629 as he endured another painful bout of gout, drinking his "liquor straight." One hopes that on repatriation to France, he found solace and comfort in a reunion with his much younger wife Christine, who was still alive in 1677.

Poutrincourt, The Sieur Jean de

After the retreat from Acadia in 1607, Poutrincourt once again took up residence at Port-Royal in 1610. At that time he undertook an ambitious agricultural and missionary program and for a decade, this hero of New France worked hard to create an Acadian and Catholic empire. Unfortunately, his efforts ended in personal bankruptcy and a prison term. In 1615 at the age of fifty-eight, Poutrincourt was buried at Champagne. There is a monument erected in this community to honor his memory.

Prévert, The Sieur Jean de

Only a note to finish the life of storyteller Jean de Prévert. Having spun tales of Gougou monsters and persuaded everyone into chasing all over Acadia for the great copper bonanza, Prévert fades like a magician from the scene after 1607, but in one last puff of smoke, Prévert acknowledged the notarized receipt of a payment of cash in advance for a guarantee to deliver 200 beaver skins to a Paris merchant in 1609. One hopes that his performance on this matter was better honored than were his promises of wealth in Acadia, which likely did much to discredit colonial support. Long before his meeting with Champlain in 1603, Prévert had married Françoise Richomme of Saint-Malo in 1591. On his death Jean de Prévert was buried in that same seaport in 1622.

Razilly, Captain Isaac de
Having not only rejected Richelieu's offer to assume Champlain's position in 1632, Isaac de Razilly stands as one of the few real heroes in the early epic years of the colony, cast in the same mold as de Monts, Pontgravé, Poutrincourt and Champlain, all of whom promoted permanent settlement in New France and forged successful trading alliances there. Champlain's praise for his colleague was unqualified; he was "prudent, wise, laborious, and impelled by a holy desire to increase the glory of God, and carry his courage to the country of New France." After a brief tenure as a governor in Acadia, the noteworthy officer died in the same year as Champlain, 1635.

Richelieu, Cardinal
The first minister of the land under Louis XIII, after an amazing career as churchman, soldier, statesman, politician extraordinaire, and cultural arbitrator of all that mattered in France, who even on his deathbed was dictating five proposals as to how the King should behave after a year of ill health, died in 1642.

Sully, Maximilien de Béthune, duc de,
The first Minister of France under King Henry IV, after a dutiful and constructive career as the King's administrator and architect of economic reform, after a brief stint in the service of the Regent, Marie de Médicis, was forced to retire in 1611. For the next twenty-seven years he devoted his life to the writing and publishing of his remarkable *Memoires*, an exposé of King Henry's reign and the economic activity of the period. Honored with the position of Marshal of France in 1634, Sully, the man who was skeptical of New France, died at Villebon in 1641.

The French Language in the Seventeenth Century

WHEN CHAMPLAIN FOUNDED QUÉBEC IN 1608, many of the guardians of French society were involved in a vigorous struggle for control of the French language. It was during this period that the French language was beginning to take its place as the engine that was to drive French culture.

At the time, Paris, the nation's center, bristled with institutions designed to protect and promote the welfare of the language. One of these that thrived during the early years of French colonial development was the Pléiade. The Pléiade was a consortium of poets who preached exhaustively on the need to reform French along classical lines. The wordsmiths of the period were a part of the group that urged reform and they wrote voluminous briefs in defense of French. These craftsmen wallowed in erudition and puritanical extremes and, even though they were ridiculed for their slavish devotion to pedantry and trivia, the Pléiade was the institutional backbone for French cultural survival in the sixteenth century.

By contrast, the exact opposite was occurring in England. While the French intelligentsia struggled for "purity" of language, Shakespeare wrote in *Love's Labour's Lost*, "They have been at a great feast of languages and stolen the scraps." These two quite different attitudes toward language held by the two colonizing nations are relevant to the history of the language conflict in Canada today.

Today, the philosophy of the Pléiade survives in Canada. In December 1983, Pierre Trudeau, then Prime Minister, accepted the Ordre de la Pléiade, an honor awarded by an international association of French-speaking parliamentarians.

In 1618, a new group concerned with language appeared in Paris. This group owed its existence to Catherine Rambouillet, the widow of a prominent noble. Madame Rambouillet turned her attentions from the grand château that bore her family name to her lavish townhouse in Paris. This she converted into a prestigious social club with a broad membership from the arts community. Here poets, grammarians, social wits, and the like gathered to banter. The Rambouillet salon with its bright decor, checkered floors, and magnificent tapestries became a center of fine conversation and spirited debate, where the participants were invited to share their best *bons mots*. In this salon one spoke not of sore feet, but of the "dear suffering ones," and rain was called "the third element descending." This was also the year in which Champlain was beset with intrigues for the survival of the colony, and the year before which he published his 1613 correspondence to King Louis, calling for the use of the French language in the seduction of North America. For the geographically vulnerable French, further fragmented by war and religious differences, language was no trifling matter.

Toward the end of the Champlain era, the politically motivated Cardinal Richelieu determined in 1630 that language and literature should be wards of the state. In 1634, with some forty individuals, he formalized a secret society initiated earlier into the Académie Française. Richelieu's men constituted a Spartan assembly of literary censors and language advocates who discouraged innovation and other forms of unbridled creativity. Under the Cardinal, who was also Champlain's commander-in-chief, all the arts in the homeland were now vetted to reflect political, spiritual and philosophical purity. For over three centuries this institution thrived as a powerful body of language inquisition. Caprice and whim often governed where grammarians, drama critics, and censors of all sorts dissected the published material of the day. Even René Descartes was excluded from this select circle, as was the nation's leading dramatist Pierre Corneille, whose classic work *Le Cid*, was deemed unworthy of acceptance by the state. Although French at this time was the national tongue and had been since the thirteenth century, the language conquest of the country was far from complete, and this was reflected by many writers of the ancien régime. Joachim Du Bellay (1522–1560), a noted member of the Pléiade, wrote a defense of the French language. Guillaume du Vair (1556–1622) wrote a treatise on the eloquence of French, and François de Malherbe (1555–1628), the best-known poet of the land, was so deeply engrossed as a word swordsman that when he heard a language infraction while he was on his deathbed, he was so roused that he reprimanded his nurse! In addition to writers there was a roster of activist grammarians, such as Claude Vaugelas (1585-1650) and Vincent Voiture (1597-1648) all ready to defend and promote French on any occasion. In 1609, Marc Lescarbot (see Chapter Nine) mocked Champlain as much for his want of language skills as for the limits of his geographic accomplishment. Champlain's period of colonial development was the same period in which the French initiated their most relentless effort: the business of language conservation, purification, cultivation, and promotion.

For those who might think such history irrelevant, Pulitzer-Prize winner De Gramont sums up for the present generation: "French . . . is carefully tended and protected from improprieties like the most delicate orchid, and it is sent to proselytize through the world like a sturdy pilgrim." After more than three hundred and fifty years, not a year passes without the international press reporting on the progress, or lack thereof, of the Académie Française's efforts to complete the ninth edition of the standard French dictionary. Richelieu's guardians are alive and well. Even though they could only advise completion as far as the letter "A" in 1986, those who would scoff should also note this institution's caveat: "Many will smile at the slowness of the work . . . [but] one should not laugh at the care we have taken. This is a very serious matter."

APPENDIX II

The Testament of Guillermo Elena

IN 1975, THE PUBLIC ARCHIVES OF CANADA ACQUIRED an extremely important document from the Archivo Historico Provincial in Cádiz, Spain. The information in it casts an entirely new light on Samuel de Champlain for it reveals a fact previously unknown: Champlain was a wealthy man who could comfortably afford to devote his life to colonial development. Indeed it is reasonable to assume there were times when he used his own funds to support colonial development activities. The story of this Spanish document and its contents are now an intrinsic part of the Champlain saga.

Ordinarily, this important document should have been included in the Public Archives of Canada's Centennial project of 1967: *Champlain et son époque, Volume I*, a collection of papers relevant to the Champlain saga from 1560 to 1622.

In early 1984, I was notified about an affidavit by Victorin Chabot, then Chief of the French Archives Section of the Manuscript Division of the Public Archives of Canada. Apparently it had lain around for years but it had gone unnoticed. The story of its discovery began some time in the 1950s, when an archivist at the Provincial Archives of Québec wrote to the Archivo Historico Provincial in Cádiz asking if they had, or had knowledge of, such a document. They did indeed, but for some reason they did not reply for a couple of decades. Apparently, one day, a newcomer at the Archivo stumbled across some unanswered letters, and among them was the request from Québec. He responded by forwarding the document itself. Thus, in 1975 the Public Archives of Canada came into possession of this affidavit, one of the most important historical discoveries regarding Champlain made in this century.

Having read the journal, I then wrote to Cádiz myself, but received no reply. In 1984, however, I received a copy of the document from Ottawa and immediately arranged to have it translated from its original Spanish into English.

The author of the affidavit was Guillermo Elena of Marseille, and he resided in Cádiz in 1601. Elena was Champlain's uncle and was identified by him in his journals as the "Captain Provençal." Among other important matters, this treasure trove of information provides additional evidence of Champlain's voyage to Spain, evidence that supports some of the facts in Champlain's *Brief Narrative*, and gives credibility to the reality of his sometimes challenged West Indies voyage.

Just as exciting, and contrary to the general perception of Champlain as a pensioner perhaps in need of employment, or as a man who accepted a position as a semi-public civil servant of modest means, is the fact that Champlain was a man of considerable personal wealth, thanks to the substantial estate that he inherited from his uncle in La Rochelle, France. In the light of this document, historians must now re-examine that off-the-cuff remark made by Champlain in 1615 in reference to his partners that he was "not dependent on them" (IV: 362).

Those who are looking at this letter as at me, Guillermo Elena, from Marseille, natural born from Marseille, at present living in the city of Cádiz, I say that I have very much love and bequeath to the Frenchman, Samuel Zamplen born at Brouage in the province with the name Santonze [Saintonge], that he is my heir, for much good work that he did for me in my illness; and he came when I needed him. And also for the great love I feel for being married to his aunt, his mother's sister and also for other reasons and for the just respect I have for him; this moves me to prove for all these reasons of my own free will and in the greatest way that I can give, and I know that I do thank him with a donation as much as is necessary for the said Samuel Zamplen, and present for him and for who he wants an inheritance of vineyards measuring seventeen carties [*sic*] French measure, coupled with the houses and warehouses and land to plant an orchard; that all this is part of the same inheritance in other words [the hacienda] which is more or less in the City of La Rochelle and located between the hacienda of Señor De La Zarna and Señor Desuse on the other side.

With this inheritance, I give to him all its access and exits, uses, customs and servants: as much as the hacienda has; houses and orchards and all I said before that he owns and all that he will own with the attendant rights and customs and the income that upon completion is to be paid to the said Samuel Zamplen and all the interests that he will possess in the future; and this donation I give to Samuel Zamplen is for him to enjoy from the day of my death and in the future, but not until I finish the days of my life, during which time I have the right to enjoy the same as my own.

Notwithstanding, I leave the hacienda and all the furnishings thereto to him, Samuel Zamplen, as I originally covenanted.

And also I have rights to some monies that are in Viscaya in the village of San Sebastián, that is funds that are deposited for goods I left to Señor Ojelde Zolan Viscayno. This merchandise came from a ship that I had left with him, a vessel of one hundred and fifty tons, and these were the funds, that as a result, I shipped to San Sebastián.

I left this money in trust with María Augustín, who was my hostess. I also advised that I had given this donation to Samuel Zamplen as an inheritance for his own fortune. All of this resulted because of a voyage that I made in a ship, the San Julián of 500 tons and the fact that I owned an eighth of her and the rest was owned by Señor Landricart Endebanes in Bretaña, and it was in this vessel that I came to Spain as a captain and was sent by His Majesty, for his officers and came to this bay with soldiers which were brought from the third Del Cavete in the army that was brought by general Pedro de Suviaure and also they owe to me the cargo and supplies. From the proceeds I give all this to him, for him to enjoy after the day of my death.

Of everything which I give in this donation for the reasons already mentioned and because this is my will and because any donation made that is greater than five hundred salaries does not have any value if it is not described, I say that this donation exceeds the quantity mentioned of five hundred salaries plus donations I make which I now renounce by law by stating it and the amounts that I could make from the ones that in this case I can take advantage of; they are mine until my death, at

which time I give the rights I have on these goods to Samuel
Zamplen from now and until the end of my life and I give these
goods in the greatest form that is necessary and I hereby give an
irrevocable undertaking and understanding for now and then I
give to him this script so that he will have this as absolute proof
of the title to these things. Samuel Zamplen can go to each
person and ask for a counting of the inheritance from the persons I left the property with; including the details of the property I left in their power, the cash, the fruits and rents from
everything from the time they have had them in their possession and at the same time, he can cash in the quantity of
money that I said I have in the village of San Sebastián and
also everything the hostess Ojelde Zalan owes me. He will be
able to cash the goods that I have left in trust with María
Augustín who was my hostess and he can ask for everything on
account of the agreement now made for my convenience and
he can cash in on the hacienda real del Rey nuestro Señor and
the quantity of maravedís [coins] that appear to be mine and
for the boat that I said I came in with the soldiers and the car-
gos and supplies.

For everything I have listed above, he can liquidate in any
way convenient to him and he will provide receipts as that
proof of payment according to law and on these conditions I
have given him my trust and transferred my rights to him.

I made a will four years ago, more or less, in Quiripercorant,
located in Bretaña and the inheritance I gave in this previous
will, I hereby revoke and now give all those goods specified to
Samuel Zamplen, because it is my wish to do so. Furthermore, I
want this new will to be in effect and I will not change it . . . .

In testimony of this, I give my covenant on this date, the
26th of the month of June, 1601, in the city of Cádiz, being at
the purple house [sic] of Antonio de Villa, a resident of this
city.

Witnesses that were present; Bartolomé Gariboy and
Jacques Alemán, residents of Cádiz, who certified that they
knew Guillermo Elena and that everything written in this affidavit was true and as certified by other witnesses present from
this neighbourhood including Antonio de Villa and Pedro
Bautista Asirio Grinovés and Françisco Sanchez Ahumada,
residents, and all in the presence of Samuel Zamplen. On these

conditions, Samuel Zamplen agreed to take the donation and he thanked me for the favour.

The same witnesses stated that they knew Samuel Zamplen and these persons also testified to this knowledge in the registry.

(Signatures) Bar. Gariboy. Guillermón Elena.
(Witnesses) Jacques Alemán. Champlain.
Marcos Rivera. Public Writer.

APPENDIX III

Champlain's Voyage to the West Indies and Spain: 1598-1601

OVER THE YEARS, CHAMPLAIN'S VOYAGE TO SPAIN and the West Indies has become a source of debate and argument among historians and Champlain buffs. The *Brief Narrative* is certainly a less than reliable source of information. The confusion swirls around three manuscripts of watercolor sketches, each supported by a handwritten diary of disjointed text. According to some scholars, all three manuscripts are copies of an original that has "disappeared".

In response to a letter in January 1986, Professor Luca Codignola of Pisa, Italy kindly provided me with welcome assistance regarding the current status of the debate:

> As to your question relating to Champlain's manuscript, the answer is simple. There are three copies of the MS [manuscript] in the world, all of them copies from a disappeared original. The earliest seems to be the one in Bologna, the second earliest the one at the John Carter Brown Library, and the latest (possibly 18th century), the one at the Archivio di Stato in Turin, Italy.

Adding to the problem, all these "copies" of the diary are incomplete on at least two counts: the journal entries regarding the events are incomplete; and there are illustrations that are numerically identified, but not included. Arguments continue as to the intent of the material that has survived; but regardless of one's opinion, there is no evidence that any of the material was intended for publication. Frustratingly, too, Champlain never vouched for or referred to a single word or brushstroke of the small volume.

279

Taking all arguments into account, I do not see sufficient reason to alter the position adopted by the Champlain Society, which chose for publication the manuscript treasure of the John Carter Brown Library (JCB), entitled the *Brief Discours des choses plus remarquables que Samuel Champlain de Brouage a reconnues aux Indes Occidentals*. Among the many reasons for this choice is the fact that the JCB manuscript is the most complete, whereas the Bologna manuscript is missing eleven sketches. And, in spite of the theory of the "copies" (a notion posed without any concrete evidence some thirty years ago), there is no evidence to suggest that the JCB artifact is not an "original," by whichever author undertook the task of its preparation. In fact the term "copy" is misleading when dealing with works of art, and in the absence of clarification, it is a bothersome frame of reference for the Champlain manuscript. At least in the world of art, the many draft sketches of Rembrandt and Leonardo da Vinci are not so classified. Part of the problem in this case may well be related to this form of classification.

And Champlain's uncle's affidavit from Spain (see Appendix II) has given us more direct evidence concerning Champlain's connection and contact with Spain, the first lap of the journey to the West Indies. This affidavit, for example confirms that on a specific date — June 26, 1601 — Champlain was in that country in a specific location; and, more importantly, this document, witnessed and signed by many, corroborates some key facts. It provides evidence, for example, that Champlain's uncle "Provençal" was a part owner of a vessel, the *St. Julien* of the exact same tonnage and name as that noted in the opening lines of the *Brief Narrative* manuscript. As well, information regarding the circumstances of Provençal's coming to Spain are also repeated. But even without these indications of Champlain's authorship of the *Brief Narrative*, there are many other persuasive points: the style of writing, the language chosen, the method of organization, the combined use of charts and illustrations in support of the field notes, and the author's expressed attitude toward the Indians.

Another piece of convincing circumstantial evidence regarding the so-called "copies" is the fact that John Carter Brown's legal title to its manuscript rarity can be traced directly to the Mayor of Dieppe, who owned the document in 1859. Dieppe is the same port in which Admiral Aymar de Chaste resided as the governor of the town and castle in Champlain's time. This is particularly interesting in the light of Champlain's published review commentary in 1632, covering his immediate post–Spanish and West Indies voyage:

In the meanwhile I reached court, having recently arrived from the West Indies, where I had spent nearly two and a half years after the Spaniards left Blavet, and peace had been made in France . . . calling upon the said Commander de Chaste from time to time and believing that I could be of help to him in his plans, he did me the honour, as I have said, to communicate to me something on the subject, and asked me if I should care to make the voyage in order to see the country, and what colonizers might accomplish there (III: 314-15).

It has been suggested by some that the John Carter Brown Library manuscript of sixty-two illustrations and charts was written, sketched, and used by Champlain as a sort of curriculum vitae to secure career advancement in his chosen field of geographic exploration. The commentary in the *Brief Narrative* manuscript itself is at least consistent with the notion that the author intended to communicate the results of the two-year journey to His Majesty the King of France. Along these lines, should the JCB artifact be, as suggested, a "copy," then it's entirely possible the primary manuscript was sent on to the King and hence the "disappearance." In any case, it seems more than coincidence that such a manuscript "copy" just happened to turn up in Dieppe.

Today, the last word can still be given to the former librarian of John Carter Brown, Thomas Adams, who wrote in 1973 in response to a challenge that the JCB manuscript was not the original Champlain manuscript: "We are satisfied that a good deal more work needs to be done before a decision is made on that point."

APPENDIX IV

Champlain's Marriage

THE SUBJECT OF CHAMPLAIN'S MARRIAGE HAS given rise to considerable controversy among his historians. Champlain betrayed no intention of marriage in his journals, nor was the bride or her family mentioned prior to the event. The marriage, moreover, occurred only three months after his return to France.

By any standard, this marriage was decided on quickly. In this race to the altar, no time was allowed for the niceties of a courtship. Champlain had only been back in France thirteen weeks; even the marriage contract on December 27, three days before the wedding, made the point that these two were to "take each other in lawful wedlock within the briefest space of time possible" (II: 317).

The fertile imaginations of historians have provoked many theories. Aside from speculation though, there are some facts that do seem pertinent. First, Champlain was twenty-eight years older than Hélène; second, from events that transpired within a few months after the marriage ceremony (see Chapter 23), it is clear that this was a loveless match — at least initially — and likely throughout, though such matches were the rule rather than the exception. To date, most historians have concluded that the reasons for the union were largely financial, or of a business nature, because the dowry sum was sizable. (In later years, a viceroy of the King would buy the whole colony of New France for this sum.) But this theory begs the question: Why did Champlain need money? Champlain, we now know, was at this time a man of substantial wealth and property.

In view of the upheaval at the death of King Henry, it is more likely that Champlain was making this move for political reasons. Plainly, he sought to broaden and solidify his political power base in Paris and this "remedy" would make some sense in view of his years of absence and vulnerability while away on exploration duties. And, in retrospect, over the long term, Hélène Champlain did prove to be an asset as she looked after her husband's many interests on the home front.

It is also possible that, as Champlain was getting on in years, he had some thoughts of retirement, and may have wanted to have children. The events that he witnessed at Sorel, and his several brushes with death, were enough to make any sane man have thoughts about his own mortality.

APPENDIX V

Champlain *vs.* Lescarbot

INFORMATION CONCERNING THE FEUD BETWEEN Champlain and Lescarbot is scant, but tradition holds that the conflict resulted from their different backgrounds.

Champlain's expeditionary role was to keep a detailed journal for the King, at the same time reporting to de Monts. The terms of reference for Lescarbot's one-year sortie in New France were never clear. He was known to have been a somewhat discredited solicitor who had recently lost an important legal action in France and was unemployed and at loose ends.

Like Champlain, Lescarbot had many varied skills to offer a New World starved for talent. In 1598, the same year that Champlain had broadened his practical education with a voyage to Spain for further venture to the West Indies, Lescarbot began to practise law. Thereafter, he became a parliamentary advocate in legal service for the Crown of France, his responsibilities including international treaty negotiations.

Lescarbot was highly educated having attended France's better schools whereas Champlain appears to have been self-educated. By the time he arrived at Port-Royal, Lescarbot was proficient in Greek and Hebrew and had translated works of history from Latin into French. He was also well versed in the *Chanoine*, the Canon law of the church. Class differences may therefore have contributed to their rivalry as well as intellectual rivalry. In fact, both men were dynamic individuals with many parallel skills. Both, for example, were experienced writers: even at the time of their first meeting in 1606, Champlain was already a published author.

The conflict between them evidently stemmed from de Monts' cavalier approach to the expedition's management, as both men assumed that they were responsible for precisely the same work. Lescarbot's written apologia that he was really on some sort of sabbatical leave to, "flee a corrupt world" hardly seemed credible as his only motive. The dream that he had was much bigger than this, and it paralleled Champlain's own. On the title page of his famous work published in 1609, *The History of New France*, Lescarbot states that he is an "Eye Witness to Matters, Moral, Natural and Geographical . . . " and that the volume contains the *requisite* tables and maps. Without hesitation, lawyer Lescarbot sets himself up in direct competition with Champlain.

The researcher who must intently read between the lines of both published works must indulge in considerable speculation in trying to understand the circumstances of the feud.

There is also uncertainty as to the *timing* of the published writings of each man. Both hint in their writings that the disagreements between them might have resulted because of an oversight on Champlain's part. In his published journal *Les Voyages* (1613), he failed to note the arrival of such a notable personage as Lescarbot at Port-Royal. Given Champlain's usual tact and diplomacy, the omission *is* a little surprising.

On the other hand, by the time that Champlain's account of this period at Port-Royal was published in 1613, Lescarbot had already published an attack against him. Perhaps this salvo was the first shot that rocked the relationship. The battle that ensued consists solely of oblique references and whispers.

Lescarbot first appears in Champlain's journal on the latter's return from Cape Cod to Port-Royal. He reported that "Upon our arrival, Lescarbot who had remained at the settlement along with the others who had stayed there, welcomed us with sundry jollities." The name Marc Lescarbot appears here for the first time without explanation. Only through other later sources do we learn, that the "sundry jollities" to which Champlain so casually refers were in fact Lescarbot's extraordinary theatrical work; *The Theatre of Neptune*, written and presented for the first time at the Acadian settlement. The drama was no trivial effort, and it deserved more than an aside. It was, in fact, the first European drama ever performed in North America, and it was published in 1609 and widely circulated in France.

Lescarbot's drama that opened on November 14 with a "Hail to

you, Sagamos" took the form of a ballad, with many greetings and
verses chanted in different languages from various vantage points and
it was performed at the water's edge in front of the habitation. The
extravaganza included the god Neptune likely played by Lescarbot
himself, six tritons (minor seagods), and a parade of Indians. Even the
shallop was employed as one of the props. Yet, we learn no details of
the performance from Champlain's journals.

Matters between the two worsened when Lescarbot published his
History of New France in 1609. In this first of four editions of the book,
the battle proper first breaks into print. Champlain was slyly accused
of stealing Jacques Cartier's thunder for the discovery of the St.
Lawrence River: "So is it with the deeds of many notable persons,
whose memory often dies with them and who are deprived of their
due need of praise . . . To go no further for examples, the voyage of our
friend Captain Jacques Cartier . . . was unknown in our age. Champlain thought himself first to gain the prize. But one must give every
man his due and therefore say that Champlain has ignored the
account of Cartier's voyage" (CW-L: 111).

The charge lacks sense. How could Champlain have been guilty of
ignoring Cartier's achievement if, as Lescarbot stated, the voyages
were unknown? And, more important, up to this point, Champlain
never claimed to be an expert on the subject of prior discoveries,
though clearly he would have had some knowledge of some expeditions.

Lescarbot's narrative followed Champlain on his 1603 voyage up
the St. Lawrence River: "in the last four chapters, we have seen that,
contrary to the opinion of Champlain, Captain Cartier pushed up the
great river as far as it is possible to go . . . [by boat] even if Champlain
has not done it and the marvels he tells of this river are not greater
than those which we heard told by Cartier." This was the first and
gentlest of the barbs in Lescarbot's dictionary of vindictive.

Lescarbot's most devastating attack, however, challenged Champlain's intelligence, his credibility as an observer, and even his sanity.
In a blistering volley of words he ridicules Champlain's belief in the
GOUGOU Monster of the Gaspé: "I leave the credibility to the
reader, for though a few savages speak of [the monster] and hold it in
dread, it is in the same way that some feeble-minded folk at home
dread the Phantom Monk" (CS-L: 172).

By the time that Lescarbot's history was published in 1609, Champlain had two grievances: he'd been libeled and he had been beaten

into print. And possibly a third grievance also existed. It was not unlikely that Lescarbot had stolen some of Champlain's primary cartographic research. Lescarbot's map of New France (fig. 22) provides the evidence. On this chart, the most scientifically accurate for the period, Lescarbot depicted the St. Lawrence River basin with all the same major geographical markings identified publicly only in writing to date by Champlain in his first journal of 1603. The original of Champlain's missing summary survey chart of 1603 was given to King Henry IV.

In 1609 Lescarbot had never been on, or even near, the St. Lawrence River. There is no other evidence that the lawyer had any cartographic or navigational skill, let alone an inventory of detailed mapping information from any other source. It is equally unlikely that Champlain would have so readily aided his rival. The circumstantial evidence is sufficiently persuasive to suggest that Lescarbot may have been somewhat deceitful. He had motive and opportunity, and was capable of deceit.

Whereas Champlain claims that he had drawn a "correct map" of all that he had seen and discovered for the period, the only other cartographic evidence of his first journey along the St. Lawrence is to be found in the cartography of Guillaume Nautonier in a survey published about 1605. In that atlas, the noted scientist acknowledges information provided by Champlain in the form of letters updating information of the coast of New France. It is unlikely that Lescarbot was aware of this exchange.

Whether or not Lescarbot was indeed guilty of blatant plagiarism, Champlain seemed dumbfounded by Lescarbot's insults. He made a guarded retort in *Les Voyages*, published in 1613, which covered the period from 1604 to 1612, and it was placed in the journal record for the year 1607, some eight months after his first casual observation of Lescarbot's presence at Port-Royal on November 14, 1606. Even this Champlain response wasn't published until 1613. Only at this late date did Champlain pointedly and in print retaliate with the claim that Lescarbot had only traveled to Île Sainte-Croix (fig. 11) and the Saint John River (fig. 9): "This the farthest he went which is only fourteen to fifteen leagues [c. 70 km.] beyond the said Port Royal" (I: 452). The remark was carefully placed in the text — an evident warning to the reader about Lescarbot's lack of integrity.

If this was Champlain's entire defense to Lescarbot's questionable activities — as it seemed to be — then it was a feckless effort, because he had left unchallenged the substance of Lescarbot's attack. It seems that instead, in a circumspect move, years later, in 1632, Champlain directed his anger elsewhere in a written attack of de Monts. In an attempt to show off a knowledge of history that Lescarbot claimed was lacking, in those later years, Champlain may have fallen into a trap. There is evidence that perhaps he was being restrained in his recognition of Jacques Cartier's legacy, thereby lending credibility to Lescarbot's earlier charge, which had been totally unfounded at the time.

Lescarbot enthusiastically noted Champlain's error and in the subsequent editions of his history, played the injured innocent, whining "I do not know why Champlain, in his account of his voyages printed in 1613, goes out of his way to say that I did not go farther than St. Croix, seeing that I do not say to the contrary" (CS-L: 359). Champlain's flimsy defense was, however, only an invitation to more abuse. In the final editions of Lescarbot's history, published in 1617 and 1618, there was more poison penmanship: "As for Champlain" was the sarcasm used to preface a recap of his observations; in the end, Champlain was even accused of taking credit for the naming of Port-Royal, credit which belonged to de Monts. Lescarbot claimed that Champlain's writing was "less literary and smooth than ordinary," and as a result it was necessary to "strike" out some "trivialities" (CS-L: 76). In one ludicrous charge, he even ridiculed Champlain for updating his maps by adding discovery information about Hudson Bay (fig. 30) to his grand survey map of 1612 (fig. 31). "He [Champlain] had no right to foist on us a map of New France in which in his desires to follow the English of their latest discovery in 1611, he has directly contradicted his own writings [Des Sauvages, (1603)] . . . and further I am unwilling lightly to attach credence to the English who speak of an inland sea on the fiftieth degree." And how wrong could he be?

The consequences of this bickering are difficult to assess more than four and a half centuries later; but there is little doubt that their feud damaged the reputations of both men. Setting aside the petty posturing concerning Champlain, Marc Lescarbot's monumental History of New France was the first work of its kind, and an important contribution to the history of New France. Yet, undoubtedly a number of influential people of the day read the two volumes and became wary of both men, perhaps thinking Champlain a gullible idealist and Lescarbot a troublemaker. Despite the fact that Lescarbot's history was published in four French editions and was translated into German and Latin, in his lifetime, the name Lescarbot today is not found in any comprehensive anthology of such works. Nor, despite his literary status, has he been credited as even a minor figure in French literature, or as a contributor worthy of a footnote. The remark of one modern historian, Morris Bishop, that Lescarbot was a "piddling scholar" indicates just how completely his work has been dismissed.

Champlain's career also suffered. In the future his writings were more defensive. This intellectual jousting was undoubtedly one reason for the verbal assault that Champlain directed at his former commander-in-chief, de Monts, in the 1632 journal for permitting Lescarbot to go to New France in the first place. There was another side effect. In Champlain's subsequent journals after *Les Voyages* (1613), there was a collection of mundane historical overviews that contributed nothing to the account.

APPENDIX VI

The Champlain Astrolabe

O N JUNE 6, 1613, THE CHAMPLAIN PARTY WAS HEAD-
ing to the base camps of the Algonquin chiefs Nibachis and
Tessouat on the Ottawa River. The group "crossed to the west of the
river . . . and took the latitude of the place, which was 46 degrees 40
minutes. We had much trouble in taking this route overland, being
laden for my part alone with three arquebuses, an equal number of
paddles, my cloak, and some small articles" (II: 273).

This field note from the pages of his journal which confirmed the
details of his personal exploration of Ontario, roused great interest in
1867 when the most celebrated artifact of the French exploration
period in America, the Champlain Astrolabe, was recovered near this
site surveyed by Champlain. Having been found in this particular
location, the now-famous navigational instrument is now automatically identified with Champlain himself.

No other artifact in the discovery history of North America has
attracted such a collection of negative inferences and speculation as to
its authenticity or origin as has this small treasure from the past.
Indeed, the parade has been led by those that should know better. The
result has been the circulation of some decided nonsense. In 1982, for
example, while researching the subject, I was provided with a letter
written to a third party from the Smithsonian Institution in Washington, D.C., that gratuitously offered this bit of misinformation about
the astrolabe: it was "lost inland in upper New York near the Canadian border . . . . [and] it was dated 1602." Dated 1603, the Champlain astrolabe was discovered near Cobden, Ontario in Canada!

Far more interesting, however, is the colorful story of the recovery of the treasure. The archaeological event that has triggered decades of controversy began on a summer day in August 1867, near Cobden, Ontario, just a few weeks after the passage of the British North America Act, which proclaimed Canada's nationhood. On that summer afternoon, John Lee and his fourteen-year-old son, Edward George, were employed by a certain Captain Overman to clear land at the edge of Green Lake, an offshoot water body of the Ottawa River system. Overman also ran the local steamboat ferry for the Ottawa Forwarding Company. A year later, Edward George Lee relayed his teenage experience to Charles MacNamara, a journalist from nearby Arnprior, Ontario. Lee's verbatim account was reproduced in *The Cobden Sun* on July 3, 1952:

One day we were working just below Green Lake, in a bush of
mixed hardwood and pine . . . . Pa sent me home for his dinner and when I got back with it he sat down to eat it, while I
went on drawing the logs with our team of oxen . . . . There
was one old fallen red pine that lay downhill . . . . Pa had
chopped the trunk of this tree into three logs and I drew two of
them away with the oxen, but the third log just below the
branches was not chopped clean off and I hitched the oxen to it
and pulled it around sideways . . . . I had to dig away the moss
and marl that the old tree lay in . . . and when the log swung
around it rolled back the moss like a blanket, and there on the
ground I saw a round yellow thing, nine or ten inches across
[c. 23 or 25 cm] . . . . I showed the compass to Pa and he put it
on a stump just a little way up the hill. Just then Captain Overman came along to see how the work was going, and Old Captain Cowley was with him. Pa showed them the compass and
they took it away, and Pa said they promised to give me $10.00
for it, but I never got a farthing nor saw hide or hair of the
compass since. Poor Pa let them have it, but if I had got it up to
the house, Ma would not have given it to them that easy. The
compass was lying about two or three rods [c. 10 to 15 m] from
the edge of the creek. I never saw water enough in the creek to
float a canoe.

In the events that followed Captain Overman donated "the compass" to Richard Scougal Cassels of Toronto, his employer and the
President of the Union Forwarding and Railroad Company of
Ottawa. On Cassels' death in 1896, the astrolabe — for that is what it
was — became the property of his son, Walter Gibson Cassels, a man
described in the published *Records of the Family of Cassels and Connections* as having a "kindly and retiring disposition." In 1897, the new
owner offered the curious treasure to the City of Québec. The archival
records of that city however, state that there were not sufficient funds
available to meet the sale price of one thousand dollars at the time the
proposal was considered. According to the Cassels family records,
(kindly provided to me by Chris Barron of Toronto), the astrolabe was
also offered to the federal government of Canada, but apparently they
too had insufficient funds to purchase the invaluable heritage artifact.

Four years later, the dissatisfied owner, Walter Gibson Cassels,
dropped the sale price by one half, and turned away from potential

institutional buyers to private collectors. He approached a New York State resident, one Samuel Verplanct Hoffman, an antiquarian collector of astrolabes. On September 10, 1901, in a no-nonsense business letter to the seller, Hoffman verified the terms of sale and the details of the transaction. "I have determined to send you a check and accordingly enclose my check #1768 on the Second National Bank of New York to your order for Five Hundred Dollars ($500.00) in settlement of the price named by you for the astrolabe delivered in the United States and will thank you to see that the astrolabe is carefully & securely packed in a box of suitable strength to stand transportation."

On September 19, 1901, a satisfied Mr. Hoffman was able to write from "Camp Hoff," Paul Smiths, N. Y. to Gibson Cassels in Toronto that he had received the astrolabe in "good condition."

The new owner, Samuel Hoffman, was more than just a collector. He was a Champlain buff, who attended the New York State tercentenary celebrations in 1909 of Champlain's discovery of Lake Champlain at the site of his first battle against the Iroquois. More important, concerning the future for the Champlain Astrolabe, however, he was also a member, director, and past president of the New York Historical Society. When he died in 1942, he willed the Champlain Astrolabe to the Society that he loved. That organization has owned it ever since.

Today, at the Society headquarters in New York City, the Champlain Astrolabe can occasionally be seen on display in the Americana exhibition area — that is, after one disembarks on the appropriate floor from an elevator the size of a shallop. Most of the time, however, the graduated metal circle, measuring only 5.63 inches [14.3 cm] in diameter is to be found within the archival dungeons of the institute, carefully stored in a wooden box as one of its most valued treasures.

NOTES

CHAPTER ONE

p. 11   **The Promotion of the French Language in North America**

Today it is in the area of French language survival and promotion that the ancien régime thrives in North America. In 1987 the Alliance Française, France's internationally accredited institute of language and cultural promotion, listed 16 branches in Canada and 205 in the United States.

Canada, however, is the forest primeval for this language harvest first seeded in Champlain's time. In defense of this language fortress, there are now more than a dozen agencies at the federal level of government, secretariats, departments, and branches, and even an Official Language Commission where loyal legionnaires daily mill around the maze of the language labyrinth for the purpose of protecting French language rights. The annual report of the nation's Official Language Commissioner trumpets his conviction with the certainty of an inquisitor. Like the Supervisor of Weights and Measures in Jean Giroudoux's play, *The Enchanted*, the commissioner lauds the little that is achieved; but, garbed as he is in the robes of the seventeenth century, he laments the larger failure of the whole enterprise.

With the aid of numerous members of the legal craft, this language promotion in the government is now a naked power struggle well advanced into its fourth century. The warning of U.S. communications expert Neil Postman is worth remembering: "When, in short, a people become an audience and their public business becomes a vaudeville act, then a nation finds itself at risk; culture death is a clear possibility." For Canadians, the enduring frustration from this cultural confrontation is deeply rooted, but as a solution one is reminded of one suggestion: "The first thing we do, let's kill all the lawyers" (*Henry VI*: Part II, Act IV, sc ii).

CHAPTER TWO

p. 16   **Brouage**

It has been suggested that the name Brouage came from the Celtic word "boue," meaning mud. But whether or not this name originally applied to the individual community there or to a larger geographic area is uncertain. A published map of the region by the nobleman Don Petro Rogiero and dated 1597 shows Brouage as only a coastal channel between the mainland and Île D'Oleron.

p. 20   Ducornet Portrait

Louis Cesar Joseph Ducornet, who managed to perpetrate many similar historical misrepresentations, was a painter without arms and with only one foot with four toes. The story of this artist and his far-reaching skill is more interesting than his farfetched faking of Champlain's image in history.

CHAPTER FOUR

p. 37   The Admirals Montmorency

There is much confusion about Champlain's contacts with the illustrious Montmorency family of peers, marshals, and admirals of France. For example, it has been the practice of a number of biographers and editors to either conclude or to leave the impression by omission that Champlain had contact with only Henri II, duc de Montmorency (1595-1632), an Admiral of France who was also Viceroy of New France from 1620 to 1625. The common misconception is that this nobleman is the same person as Charles de Montmorency (c. 1537-1612) of the same family who held the same military rank and was the former Admiral of France and Brittany. Biographers Bishop, Morison, and Dionne (see Bibliography) are all either vague or incorrect in identifying the two relatives. *The Dictionary of Canadian Biography*, too, is in error through an inaccurate index reference.

The error is compounded in references to Champlain's naming in 1603 of Montmorency Falls, the largest waterfall in the province of Québec, ten kilometers east of Québec City at the mouth of the Rivière Montmorency. It is clear from the Champlain journals that he named the falls after Admiral Charles de Montmorency and not, as stated in *The Canadian Encyclopedia* (Hurtig) or *The Encyclopedia Americana* (Grolier), after Viceroy Henri de Montmorency, who was only eight years old at the time.

CHAPTER FIVE

p. 44   The French Trading Companies

The trading company of the sort for which de Monts was granted a licence was an important part of the process of exploration and colonization. Without becoming too involved in details, its operation was as follows:

For many years independent merchants of France's coastal ports, Saint-Malo and La Rochelle, for example, had financed yearly voyages to the coast of North America. Fishing was one endeavor, and the second was trading furs with the coastal Indians. From time to time, the Crown would attempt to control trade by granting a monopoly to a favored nobleman who would, in turn, form a consortium of investors to finance expeditions. Sometimes the monopoly would apply only to furs, sometimes to both fishing and furs. This angered the independent entrepreneurs, who both ignored the monopoly and lobbied at home for its dissolution. Moreover, given the area in question, a monopoly was virtually impossible to enforce. During Champlain's time, several commissions were granted and several attempts were made to involve the merchants in order to reduce the competition. And there were periods of "free trade" when it was every man or group for itself. One of the advantages of a colony up the St. Lawrence River was that the company that ran it would have the opportunity to trade before the furs reached the coast, where the competition included the ships sent by France's other merchants as well as vessels sent by the Basques and the Portugese, who, with the French, had long fished the Grand Banks. Later, of course, the British and the Dutch would also provide competition.

Although Champlain devoted himself to the building and maintenance of a settlement up the St. Lawrence at Québec, the fur trade seemed to interest him only because it provided a means to an end. In short, it kept others interested. It seems clear, however, that exploiting the fur trade was not Champlain's primary concern. In fact, only once in all his years in North America is it recorded that he attended the great trading meeting that took place yearly at Trois-Rivières.

p. 52   **Mount Desert Island**

In December of 1983 an international agreement was signed by Canada and the United States recognizing the historical significance of this island. It was declared in the treaty that de Monts' and Champlain's Île Sainte-Croix is an "international site" of interest to both nations. For the future, plans are under way to better recognize and improve access to this North American heritage site.

CHAPTER SIX

p. 87   **Champlain Monument at Chatham Harbor, Massachusetts**

The most curious of all Champlain monuments on the North American continent was erected at Chatham Harbor on the

roadside, just before what is now known as the Chatham Sailing
Club. Barely visible, rising above the grassy shoulder of the road
and not more than three feet above the ground, there is an out-
cropping of granite with an inscription which reads: Samuel de
Champlain/The First White Man on These Shores Landed Here
October 1606.

This monument was erected by Carol V. Wight, a local resident of Chatham Harbor, and a professor at Johns Hopkins
University. While ensuring that there was a solid foundation
underneath the memorial cairn, the professor had the gravel bed
layered with broken bean pots. Years later, this action prompted
one concerned scholar, Professor Lorne Petrie of Cornell, to
exclaim: "Some future archeologist will conclude that Champlain
introduced baked beans into New England."

CHAPTER TEN

p. 101   **Québec City, a U. N. Heritage Site**

Today, the city that Champlain founded in 1608 is included on
the UNESCO World Heritage List as a "site of outstanding uni-
versal value." With its famous original fortress walls still intact, it
joins some 200 other world class heritage monuments such as the
Taj Mahal and the Great Pyramids of Egypt. In this city there is
much to see. The most celebrated Champlain festivities that ever
took place in Canada, however, were those of the 1908 Champlain Tercentenary at Québec. This was a festival appropriately
named Lord Grey's Imperial Birthday Party. As the story goes,
aware of a lack of national pride and the antagonism between the
English and the French, Grey idealized a solution — a festival of
Britain on the Plains of Abraham. On this extraordinary occasion, no less than eight warships of the British Atlantic fleet
including the flagship, two battleships, and several cruisers sailed
the Atlantic under the command of the Prince of Wales where
they were joined by ships from the French and U. S. navies along
with some twelve thousand Canadian troops. Some $75,000 was
set aside for the festivities which offended many Francophones.
Coming to the rescue, Prime Minister Wilfrid Laurier and the
Prince of Wales, acting on behalf of King George V, addressed the
assembled multitude of several hundred thousand people in
French. It was reported that momentarily the bitter politics
between the French and the English were put aside in favor of a
grander vision. Champlain would have been pleased.

p. 113   **Champlain Monument at Crown Point, New York**

At Crown Point in New York State, the site of Champlain's first
great battle against the Iroquois (fig. 26), there is one of the finest

monuments to Champlain to be found anywhere, an Italian renaissance structure known as the Champlain Memorial and Lighthouse at Crown Point. This tercentenary monument commemorating Champlain's visit in 1609 is to be found on Lake Champlain just north of Ticonderoga. The New York and Vermont State 1909 celebrations were certainly the most expansive ever held to honor Samuel de Champlain. To celebrate the occasion, gold, silver and bronze medallions were struck, certificates printed, and invitations were sent far and wide. On July 6, 1609 President William Howard Taft and Vice-President James S. Sherman as well as the governors of New York State and Vermont participated in three days of festivities, including many banquets and other activities.

p. 117   **The Iroquois Fortress, Sorel, Québec**

From Champlain's journal, there is any number of conclusions one could draw as to where the Iroquois fortress might have been. He refers to an island, a journey by canoe and a trek of "about half a league through thick woods", which could mean anything from a journey southward on the Richelieu River and then inland, to a simple rearguard action ploy near the river mouth. Although a definitive location cannot be pinpointed, some historians have blandly accepted that Cap de la Victoire on the Richelieu River is the site (no longer on Québec road maps). A more likely choice would be the later site of Fort Richelieu, erected in 1642 by the French and then destroyed in 1647 by the Iroquois. If this is indeed the case, then the town of Sorel today is the battle site which should be remembered.

CHAPTER FOURTEEN

p. 127   **Savignon in France**

Marc Lescarbot gives us a hint of the enormous cultural chasm between the French and the North American native peoples after observing the "savage" Savignon in Paris: "Often when he saw two men quarrelling without coming to blows or killing one another, he would mock at them, saying they were naught but women, and had no courage."

CHAPTER SIXTEEN

p. 146   **Champlain Monument in Ottawa**

For the visitor to the Ottawa region there are many Champlain highlights to see, but the nation's most curious is the great statue of Champlain to be found at Nepean Point in downtown Ottawa

near the new National Gallery of Art. The sculpture was
unveiled on May 27, 1915 by the Governor General, the Duke of
Connaught in the presence of Prime Minister Sir Robert and
Lady Borden.

The statuary is the work of Hamilton Plantagenet MacCarthy,
who was born in England and came to Ottawa in 1899. Although the artist was recognized as the dean of Canadian sculp-
tors of the day, his "Champlain" is now one of the most contro-
versial sculptures in the nation. The famous artist fashioned the
figure of the great navigator holding the tool of his craft, the
astrolabe, upside down!

p. 149   **The Nicolas de Vignau Controversy**

Giving de Vignau the benefit of the doubt for at least some of his
actions, it seems reasonable to conclude that he was confused
and had relayed to Champlain a mixture of facts based on experience, plus information gained from the Indians, which may or
may not have been true. He may also have added his own impressions to embellish the account given to Champlain, hoping to
profit if all went well, as he might have expected it would. It is
equally possible that de Vignau did acquire some direct knowledge of the fate of the Hudson party from the Indians. The problem today is in discovering his sources. After raving for pages on
the subject, Champlain himself finally left the matter open. Not
until two years later when he voyaged to Huronia in 1615 was
Champlain in a position to fully appreciate the fact that the
Algonquins were masters of disinformation.

No matter how de Vignau's story is interpreted, it was clear
that the Algonquins succeeded in completely stalling Champlain's mission westward in 1613. Totally frustrated by the de
Vignau incident, Champlain did a complete about-face and
returned to the St. Lawrence River: "My journey in this direction
westward having ended, and without any hope of seeing the sea
in those parts except by surmise, there remained to me nothing
but the regret of not having made better use of my time." That
year the only memorable mark left by the expedition was at Tessouat's camp on the shore of Lake Allumette, "a cross of white
cedar, bearing the arms of France" (II:296-97).

p. 163   **The Champlain Landfall in Huronia**

The accepted view now is that Otoucha is the same word as
Toanche, meaning the "double landing place," which, inciden-
tally, is not to be confused with the location of the present-day
community of Toanche. Rather, it was most likely that Champlain landed at the double-sided promontory of Methodist Point

in Awenda Provincial Park. However, pinpointing Champlain at any specific spot in Huronia is like trying to lift globules of mercury with a fork. With rare exception, it is impossible to pinpoint any of the locations of Indian villages Champlain visited on today's map simply because there are no remaining demographic landmarks. According to archaeological expertise, Huronia at this time in the seventeenth century had the largest concentration of Indians anywhere in North America (now estimated to have been about 20,000), but most Huron villages moved any time after a period of ten years and one record suggests there were as many as four hundred villages in the region. Having abandoned the practice of providing regional maps, with geographical points of reference, Champlain isn't much help. However, what is lost in geographical detail is made up for with entertaining ethnographic observations.

CHAPTER EIGHTEEN

p. 164   **Cahiagué**

Until recently and without archaeological or other scientific information for decades, historians have assumed that this large Huron settlement was located at present-day Hawkestone on the western shoreline of Lake Simcoe. However, there is now a substantial body of archaeological evidence which points to the more likely location of either of two, or both, other sites: Warminster and now the Ball site, both on Highway 12, about ten kilometers west of Orillia, Ontario. Challenging the earlier acceptance of Warminster as the likely candidate, the experts are now searching more diligently for the answer. Just as intriguing as the possibility of one or both of these locations being Champlain's winter home in 1615 and 1616 is the astonishing inventory of European artifacts that have been found on these sites. Items include a shoe-buckle, cutlery, metal arrowheads, pins, clay pipes, beads, and various tools. This extraordinary cache, Canada's finest for the early French exploration era in Ontario, has only been cataloged in part and, sadly, has never been open to public display.

CHAPTER NINETEEN

p. 169   **The Iroquois Fortress, Syracuse, New York**

One curiosity of the illustration was the well-constructed cavalier made of planks rather than cut trees and poles. To date, scholars have consistently taken the position that this artistry was rather fanciful and that such craftsmanship at this site doesn't make sense. Perhaps. But it is well to reflect that earlier in the year,

Champlain as before, did sail from Honfleur, the carpentry capital of France. In the past the French had transported prefabricated buildings, such as the Québec Habitation and the Port-Royal Habitation, from Île Sainte-Croix (figs. 25, 17, and 10), over great distances. The fact that this well-made military device suddenly appears on the second day of the conflict might well indicate that some of the parts for the cavalier, including the platform, were transported the full distance from Québec. For many decades there has raged a great battle amongst researchers as to the location of the Onandaga fortress of the Iroquois (fig. 34). There are those, for example, who claim that the site was that of Nichol's Pond in Madison County. A certain General James S. Clark, a member of the illustrious New York Historical Society, offers these words of assurance regarding his findings:

> I claim especially to understand the record of Champlain by following his narrative *verbatim et literatim*, and accepting his estimates of distances, his map and illustrations. I stand on no uncertain ground. I understand the question thoroughly. I know that I am right. I desire no misunderstanding on this question. I take the affirmative and throw down the gauntlet to all comers; and if any choose to enter the list, I have the most unbounded confidence that it will not be me that will be born [sic] from the field discomfited. I identify the site [Nichol's Pond] as certainly as any gentleman can identify his wife at the breakfast table after ten years of marriage.

In spite of this bravado, however, the archaeological evidence now weighs rather heavily against the Nichol's Pond site. The leading authority on the subject is anthropologist Dr. Peter Pratt, who in response to my query on the matter in 1986, kindly responded with this assessment:

"In sum while Nichol's Pond is stockaded, its stockade does not match that described by Champlain. Furthermore, the site antedates the battle by a little more than a century. The most likely site of the battle was at Onandaga Lake. That site has probably been largely destroyed with possibly a morsel of it preserved under Hiawatha Boulevard in Syracuse."

CHAPTER TWENTY

p. 173   **A Carolina Parakeet in Ontario?**

Not since the tales of the Gaspé "GOUGOU" monster and the days of drawing dragons for the *Brief Narrative* had Champlain written of things that had left him open to ridicule by Lescarbot. There may, however, be a plausible explanation.

Experts now have evidence of the existence of the Carolina parakeet in the modern history of Ontario. This bird is strikingly similar in description to Champlain's ornithological wonder and, although the last sighting in North America of this now extinct creature was recorded by the U.S. Department of Agriculture in Florida in 1920, there was a report of one being shot in London, Ontario in 1877. In recent years, archaeologists have discovered in Ontario the bones of a Carolina parakeet, and, at the Smithsonian in Washington, there is an Indian clay pipe that was unearthed in upper New York State that has a parrot in the design. Although Champlain's description of his parrot does not completely fit that of the Carolina species, the similarity of bird coloring — the Carolina parrot has a head of yellow and red feathers with bluish-green wings — is enough to raise the question as to whether or not this was what Champlain saw.

p. 186   **Champlain's 1616 Summary Survey**

With regard to the unknown map, by stroke of fortune, in July of 1953, The John Carter Brown Library of Providence, Rhode Island, the home of so many Champlain treasures including the manuscript, the *Brief Narrative*, acquired a single proof sheet from an unfinished plate of a previously unknown map by Champlain. As the tale unfolds, this unique print was discovered by an antiquarian bookseller in Paris who found it bound in a seventeenth-century atlas which was up for sale. It is not known why this survey was not included in any of the published works, especially the last volume in 1632, but most likely the chart was intended for inclusion in the great cultural treatise *Les Voyages*, published in 1619. This at least would be consistent with Champlain's practice of providing a large overview survey summary at the end of each phase of his activities. Perhaps the death of his publisher Jean Bergon in 1617 frustrated its completion. It is also possible that Champlain was waiting on Étienne Brûlé's report; but that when the information came it was too vague to warrant a complete overhaul of the chart, thus leaving Champlain by publication date with a map that he viewed as obsolete and potentially embarrassing.

CHAPTERS TWENTY-ONE, TWENTY-TWO AND TWENTY-FOUR

pp. 196, 209, 221   **The Two Murderers**

The amount of documented confusion about the circumstances and identity of the two Indians accused of the first two murders has accumulated from historians, biographers, and editors over the years. Two historians, for example, Morris Bishop and Samuel Eliot Morison, have chosen to sidestep the issue by reducing the story to the point where there was really only one murderer. It is not clear how this theory first began, but one suggestion may involve the editor of the original Champlain Society translation of the Champlain journals. In the index under "Cherououny", the entry reads "He [Cherououny] was called earlier "the murderer" (VI: 393). In view of the fact that there were two culprits originally mentioned by Champlain himself, this entry is at best misleading.

In fairness, however, the vagaries of Champlain as chronicler must also be taken into account. In his account of the conviction of the one accused who did present himself at the trial in 1618, Champlain does not mention his name nor describe his exact role in the crime. Indeed, it is not until July of 1623 that he offers any more insight into the matter.

In my opinion, his words at that time allow for the more legitimate speculation that the accused and convicted man at the 1618 trial was merely the accomplice and not the same person to whom Champlain later refers as "the Reconciled", "the murderer", or "Cherououny", a Chief of the Montagnais Indians. Champlain subsequently admits in the journals that his anger against the "murderer" who was brought to trial was, on at least one occasion, stage-managed. Then adding confusion to this inconclusive description of 1623, Champlain reports that: "the murderer, who had always enjoyed renown, . . . had been made a captain [chief] by the savages for having killed our men. The said murderer was required to stand in the midst of the assembled tribes, and with him the man who had assisted him in the murder" (VI: 105). There are also several other factors deserving of consideration, but they are beyond the scope of this book.

CHAPTER TWENTY-FIVE

p. 226   **The Huguenot Uprisings in La Rochelle, 1627-1628**

Beginning in 1627, the Huguenot stronghold of La Rochelle was under siege by the Catholic monarch King Louis XIII with Cardinal Richelieu at his side. But by 1628, the half-hearted rebellion had become a bitter personal struggle between the Huguenot leader of La Rochelle, Jean Guiton, and his protagonist, the eminent King's First Minister. Guiton placed his knife in front of him on a desk as a symbol of his target, the jugular vein of absolute authority in Paris. At the end of the bloodbath which followed, only 5,000 out of 28,000 who had rebelled survived to receive the King's pardon at 3 p.m. on October 28, 1628, after a fourteen-month siege.

The monarch's decree read on the date of this victory clearly revealed to what extent the Huguenot bastion had preoccupied the nation's government and robbed the royal treasury of resources that might have been deployed to better protect New France: "Let all the towers of La Rochelle be razed such that a plough can go over it. Save only the shoreline fortifications to fend off the English." It was no wonder that the Kirkes were so readily able to conquer the colony overseas.

CHAPTER TWENTY-EIGHT

p. 258 **Richelieu's Rise to Power**

Richelieu's rise to power accelerated when King Louis' mother, Marie de Médicis, who was Regent after the death of King Henry IV in 1610, ensured the appointment of this priest as a secretary of state in 1616. At first he was loyal to the Regent in the power struggle between her and her royal son, even following her into exile in 1617. But, at an opportune moment, Richelieu switched allegiance to the King he could manipulate. Even so, he still performed services for his former patron and by 1622, while effectively playing all sides to personal advantage, Richelieu became a Cardinal. By 1624 he was the first minister of the land and by 1630, in the final phase of gaining complete control of the government, this prince of the church engineered the final exile of the King's mother.

pp. 251, 266 **La Compagnie de la Nouvelle France (1627-1663)**

Richelieu envisaged La Compagnie de la Nouvelle France, known also as the Hundred Associates, as a vertically integrated enterprise that reached into every conceivable activity from armaments manufacturing to schools of navigation. The new company was not merely a domestic corporation for avaricious entrepreneurs, but a multinational land bank granted in spite of reality the title to all lands in North America from Florida to the Arctic and for time immemorial. For Richelieu, Paris, not the region, ruled. He was a curious mixture of the leader who can on occasion delegate authority and even pick talent, but then can also be crippled by the peevish distractions of provincialism and religious paranoia.

p. 264 **Champlain's Gravesite**

There is no certain knowledge as to Champlain's final resting place. The most likely location of the grave for the man known as the Governor would certainly have been a crypt within his beloved spiritual sanctuary, Notre Dame de la Récouvrance, the house of worship built during the last years of his residency. Unfortunately, this house of God was destroyed by fire in 1640. Nevertheless, the question has been asked as to whether or not a box filled with bones preserved in the crypt of the Basilica of Québec now contains the skull or other remains of Champlain, these purportedly having been transferred from the vicinity of the original site of the settlement. From the archeological evidence available, this is unlikely.

Selected Annotated Bibliography

Biggar, H. P., ed. *The Works of Samuel de Champlain*. 6 vols. Toronto: University of Toronto/The Champlain Society, 1936. Primary reference material essential to any study of Champlain.

Biggar, H. P., and Litt, B. A. *The Early Trading Companies of New France*. Reprints of Economic Classics. Clifton, N.J.: August M. Kelley, 1901; reprint 1972. Valuable background.

Bishop, Morris. *Champlain: The Life of Fortitude*. New York: Alfred A. Knopf, 1948. Scholarly and a bit fanciful; a good read.

Bloch, Marc. *French Rural History*. London: Routledge and Kegan Paul, 1966. The classic on the subject.

Blunt, Anthony. *Art and Architecture in France: 1500-1700*. The Pelican History of Art. London: Penguin Books, 1982. Superb, insightful work.

Briggs, Robin. *Early Modern France: 1560-1715*. Oxford: Oxford University Press, 1977. Useful background to the age.

Brown, George W., ed. *Dictionary of Canadian Biography*. Vol. I. Toronto: University of Toronto Press, 1966. A tremendous contribution to Canadian history.

Davis, Natalie Zemon. *Society and Culture in Early Modern France*. Stanford, California: Stanford University Press, 1986. Brilliant and fascinating.

Dickason, Patricia Olive. *The Myth of the Savage*. Edmonton: University of Alberta Press, 1984. A valuable examination of Amerindian culture in the early years of the French colony.

Dionne, N.-E. *Champlain*. The Makers of Canada. Toronto: Morang and Company, 1906. A shorter, edited version of the author's classic work.

Goubert, Pierre. *The French Regime: French Society, 1600-1750*. New York: Harper & Row, 1973. A welcome lamp that illuminates the dark era that produced Champlain.

Heidenreich, C. E. *Huronia*. Toronto: McClelland and Stewart, 1971. A history and geography of Ontario's Indians from 1600 to 1650. Scholarly and packed with regional details.

————. *Explorations and Mapping of Samuel de Champlain, 1603-1632*. B. V. Gutsell, Department of Geography, York University, Cartographica series, monograph #17, 1976. An important and unique evaluation of Champlain's North American cartography.

Lescarbot, Marc. *The History of New France*. Trans. and ed. W. L. Grant. 3 vols. Toronto: The Champlain Society, 1907-1914. Another essential primary work.

Macnamara, C. "Champlain's Astrolabe," *Canadian Field Naturalist*, vol. 33, no. 6, 1919, pp. 103-9. The story of the discovery of the famous instrument.

Morison, Samuel Eliot. *The European Discovery of America: The Northern Voyages, 1500-1600*. New York: Oxford University Press, 1971. The classic work on exploration of this continent before the era of Champlain.

――――. *Samuel de Champlain: Father of New France*. Boston: Little, Brown and Co., 1972. An important biography by the noted American naval historian.

Parker, T. H. L. *John Calvin*. Sutherland, Australia: Lion Publishing, 1975. Useful background about the architect of the Huguenot religious movement.

Parkman, Francis. *The Jesuits in North America in the Seventeenth Century*. Vol. II, France and England in North America. New York: Frederick Ungar Publishing Co., 1965; reprint from 1867 edition. The American nineteenth-century classic.

Public Archives Canada. *Nouveaux Documents sur Champlain et son époque*. Vol. I, 1560-1622, Publication no. 15. Essential primary source material.

Ranum, Orest. *Paris in the Age of Absolutism*. Bloomington and London: Indiana University Press, 1969. Excellent examination of Champlain's France.

Sagard, Father Gabriel. *The Long Journey to the Country of the Hurons*. Ed. B. M. Wrong; trans. H. H. Langton. Toronto: The Champlain Society, 1939; facsimile edition: New York: Greenwood Press, Publishers, 1968. Essential primary source.

Salmon, J. H. M. *Society in Crisis: France in the Sixteenth Century*. London: Methuen, 1979. Good introduction to the era.

Thwaites, R. G., ed. *The Jesuit Relations and Allied Documents*. 73 vols. Cleveland: Burrows Bros., 1896-1901. Vital primary source.

Trigger, Bruce G. *Natives and Newcomers: Canada's "Heroic Age" Reconsidered*. Kingston and Montreal: McGill–Queen's University Press, 1985. A fanciful and provocative work by the noted anthropologist. A good read.

Trudel, Marcel. *The Beginnings of New France, 1524-1663*. Toronto: McClelland and Stewart, 1973. A comprehensive modern work by the eminent scholar of French Canada.

Illustration Credits

Champlain's works	Credit
FIGS. 1, 2, 3, 4, and 39	John Carter Brown Library at Brown University

FIG. 5 - NL 15315	Public Archives Canada,
FIG. 6 - NL 15313	National Library, Ottawa
FIG. 8 - C 130981	
FIG. 9 - NL 12422	
FIG. 10 - NL 15306	
FIG. 11 - NL 15319	
FIG. 12 - NL 15311	
FIG. 13 - NL 15304	
FIG. 14 - NL 15310	
FIG. 15 - NL 15317	
FIG. 16 - NL 15325	
FIG. 17 - NL 8760	
FIG. 18 - NL 15324	
FIG. 19 - NL 15322	
FIG. 20 - NL 15323	
FIG. 23 - NL 15312	
FIG. 24 - C 129201	
FIG. 26 - NL 6643	
FIG. 27 - NL 15318	
FIG. 28 - NL 15316	
FIG. 32 - NL L3127	
FIG. 33 - NL 15309	
FIG. 34 - NL 15320	
FIG. 35 - NL 15321	
FIG. 36 - NL 15305	
FIG. 37 - NL 15308	
FIG. 38 - NL 15307	

FIG. 22 - NMC 97952	Public Archives Canada,
FIG. 25 - NMC 17446	National Map Collection
FIG. 40 - NMC 51970	

FIG. 21	The Library of Congress, Washington D. C.

FIGS. 7, 29, 30, and 31	Joe C. W. Armstrong CANADIANA COLLECTION

Other Works

Fake Portrait of Champlain   Public Archives Canada
by Louis C. J. Ducornet - C 6643

The Champlain Astrolabe   Courtesy of The New York
- 43510   Historical Society,
          Washington D. C.

INDEX

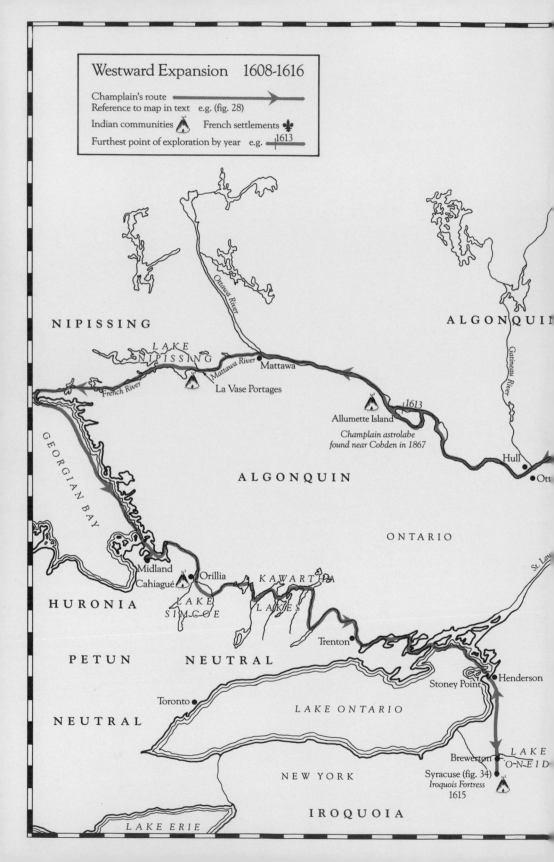

Westward Expansion   1608-1616

Champlain's route
Reference to map in text   e.g. (fig. 28)
Indian communities   French settlements
Furthest point of exploration by year   e.g. 1613

NIPISSING

ALGONQUIN

Ottawa River

LAKE NIPISSING

Mattawa River   Mattawa

French River   La Vase Portages

Gatineau River

1613

Allumette Island

*Champlain astrolabe
found near Cobden in 1867*

Hull

Ott

ALGONQUIN

GEORGIAN BAY

ONTARIO

Midland
Cahiagué   Orillia

KAWARTHA

St. Law

HURONIA

LAKE SIMCOE

LAKES

PETUN   NEUTRAL

Trenton

Stoney Point   Henderson

Toronto

LAKE ONTARIO

NEUTRAL

Brewerton   *LAKE O-N-E-I-D*

NEW YORK

Syracuse (fig. 34)
Iroquois Fortress
1615

IROQUOIA

LAKE ERIE